Culture, Mind, and Society

The Book Series of the Society for Psychological Anthropology

The Society for Psychological Anthropology—a section of the American Anthropology Association—and Palgrave Macmillan are dedicated to publishing innovative research that illuminates the workings of the human mind within the social, cultural, and political contexts that shape thought, emotion, and experience. As anthropologists seek to bridge gaps between ideation and emotion or agency and structure and as psychologists, psychiatrists, and medical anthropologists search for ways to engage with cultural meaning and difference, this interdisciplinary terrain is more active than ever.

Titles in the Series

Adrie Kusserow, *American Individualisms: Child Rearing and Social Class in Three Neighborhoods*

Naomi Quinn, editor, *Finding Culture in Talk: A Collection of Methods*

Anna Mansson McGinty, *Becoming Muslim: Western Women's Conversions to Islam*

Roy D'Andrade, *A Study of Personal and Cultural Values: American, Japanese, and Vietnamese*

Steven M. Parish, *Subjectivity and Suffering in American Culture: Possible Selves*

Elizabeth A. Throop, *Psychotherapy, American Culture, and Social Policy: Immoral Individualism*

Victoria Katherine Burbank, *An Ethnography of Stress: The Social Determinants of Health in Aboriginal Australia*

Karl G. Heider, *The Cultural Context of Emotion: Folk Psychology in West Sumatra*

Jeannette Marie Mageo, *Dreaming Culture: Meanings, Models, and Power in U.S. American Dreams*

Casey High, Ann H. Kelly, and Jonathan Mair, editors, *The Anthropology of Ignorance: An Ethnographic Approach*

Kevin K. Birth, *Objects of Time: How Things Shape Temporality*

Andrew Kipnis, editor, *Chinese Modernity and the Individual Psyche*

Katie Glaskin and Richard Chenhall, editors, *Sleep Around the World: Anthropological Perspectives*

Naomi Quinn and Jeannette Marie Mageo, editors, *Attachment Reconsidered: Cultural Perspectives on a Western Theory*

Rebecca Seligman, *Possessing Spirits and Healing Selves: Embodiment and Transformation in an Afro-Brazilian Religion*

Karen J. Brison, *Children, Social Class, and Education: Shifting Identities in Fiji*

Katie Rose Hejtmanek, *Friendship, Love, and Hip Hop: An Ethnography of African American Men in Psychiatric Custody*

Friendship, Love, and Hip Hop

An Ethnography of African American Men in Psychiatric Custody

Katie Rose Hejtmanek

FRIENDSHIP, LOVE, AND HIP HOP

First published 2015 by
PALGRAVE MACMILLAN

The author has asserted their right to be identified as the author of this work in accordance with the Copyright, Designs and Patents Act 1988.

Palgrave Macmillan in the UK is an imprint of Macmillan Publishers Limited, registered in England, company number 785998, of Houndmills, Basingstoke, Hampshire, RG21 6XS.

Palgrave Macmillan in the US is a division of Nature America, Inc., One New York Plaza, Suite 4500, New York, NY 10004-1562.

Palgrave Macmillan is the global academic imprint of the above companies and has companies and representatives throughout the world.

Hardback ISBN: 978–1–137–54472–8
E-PUB ISBN: 978–1–137–54474–2
E-PDF ISBN: 978–1–137–54473–5
DOI: 10.1057/9781137544735

Distribution in the UK, Europe and the rest of the world is by Palgrave Macmillan®, a division of Macmillan Publishers Limited, registered in England, company number 785998, of Houndmills, Basingstoke, Hampshire RG21 6XS.

Library of Congress Cataloging-in-Publication Data

Hejtmanek, Katie Rose.
Friendship, love, and hip hop : an ethnography of African American men in psychiatric custody / by Katie Rose Hejtmanek.
pages cm.—(Culture, mind, and society)
Summary: "Friendship, Love, and Hip Hop investigates how young Black men live and change inside a mental institution in contemporary America. While the youth in Hejtmanek's study face the rigidity of institutionalized life, they also productively maneuver through what the author analyzes as the "give"—friendship, love, and hip hop—in the system"—Provided by publisher.
Includes bibliographical references and index.
ISBN 978–1–137–54472–8 (hardback)
1. Adolescent psychotherapy—United States. 2. African American young men—Psychology—United States. I. Title.

RJ503.H36 2015
616.8991408996073—dc23 2015015112

A catalogue record of the book is available from the British Library.

For my parents, Michael J. and Jeanne M. Hejtmanek

Contents

Figures and Table

Figures

Table

Series Editor's Preface

Psychological anthropologists study a wide spectrum of human activity: child development, illness and healing, ritual and religion, selfhood and personality, political and economic systems, just to name a few. In fact, as a discipline that seeks to draw the lines connecting persons and culture, it would be difficult to come up with examples of human behavior that fall outside the purview of psychological anthropology. Yet, beneath this substantive diversity lies a common commitment. The practitioners of psychological anthropology seek to answer broad questions about how peoples' inner worlds are interwoven with their outer ones. And, while psychological anthropologists may focus on emotions or human biology, on language or art or dreams, they rarely stray far from the attempt to understand the mental and physical possibilities and limitations that ground human experience.

In *Friendship, Love, and Hip Hop*, Katie Rose Hejtmanek attends to processes of healing the psyche, and on the broader problem of how the very self can be transformed. Taking as her subject young African American men confined at an inpatient mental health facility, Professor Hejtmanek shows us how intimate social relationships with the staff at the institution can heal. Those relationships are realized, in part, in the idiom of hip-hop culture, a counterhegemonic ideology that has taken shape in the broader African American community. In this study, the author points us toward an evolving understanding of how a culture—and the identities it allows men and women to build—is the foundation of mental health.

Peter G. Stromberg

Acknowledgments

First and foremost, I want to thank the boys, men, and woman of Steele Cottage. It is not easy to have an anthropologist hanging around all of the time, writing down what you do and say. And yet, you not only allowed my presence but you opened your hearts to me. I am forever grateful for all of the laughter, fun, and real talk/real walk I shared with you. I hope this book does justice to what I heard, saw, and lived through, next to you.

I want to thank the people of Havenwood for allowing me to live and conduct ethnographic research at the institution. Although I had permission to do so, real data and knowledge comes when people include you in their lives. I am not sure you realize how much it meant to me when you finally started inviting me to attend meetings, hang out in cottages, ride along on off-campus activities, come to lunch, and trust me with your knowledge. Thank you so very much.

Research requires money and I was fortunate to procure generous support for the research and writing of this project. The research for this book was funded by a dissertation improvement grant from the National Science Foundation, Cultural Anthropology (DDIG # 0648590). The period for writing this book was generously funded by fellowships and programs at Brooklyn College and the City University of New York. First, I want to thank the Whiting Foundation for the generous teaching award and fellowship that allowed me to focus solely on writing this book for an entire semester. Thank you to the CUNY Faculty Fellowship Publication Program, which provided released-time and a weekly place to share and engage with others' work. In particular, I want to thank my cohort of interdisciplinary critical race scholars from across CUNY including Lourdes Follins, Elissa Bemporad, Angie Berman, Sheldon Applewhite, Jennifer Morton, Tamisha Bouknight, and Stephen Steinberg, who read and commented on very early chapter drafts. Thank you for your insightful and supportive feedback. I also want to thank the Professional Staff Congress research foundation of CUNY (PSC-CUNY) for funding my summer writing.

I have found a lovely home at Brooklyn College. I am so fortunate to share the hallways of the Department of Anthropology and

Archaeology and the Children and Youth Studies Program with amazing colleagues, including Arthur Bankoff, Sophia Perdikaris, Patricia Antoniello, Jillian Cavanaugh, Naomi Schiller, Stephen Chester, Alfred Rosenberger, Edward Sammons, Russell Sharman, Gertrud Lenzer, Jeremy Porter, and Elise Goldberg. In particular, this book could not have been written without the many conversations I had with Jeremy Porter, Jillian Cavanaugh, Patricia Antoniello, Sophia Perdikaris, and Naomi Schiller. Thank you for engaging with my work so thoughtfully. I also want to thank my students—who have listened to and shared their thoughts about my work—especially those in my Generation Next, Psychological Anthropology, and Culture and Transformation courses. I have thoroughly enjoyed working with such smart, thoughtful, and forthright students.

I have presented parts of this book at various places and times and obtainined critical feedback. I want to thank the PhD Program in Anthropology at the CUNY Graduate Center, the Culture, Power, and Boundaries seminar at Columbia University, and Stephanié Larchanché and her colleagues at Centre F. Minkowska and Université Paris Descartes for their helpful feedback on various chapters of this book. Bambi Chapin, Lorna Rhodes, and Anne Lovell—thank you for providing very important discussant feedback at critical junctures in the writing process. Rebecca Lester, Atwood Gaines, Paul Brodwin, Cheryl Mattingly, Eileen Anderson-Fye, John Bowen, Peter Benson, and John Baugh have been crucial to my professional growth. Thank you so much for your time and insights over the past many years. I also want to thank John L. Jackson, Jr.—without your questions, conversation, and encouragement I would not have been able to write this book. Thank you for being an incredible mentor and friend.

Many friends have encouraged me and helped keep me grounded during the process of writing. Thank you so much Angie Wassif, Lourdes Follins, Terry Perlin, Livia Stone, Lisa Isenhart, Meghan Ference, Nicole Havelka, Reggie Brown, Vanessa Hildebrand, Sharon Lennon, Nutsa Batiashvili, Meghan Hendrickson, Nadia El-Shaarawi, Kristen Drybread, and Anubha Sood. Many of you have enriched this manuscript in ways that you may not know. A huge heartfelt thank you to Stephanié Larchanché for reading my manuscript and providing essential feedback, including copyediting. In the past few years, I have returned to track-and–field, which has been a source of well-being and so much joy. I've flourished in New York City, thanks to my coach Lesleigh Hogg, teammate Michelle Cameron, and many other fellow athletes and coaches at my home away from home, The Sport Center at Chelsea Piers.

I want to thank Mireille Yanow at Palgrave Macmillan and Peter Stromberg of the University of Tulsa and the series editor for Culture, Mind and Society for seeing the promise in my manuscript and guiding the book to completion.

Thank you to my siblings and their beautiful families—Michael, Kim, Harper, and Sadie Hejtmanek, and Jenny and Craig Robin—for your encouragement, support, and visits over the past few years while I was writing. It isn't easy to watch one's child study genocide orphans in Rwanda, child soldiers in Uganda, or to move into and study life in a mental institution. My parents, Mike and Jeanne Hejtmanek, may not have always understood my motivations but they did everything in their power to support and encourage me as I struggled to realize my goals and dreams. My mom read countless drafts of this manuscript, offered gifts, advice, and a comforting shoulder when I felt discouraged, and made sure that Laramie was loved and cared for. My father, a role model for doing what one loves and for always learning and being adventurous, reminded me to "bull my neck" when the going got tough. I feel so very fortunate to have parents who let me be and *do me*. Thanks Mom and Dad.

Finally, although many people contributed to this book, any errors, omissions, or misinterpretations are my responsibility alone.

Introduction

The "Black Box" of Psychiatric Custody

"Residential is like a black box," a therapist tells me. He uses the informal "residential" to indicate residential treatment for mentally ill youth. "You have all of these services and interventions but you never know which one is working. And each kid is different. You just hope something sticks." We are walking across Havenwood's large college-like campus, from one clinical meeting to another. Havenwood is a residential treatment center, a present-day asylum, located near a major midwestern city in the United States.[1]

Residential treatment is often colloquially identified as a "black box," a metaphor linked to a common engineering concept.[2] The idea is that an input goes into a black box, something happens to this thing while in the opaque box, and an output, something altogether different, emerges from the box.[3] In this case, the input that enters the black box is locally identified as a "troubled youth," the black box is the total institutional structure of residential treatment with all of its psychiatric and therapeutic services and interventions, and the desired output is often referred to as a "productive citizen."[4] The alchemy within the total institution, the inner workings and mechanisms by which the troubled youth is turned into a productive citizen, is often described, in causal conversations or state-level reports, as somewhat mysterious, extremely complex, and difficult to pin down. However, regardless of how the process works, the goal is, as the therapist states it, to get some sort of change "to stick."

The therapist and I are headed to a weekly meeting of psychologists, therapists, social workers, teachers, and the group of people who work with a featured client in his or her living space. These individuals discuss the best ways to interact with the challenging residential clients (hereafter referred to as residents), focusing on one case study. A challenging resident is often one who is dangerously aggressive or violent and might often need to be restrained, physically held down, or confined, quarantined from the rest of the group in a small room. The meeting's agenda is to figure out what causes the resident to act in such extreme ways and to adjust his or her treatment plan to better address these causes. During the meeting, a psychiatrist asks, "How much thinking can the kid do without an adult there? My main distinction is between following rules and really changing." In addition to hoping that something "sticks," clinicians and other professionals at Havenwood often discuss and question the youth's transformation.

"Can kids make good choices without as much structure? That is always the question," a psychologist responds, voicing a central question of residential treatment. Are the residents really changing or are they adapting to the constraining social structure and culture of the total institution? These mental health professionals want to know: Is the change occurring at the level of the self, or are these young people merely adapting to institutional life?

"How do you get a resident to buy in to his or her own treatment?" Another therapist asks. In other words, how do you convince a person he has psychiatric needs, if he did not seek psychiatric help willingly?[5] Unlike outpatient treatment, where individuals seek psychiatric help due to personal distress, young people in residential treatment often do not believe they have psychiatric issues, especially those that require social abjection and institutionalization. Therefore the therapist wants to know: How do you convince a resident that he needs to live in residential treatment? How do you get youth to do the work—to talk in therapy, to share in group therapy, to not physically attack others, and to have hope for the future—of treatment? More importantly, how do you get them to believe in and want to change? How do you get them to "buy in" to the idea that they need institutionalized treatment and that they need to change who they are?

The therapists of Havenwood struggle with the task assigned to them by the State—to admit youth identified as needing residential treatment and get them to *really* change, to buy in to their need for treatment and the institution's desired changes, rather than to just follow the rules, before they become adults and can make their own decisions about their lives.

* * *

Residential treatment is a specialized mental health treatment method for young people identified as having severe psychiatric needs (Hejtmanek 2013). The first stage of treatment is institutionalization. Residential treatment is defined as a place where youth live and their daily lives are organized around their psychological treatment (Mayor 1955). Young people are socially abjected from mainstream life—including schooling, home life, neighborhood contexts, hobbies or extracurricular activities, teenage hangout time, and other aspects of conventional American childhood and young adulthood—and sent to all-encompassing psychiatric treatment.[6] Residential treatment is often court ordered and funded by the State.[7]

Once remanded to residential treatment, the young people receive a plethora of psychiatric and therapeutic services to address their mental disorders. These services include psychotropic medication regimens, milieu therapy, individual therapy, group therapy, recreation therapy, and family therapy. In addition to living in the institution and receiving therapeutic services, young people are also educated in these institutions in an alternative school designed to treat special needs populations. The overarching ideology of residential treatment is to admit into a total institution a State-identified psychiatrically disordered young person, treat him, and discharge a productive citizen. Residential treatment is the end of a long continuum of mental health care for severely behaviorally disordered and emotionally disturbed youth (Aichhorn 1935; Barker 1974; Bettelheim 1950; Cotton 1993; Magellan Health Services Children's Services Task Force 2010; Mayor 1955; Polsky 1962/1977; Polsky, Claster, and Goldberg 1968; Robinson, Gardner, Greenwood, Hagan, and Richmond 1957).

Residential treatment is understood to be the place where some of America's most problematic young people live. I often heard Havenwood youth referred to as the "worst of the worst." Residential treatment occupies a similar social location to juvenile detention. Often presenting the same symptoms, usually socially problematic behavior (e.g., fighting, truancy, and drug use), youth are placed in either treatment or detention depending on a court's decision. In fact, many of the youth at Havenwood had extensive experience in both treatment and detention. When I asked how it was decided where a young person went, the common answer from therapists, line staff members, and lead administrators (I did not speak to the judges myself), was that if a judge sees potential in the youth, determining that the youth is redeemable as a citizen, that child is sent to treatment for help rather than to detention for containment.[8] In the contemporary United States, this help comes in the form of court-mandated psychiatric living and therapeutic intervention. The child's ability to officially leave the institution is also determined by State officials—the youth must prove that he or she has really changed. Therefore, rather than "residential treatment," I prefer "psychiatric custody" to more accurately conceptualize the State-ordered psychiatric remanding of America's problematic youth. Havenwood is a site of psychiatric custody.

The Ethnographic Setting: Havenwood Campus

Havenwood is located on the outskirts of a major midwestern city. After traveling two hours by car from the major city, via interstate and local state highways, one comes upon a sign declaring "Havenwood, A Place for Youth in Need."

From the state highway, Havenwood's campus extends north along the main Havenwood drive. On the right is a large open field, big enough for multiple football games to be played. At the north end of the field is a building that houses two male living units, also called cottages, of Bradley North and Bradley South. To the left of the big field is a dense forest of pine trees and brush extending deep enough so as to obscure the other end of the forest. Still further north, across the small 30-yard wide parking lot in front of Bradley, is another large building. This building houses two female cottages Shelby North and Shelby South.

Continuing north along the main drive, to the right are three little cottage-like buildings and the circular drive at the school. The school and its buildings comprise this section of the campus. It would be common to see a single file line of mostly African American teenagers walking out of the school. To the left, the woods open up to a clearing about the size of a football field. The clearing has a large mound, which youth sled down in the winter and run around during cross-country races in the fall. Behind the mound sits a huge greenhouse, and a large industrial building. The large building houses the on-campus laundry, the home economics classrooms, the wood shop, and the auto-mechanics shop. During my time there, residents offered to change my car's oil and filters for credit in their auto class. The laundry room is filled with industrial sized laundry machines, per state hygiene codes. The school and the shop building are only a few years old, which is in direct contrast to many of the other buildings on campus.

From the school's drive, the Havenwood road bends northwest. This curving allows for another large field, a baseball field with a backstop. To the east of the field is the residential administration building, which is also attached to the chapel and gymnasium.

These buildings open up to the center of the campus, on the east side. A group of young people would probably be playing a game in the field; I would come to watch many physical education classes and therapeutic recreation group sessions on these fields. The road curves around to the right, providing a northern boundary to the open sports field. Speed bumps are located at this curve, which is also at the front of the main maintenance building. At the north end of the field are a large generator, a gas pump, and the water tower. I initially wondered if Havenwood produced its own power and water, making it autonomous from local municipal water, gas, and electricity sources. The generator is used when the local power sources fail, which happens periodically in the winter and spring, due to storms. The gas is used to fill Havenwood's vans, which transport the youth to various off-campus activities and home visits. The water tower is no longer in use except as a hazard.[9]

The road opens up into a parking lot nestled at the northern most point of Havenwood's campus. This parking lot sits between old buildings that I would later come to know as the main administration building, the female living unit known as Evelyn's Cottage, a small cottage housing therapy offices, the dining hall, the nursing station, a storage building, and a large building that housed all of the maintenance crew and equipment needed to operate such a large campus.

The road circles around past the main administration building and turns south. At this point, the small lake appears; Havenwood's eastern boundary is a lake. A small beach nestles between two cottages, complete with a covered picnic area, kayaks, and a sand volleyball court. The road continues past two more house-like buildings—Kerry Cottage and Terrance Cottage—where it finally comes to a halt at a gate behind Steele Cottage, home to 14–18-year-old boys, and Roger Cottage, referred to as the "little boy cottage," because it housed 7–13-year-olds.

The Havenwood campus is beautiful. It snuggles up next to a lake on the east and northeast side, with the woods on the northwest and west sides. Large oak trees dot the campus. A dense wooded area known as "the swamp" and well-groomed lawns and fields provide contrasts in the landscape. The concrete and gravel pathways crisscross the campus, leading from building to building. Two different jungle gyms are strategically located—one outside the dining hall for after lunch play, and one behind the elementary classrooms. Two basketball hoops are located outside the gym, near the dining hall. Picnic benches are located near the jungle gym, outside the basketball court, and outside of each cottage. Geese wander around the campus, swans swim in the lake, and periodically, deer are seen behind the big mound near the greenhouse. The sounds that fill the air are of birds chirping and water lapping.

The buildings contribute to the idyllic feel of the campus. Some of the older buildings of the 1930s have stained glass windows, dark wood interiors, and charming architectural details. The beige colored building I lived in had a rounded turret with a red door at its base. The newer buildings were also aesthetically pleasing with large dark windows, brick exteriors, and grand sloping roofs. A simple Google image search of residential treatment centers reveals a somewhat standard architectural design of the campus residential treatment centers, especially of the newer cottage buildings.[10]

Unlike juvenile detention, Havenwood is not enclosed by a fence or barbed wire. Rather, nature provides the barriers to escape. Residents told me they were afraid of the woods on the west and would not or could not swim. It was a few hundred yards to the state highway that provided the southernmost boundary and the easiest escape route. Once off campus it was miles, as the crow flies and even further by road, to the nearest fully functioning train station. Buses were largely absent from this rural part of midwestern United States. In addition, local police routinely stopped residents walking along the highway, fearing they had run away from Havenwood. It was in this setting that "troubled youth" received all forms of psychiatric therapeutic interventions in an effort to be changed to "productive citizens." In 2006, I set out to learn what life was like for American adolescents in this kind of setting.

Derrick's Take on Psychiatric Custody

"Hello, this is life history number three....Psych! Number two, for your boy D. Yes, I was mad the other day, ladies and gentlemen, but I'm back down like SmackDown.[11] You down with me? You down with me, Katie?" Derrick, aka. "D," engages with the audience of listeners, as he picks up the digital recorder off the table and talks directly into it, rocking it like a microphone.[12] Our scheduled life history interview had been cancelled two days earlier. Derrick had been upset and we had to reschedule. Today he begins the interview with his usual hip hop style and flair.

Derrick is a 15-year-old African American boy who lives at Havenwood. It is a mild March afternoon when Derrick and I sit down for this interview. I had been at Havenwood for eight months and had learned that interviews are occasionally rescheduled when a youth is upset, angry, has chosen to do something else more fun, or for a variety of other reasons.

"What should people know about Havenwood?" I ask him.

"That Havenwood makes me a better person. You got people here to help 24/7. You can talk to 'em if you upset or somethin'.[13] If you want, you get to play sports. They teach you how to, you know, work without havin' a gun or sellin' drugs, work without havin' to bring money to somebody else, cause you owin' somebody." He pauses and looks at me, "If you gotta survive, you can't just know guns and stuff. Ya dig?"

"No you can't, huh?"

"I'm getting my life together," he tells me. "I can't wait till the day when I finally live by myself. I'll show people I don't need to be locked down…nunna that."

He continues, giving me a complete answer to what people should know about Havenwood. "Living in residential, in a group home here don't make you successful. It's what you do when you come outta there that makes you successful. I do what I gotta do so I can leave. I go to school, not get restrained, wait for my placement. I don't snap on people."

Derrick lists formal treatment ideals (going to school, not getting restrained, and waiting for his placement) first, when discussing how he can leave. However, he also includes a colloquial phrase meaning to not verbally confront someone with an aggressive tone. "Why don't you snap on people?"

"I don't snap 'cause that makes other people mad. And we all gotta live together. We all gotta get along."

"How do you learn all of that?" I ask. I'm hoping Derrick can answer some of the questions posed by the therapists.

"Staff. Peers."

Derrick informs us that Havenwood has people to talk to, to help you 24 hours a day, 7 days a week. These people, he states, teach him how to survive without guns, drugs, and aggressively confronting people. Derrick tells me that he does not want to snap on people because it affects others, it makes them mad, and he wants to live and get along with others. He wants to know how to work without selling drugs or ending up owing someone else money. He wants to prove that he does not need to be "locked down," that he can take care of himself and be on his own. Derrick states that it is what he does when he is out of Havenwood that matters, the way he lives when he is not "locked down." He tells me he learns these lessons from staff and peers. For Derrick, what matters in residential treatment, or psychiatric custody, and how he learns to change is simple. It is not unknowable, mysterious, or even that complicated. He learns the lessons he needs to really change from staff and peers.

This interview provides a small window into Derrick's understanding of his psychiatric custody and his version of "buying in"—to reject guns and drugs and to get along with people. Throughout the book, I will shed more light on the ways in which young (predominantly) Black men go about their treatment and transformation in psychiatric custody. We will come to see how "staff" and "peers" matter in the learning process in ways missing from other accounts of residential treatment, psychiatric custody, and total institutional life. When Derrick, and other youth, say "staff," they refer to the adults who work directly in the living units at Havenwood, known in residential treatment parlance as "line staff." It is important to note that the shorthand "staff" did not include therapists or other kinds of staff members. The term "peers" means those young people who live at Havenwood. Therefore, the focus of this book is to take up Derrick's version of psychiatric custody, to focus on the youth's lived experience in psychiatric custody, and how psychiatric living, therapeutic practices, and important social relationships, particularly those among African American men, are integrated to cultivate self-transformation therein.

Psychiatric Custody, Therapeutic Mechanisms, and Transformation

Following Erving Goffman's (1961) foundational participant-observation study of institutional life, I wondered if an anthropologist actually *living* in psychiatric custody for youth could shed light on the quotidian life of treatment, as well as make an argument about how the youth there transformed. Therefore, I undertook an ethnographic study of Havenwood, the social location and history of psychiatric custody, and the mechanisms and processes of change that American adolescents might undergo from living in psychiatric custody. As an anthropologist, I assumed that an experience-near ethnographic approach might provide an insight into the opaque alchemy of the transformation from troubled youth to productive citizen.[14] I also thought that the young people themselves might be able to provide an insight into how it is they change.[15] My interests and research are what James Waldram (2012) has identified as an "anthropology of therapeutic intervention."

Therapeutic intervention is an unwelcome health-related intrusion into the lifeworld of a person. Therapeutic intervention is often an intrusion with patients who "may not recognize or accept that they have a medical or psychological problem, or they may accept that they have a problem but reject the official diagnosis, or they may not accept that treatment is needed, or they may reject the kind of treatment offered or imposed" (Waldram 2012:235). In many cases, these patients may be cognitively or legally powerless in the prescription of treatment. Therapeutic intervention is often coerced or forced due to "social, political and economic structures, including legal structures, [that] establish a jurisdictional right to intervene, to determine what is in the best interests of the patient and society more broadly" (Waldram 2012:235). Therapeutic intervention, then, is often a State-level coerced therapeutic context with people who do not quite "buy in"—to use the phrase ubiquitous at Havenwood—or believe that they need treatment. Therapeutic intervention is a theoretical framing for psychiatric custody.

An *anthropology of* therapeutic intervention, then, is concerned with "cultural processes to understand the dynamics, at all levels, at work in [what I call psychiatric custody], from the macro-level examination of structures of power to the quotidian experience of daily life lived out" within these particular therapeutic contexts (Waldram 2013:236). The anthropology of therapeutic intervention investigates how *individuals experience* their intervention, as much as it investigates the *structural forces* that lead to it. I focus in this book on the lived experience of those engaged in the daily practice of therapeutic intervention at Havenwood.

At Havenwood, the first important therapeutic intervention is total institutional living. Erving Goffman (1961) coined the term "total institution" to make sense of the social world where mental patients and other inmates lived. He defined a total institution as "a place of residence and work where a large number of like-situated individuals, cut off from wider society for an appreciable period of time, together lead an enclosed, formally administered round of life" (1961:xiii). Havenwood is a total institution that housed like-minded residents (psychiatrically disordered youth). It cuts them off from wider society (including parents, schools, and everyday youth activities for an average of 18 months), and organizes life around a variety of treatment paradigms (I discuss these in chapter 2).

Within total institutional life, additional therapeutic practices are used to procure change. In his work with sexual offenders in a prison therapeutic ward, James Waldram (2012) analyzes the use of group therapy sessions as important events for therapeutic intervention. Waldram illustrates how inmates learn to tell their stories of sexual violence in new ways through and within group therapy sessions. At Havenwood, milieu treatment, individual therapy, group therapy, psychotropic medication use, and behavior management are all used together to cultivate change. In this book, I focus on the use of behavior management techniques, physical interventions (restraints and confinements), group therapy, and milieu treatment as important therapeutic practices.

When I went to Havenwood, I wanted to study the system, the ways in which young people were subjected to State-level intervention, and the work of psychiatric disciplinary techniques by actually living in the institution. However, what I came to see while living there was an interesting and very powerful "give" in the structure. In her book on maximum security prisons, Lorna Rhodes (2004) concludes her ethnography with how people engaged in prison work "struggle out" what it means to work and live in such a place. Correction offices and prisoners struggle to bring into focus the humanness of the work and of the prisoner, unsettling the terrain of the rigid and hermetically sealed institution. Rhodes illustrates how small, intimate, everyday practices such as tier walks and conversations about needs might be a small "give in the system" of prison life (2004:201). What emerged during my 18 months of living at Havenwood was the pervasiveness of such a "give." Therefore, this book focuses less on the rigid, formal, ritual-like processes of therapeutic intervention; it brings into sharp focus the "give" in the structured lives of those living and working in psychiatric custody.

This "give" settled on the intimate work and relationships between those who live at Havenwood and those who work in the cottages or living units. Therefore, my analysis is what Cheryl Mattingly (2010) has identified as a focus on the dramas between people engaged in important healing work within biomedical contexts in the United States, especially with African Americans. Mattingly (2010) and Mattingly and Lawlor (2001) show that healing and transformation are often not quite what they are expected to be, that dominant biomedical narratives of healing do not quite get at the lived experiences of those engaged in the long, fraught process of living with chronic and debilitating illness. Rather, Mattingly argues that the dramatic, everyday experiences of people with chronic illness challenge the hegemony of biomedically structured accounts by "highlighting the unfinished, idiosyncratic, unpredictable, suspenseful qualities of life" and healing (2010:44). Healing is fragile and unpredictable and only through an analysis of the phenomenology of healing can we actually understand this (Mattingly and Lawlor 2001). I wish to highlight the unpredictable, intimate, and phenomenological aspects of life and "really changing" meant for the youth of Havenwood. Therefore, in this book, I hone in on the phenomenological experiences of transformation that occur due to intimate, fragile, and loving relationships that emerge between the young men who live at Havenwood (and in particular, one cottage that I call Steele) and the adult men who work with them every day of their confined lives.

"It's all about the relationship"

Throughout my time at Havenwood, I was told that a significant cause of change was what many people called "the relationship." Many line staff and therapists would tell me, "Katie, it's all about the relationship." As I lived at and studied the therapeutic elements of Havenwood, I came to realize that it was precisely this "relationship" or Derrick's "staff and peers" that truly mattered to the youth. However, I soon realized that "the relationship" or "staff and peers" were just about as murky a local concept as "the black box." As I asked my interlocutors what they meant by "the relationship," they struggled to pin it down. I would come to agree that it was this "relationship," or what I identify as intersubjectivity, that allowed for this fragile, suspenseful self-transformation.

Michael Jackson argues for the "value of intersubjectivity for ethnographic analysis" because by investigating what happens "between people," we come to see a world of "inter-experience, inter-action, and inter-locution" (1998:3). An effort to understand what it means for people to be in the world, in the phenomenological sense, we have to think about how they are in the world *with others*. Often, anthropology's focus on the self or subjectivity comes from isolated moments "artificially isolated from the flux of 'intersubjective' life" (Jackson 1998:6). While the focus on the self is important, so are the contours of intersubjective life. Douglas Hollan and Jason Throop flesh out Jackson's articulation of intersubjectivity. They argue that intersubjectivity is "held to entail processes that serve as the phenomenological and biological grounded basis for the more complex emotional, embodied, and cognitive work that is implicated in approximating the subjective experience of another from a quasi-first-person perspective" (Hollan and Throop 2008:386–387). Intersubjectivity is about orienting toward other subjects, especially by approximating one another's complex emotional, cognitive, and embodied experiences.

The intimate knowledge of how subjects orient toward and with others can tell us about broader social projects, such as institutional psychiatric healing (Jackson 1998). Derrick tells us that he learns to get along with people and to do work that does not require guns or drugs from his relationships with others, namely, his "staff" and "peers." In a total institution that contains all of life under the umbrella of psychiatric treatment and therapeutic practices, Derrick does not name a form of therapy from which he learns to change, nor does he only speak in a psychiatric or therapeutic register.[16] Rather, he indexes the institutional relationships he has with individuals—his staff and peers. It will become clear, however, that what initially looks like institutional relationships are in fact complex relationships—therapeutic and then some—built among the youth and adults of Havenwood. It is the intimate relationships that matter in the project of self-transformation and psychiatric healing. The striving for treatment success at Havenwood, it turned out, hinged on love.

On Love

Anthropology tells us that love can be many things.[17] It can be a feeling, a practice, or an interpretive framework. Love is often associated with intimacy, romance, and sexual relationships.[18] It has been identified with an "emotional community" between mothers and children, or a "resonance" that occurs between people.[19] It is articulated as ways in which war-injured soldiers heal or people in Sierra Leone made sense of life during years of war.[20] Richard Shweder (1995) illustrates that love, and other emotions, are feelings in the body that become salient when interpreted using a framework of emotion.

Love is what emerged as an interpretive framework of interaction at Havenwood. I will illustrate how this emic love plays out during the treatment process. Throughout this book, we hear residents talk about how and why important lessons are taught, and how youth come to change—staff and peers have love for one another. Love was the lynchpin in the intersubjective, fragile transformation for the youth I studied.

At Havenwood, love is something people have for someone else. It defines the reasons for intimate relationships, and it is why people cultivate new ways of being. Love at Havenwood is inherently intersubjective, and it is evinced in the things that people do and feel for one another. In addition, love emerged in my analysis of transformation, beyond just the emic framework used by the young men.

In addition to being a practice, a feeling, and an interpretive framework, Jarrett Zigon finds that love "stands as the ethical demand central to projects of transformation and remaking moral subjectivity" (2013:203–204). Zigon (2013) focuses on the romantic relationship between two former rehabilitants and how this romantic relationship, or love, helps him understand singular moral experiences. This existential way of being in the world, romantically with others, is what allows his interlocutors to change toward an ethical subjectivity. In much the same way, the young men of Havenwood work toward self-transformation. Young men come to "buy in" to their treatment and to do the work of change because other men—friends, mentors, and quasi-kin—have love for them. However, I will argue that the transformation is not easily linked to ethical subjectivity. Rather than an ethical subjectivity, I will argue that a hip hop-therapeutic subjectivity is the subjectivity cultivated through loving relationships and psychiatric custody.[21] I will make this argument, because love is not as much an ethical demand as it is a balm and politicized force against racism, prejudice, and injustice.

Hip Hop and Black Men[22]

As I briefly illustrated with Derrick's interview earlier and what will become more apparent throughout this book is that hip hop is integrated into the practice of therapeutic intervention in psychiatric custody at Havenwood. I use hip hop the way that hip hop and African American Studies scholar Imani Perry defines it: "Hip hop is an iteration of black language, black music, black style, and black youth culture…overwhelmingly and fundamentally black American" (2004:2). As Perry articulates, hip hop is its own iteration of language, style, music, and culture within African American culture.[23] She argues that hip hop is Black American because of four important characteristics:

(1) its primary language is African American Vernacular English (AAVE);

(2) it has a political location in society distinctly ascribed to black people, music, and cultural forms;
(3) it is derived from black American oral culture; and
(4) it is derived from black American music traditions.

(2004:10)[24]

To identify hip hop as Black American is somewhat controversial, due to hip hop's multiracial origins and contemporary global popularity (which I address in chapter 1).[25] However, I draw from Perry's focus on hip hop as a current cultural form, which, she states, exists "within black American political and cultural frameworks" (2004:10).

While music is the point of origin, hip hop has transcended music and has become meaningful as a culture, style, nation, and generation (Chang 2005; Forman 2012; Kitwana 2002; Neal 1999; Perry 2004; Rose 1994, 2008). The culture and nation include the music, but also the political context that has emerged around the music (Neal 1999; Rose 1994). Hip hop even has its own language according to linguist H. Samy Alim (2006). Furthermore, hip hop includes material artifacts. Hip hop is associated with branded items including shoes, clothing, alcoholic beverage, soft drinks, cars, jewelry, and so on. Therefore, hip hop is more than just rapping, it is a "national youth culture with clothing, speech, and ideological positioning" (Perry 2004:23). While hip hop has become commercialized and mainstream on the one hand, and global and multicultural on the other, the *voices* of hip hop are still "overwhelmingly young, Black, and male" (Perry 2008:166). Therefore, for the youth of Havenwood hip hop provides a sense of voice and agency in psychiatric custody. I will illustrate how this plays out in terms of group therapy session, dress style, therapeutic expression, and interpersonal interactions.

However, the youth of Havenwood must negotiate the legitimacy of hip hop, especially in more constrained psychiatric events such as individual therapy (see chapter 3). In some instances therapists and psychiatric frameworks would not recognize or value hip hop as a legitimately meaningful or positive cultural framework for the youth of Havenwood. I believe this is because of hip hop's negative image in mainstream America.

While scholars argue that hip hop "presents us with a complex masculinity" (Perry 2004:128; see also Neal 2013), mainstream hip hop is dominated by images of young Black men as criminal, violent, individualistic, and misogynistic with over-the-top consumption practices. Therefore, young Black men who practice hip hop are easily read as social problems or as villains (Du Bois 2005[1903]; Kitwana 2002; Neal 2013; Van Deburg 2004).

Often punitive measures are taken in order to address this "problem." These punitive measures play out "in every institutional arena from public education, the labor force, and health care (particularly mental health) to, most tragically, the criminal justice system, something that many of us were reminded of with the shooting death of Trayvon Martin" (Neal 2013:5). In chapter 1, I discuss how a disproportionate number of young Black men are psychiatrically confined, supporting scholars who argue that they are often stereotyped as a "problem" (Neal 2013; Van Deburg 2004). I am not suggesting that all youth in psychiatric custody are sent there because of racist stereotypes. Nor am I suggesting that many Black youth do not suffer from mental health issues, or that they do not need treatment. However, it is clear that the *institutionalization rate* of Black youth in psychiatric custody (rather than outpatient treatment) is very high, especially as compared to other racial groups (I will come back to this in chapter 1). Black youth are identified as villains or problems to be contained. Into this containment the young Black men bring with them the Black youth culture that had them identified as needing containment to begin with—hip hop.

While hip hop is identified in the mainstream using caricatures of Black men, hip hop as a cultural practice is actually a method by which Black youth challenge these caricatures, precisely the "hegemonic structures of understanding and meaning propagated by the dominant culture of white supremacy" (Perry 2004:45). Hip hop "nourishes" disenfranchised young Black men by offering membership in a community, as well as by "offering a counter-hegemonic authority and subjectivity to the force of white supremacy in American culture" (Perry 2004:44). In fact, African American youth "take up hip-hop's expressive forms in order to challenge structural authority, articulate their own agency, and define their identities in locally meaningful ways" (Forman 2012:4–5). In the spirit of counter hip hop culture, young Black men at Havenwood do not fully accept that they are "problems," despite the fact that they are institutionalized because of this reading of them. Rather they use hip hop: (1) as an African American cultural form, to give shape to daily life at Havenwood; and (2) as a counterhegemonic practice and subjectivity, to challenge the power of psychiatry's labels and custodial healing frameworks.

Preliminary Conclusions

The main thread of this book is to illustrate how African American men transform in psychiatric custody. In many ways these youth change according to the standards set by the institution: they learn to share feelings, to talk in group therapy, to not behave dangerously, and to make better choices. However, in many ways they add to these therapeutic definitions of treatment progress and success using hip hop ways of being in the world, which include *mad love* and *doing you*.[26] I like to call these additions to psychiatric practice a form of "sampling." Sampling in hip hop music is the practice of taking a portion of one song and reusing it in another. It is a way to pay homage and illustrate cultural literacy; it is an invocation of another voice to help one best articulate him or herself (Rose 1994). Let me extend this metaphor. The original track at Havenwood is psychiatry and mainstream ideals of therapeutic transformation and American citizenship. This track is made more meaningful to the young Black men who engage with it through hip hop sampling, breaks into the original track. This sampling, which includes hip hop uniforms, keepin' it real group therapy sessions, a way of life in milieu treatment defined as "kickin' it," and using African American registers to define success (*do you*) and healing processes (*mad love*), is the integration of distinctly Black cultural practices, specifically hip hop, within psychiatric custody. What results is a new track, a hip hop-therapeutic track. This track is very different than the original psychiatric custody or hip hop tracks.

The hip hop-therapeutic track is revealed through and the result of various forms of practice—language use, clothing style, and the dramatization of events (Mattingly 2010). The sampling of hip hop was not an explicit topic of conversation or official treatment model. Never did anyone say, "Here is where we will integrate hip hop into a group therapy session."[27] It happened because hip hop is a way of life for many of the young and adult African American men who live and work at Havenwood. Of course, not all of the African American men can be identified as hip hoppers. That would be an oversimplification of complex African American manhood and the power of hip hop. However, hip hop is a significant element of African American culture in contemporary America, especially for urban youth and men, and it was meaningful at Havenwood and in living units such as Steele Cottage, which we will come to know intimately in this book.

Through the use of hip hop, I believe a subtle and yet unambiguous critique of psychiatry and custodial psychiatry is being mobilized.

It is a counterhegemonic approach mixing hip hop with the power of psychiatry, especially in a custodial institution. The State has institutionalized the bodies of these Black youth in psychiatric custody, and therapeutic discourses are used at Havenwood to discipline the emotions, minds, and behaviors of these youth to make them "productive citizens." However, as we will see, this is not the main therapeutic and transformative focus of the men and boys I studied. Instead, the African American boys and men use hip hop as a counterhegemonic authority and subjectivity in opposition to the white supremacy of unequal incarceration practices (Alexander 2010; Puzzanchera, Adams, and Hockenberry 2012) and psychiatric ideologies (Gaines 1992; Guthrie 2003; Metzl 2009). Hip hop, as used at Havenwood, is an expansive and deep iteration of Black youth culture that provides a counterhegemonic experience to the oppressive white supremacy power found in the form of State psychiatric custody and American social life, more broadly. African American youth integrate hip hop with psychiatry in an effort to emerge from custody transformed, but also spiritually, subjectively, and culturally intact.

Ethnography in Psychiatric Custody; Ethnography with Confined Black Men

Few researchers, Waldram states, have ever "meaningfully ventured," especially ethnographically, into sites of therapeutic intervention, prisons, or psychiatric custody and asked to hear the stories and experience quotidian life with these socially abjected groups of people (2013:xi). This ethnography will hopefully contribute to our understanding of life within these kinds of total institutional spaces, and with the people who live their lives out in them. I agree with Waldram's assertion that anthropology and ethnography have something very important to say, if we take the time to venture in.

In August 2005 I met with the vice president of Public Relations at Havenwood for the first time. I arranged a meeting with him to discuss anthropology and what I was thinking about for field research. I gave him a formal letter of introduction and research proposal. He informed me that the president was interested in "thinking outside of the box" and would probably "seriously consider" my request to do ethnographic research at Havenwood. He then gave me a tour of the campus. I saw the insides of the dining hall, the gym, and the chapel, with an old pipe organ, stained glass windows, and mahogany pews and altar. We toured the school and one of the cottages. As he walked me to my car, he told me that he would present my documents to the president. He would be in touch.

I returned two weeks later and met with the president. She listened to my proposal and my other fieldwork experiences with orphans in Rwanda and child soldiers in Uganda and was particularly interested in my work. She wanted to be as helpful as possible. We vowed to keep in touch. The president would ask around to see what others thought of my research idea, while I would work on getting my external funding proposals together. My third visit, months later, included another meeting with the president and the vice president of Residential Services. The president asked the vice president if he had any problems with me conducting the research. He simply stated, "No." I received a letter of support signed by the president and the board of trustees.

After I received this letter of support, I went about the 8-month process of securing institutional review board clearances from my home university, the state where I conducted the research's Department of Family and Children Services, and procuring a Certificate of Confidentiality from the National Institute of Child Health and Human Development.[28] For formal interviews, the Department of Family and Children Services required that I get the Guardianship Administrator approval for all foster care children.[29] Once I received the signed consent form in the mail, I could ask the youth to sit down with me for a recorded interview. When I received all of these clearances in August 2006, I moved to Havenwood's campus, into a second-story room in a quaint cottage that housed therapy offices.

Early in my research, I was referred to as "the nosey lady who lived in the room with the red curtains." Like other anthropologists, my status as an outsider changed over time. At Havenwood these transitions were marked by nicknames. I went from "the nosey lady who lives in the room with the red curtains" to "the reporter" to "Lily White" to "Li'l Bit." It was the process of field research and living at Havenwood that allowed for me to make these transitions. These transitions allow me to tell the story that unfolds here.

I observed and participated in a variety of activities at Havenwood. I observed countless hours of meetings to discuss admittance, treatment progress, clinical dilemmas, and the overall functioning of the institution. I took detailed, verbatim notes during these meetings. I was also trained like any line staff member, which included two full weeks at the beginning of my research and on every other Wednesday morning for the first three months. I also participated in the Therapeutic Crisis Intervention (TCI) training, which spanned the course of four full days and then one-day trainings every six months. I attended clinical in-services on Fridays, as part of the training for new therapists. I observed weekly supervisor meetings and quarterly administration meetings. I had carte blanche access to the formal operations of Havenwood.

In addition to spending many daytime hours in meetings, I also spent time at the school. I observed a number of classrooms and school activities. I ended up tutoring Lamar, Mark, and Jonathon during the school day, and would observe their classrooms before and after the tutoring session. I observed physical education classes, library time, and other academic instruction. I attended on-campus sporting events and periodically traveled with the teams to away games, as Havenwood was part of a residential treatment center league in the area. I helped scare children during Halloween, in the haunted house, cheered on teams in the annual Havenwood Summer Olympics, and attended the Valentine's Day Dance, graduation, and various music recitals.

After school hours and at the end of a day filled with observing meetings, I would observe life in the cottages. I spent time in every cottage, however, I focused on Steele Cottage, a cottage for teenage boys that I will discuss at length later. I was invited to birthday parties across the campus, observed intercottage therapeutic recreation, and even traveled with six of the nine cottages to off-campus events. We went to the movies, the mall, the skating rink, college basketball games, on camping trips, and even worked on a Habitat for Humanity construction project. I met family members of many residents, if they visited campus. I participated in a wide range of cottage activities.

I was able to have the diverse experience of life at Havenwood because I lived there. For 18 months, I called a small red-curtained room on the second floor of a cottage-like building home. I ate the vast majority of my meals at the dining hall, slept on a plastic covered mattress (used by psychiatric institutions because people might soil the beds), and celebrated my holidays and birthday there. For the first 30 days I did not leave campus, which is standard procedure for all new residents. After this, I usually traveled by Havenwood van with the staff and residents. I tried my best to live as close to the life of a resident as possible.[30]

In addition to the tasks of data collection and ethnographic research, building relationships with people was very important. This is true for anthropological fieldwork in general. However, I found that research in psychiatric custody was unique for two reasons.

First, I observed and analyzed the daily life and work of people observing and analyzing people. While I was looking for dynamics of culture, power, history, and individual experience, people wanted to know what was wrong with the youth, how they were bonding with others, what their motivations were, and how they were changing. Never before could I ask the anthropological "why" with the expectation that I would receive well thought-through answers from almost everyone.

Of course this analytical gaze was turned toward me as well. People wanted to know why I would suspend my "real life" to live at Havenwood, and for no pay! This bizarre choice, in their minds, became the topic of much speculation, gossip, and an "intervention."

My intervention is what I identify as the second unique part of my research in psychiatric custody with African American men. Research with or on African American populations has a problematic, racist history. Most people are familiar with the Tuskegee Syphilis Study, however African Americans have been unwitting subjects of medical experiments and research studies for centuries (Washington 2006). A few of the men at Steele Cottage, who I ended up talking to about these subjects, were suspicious of my research. And it took them time to confront me directly about my motivations. I did, after all, have the consent of the president. Finally, one day, Arthur, an African American staff member at Steele Cottage, decided that if I was going to hang around Steele he wanted a say in what I was learning and how I was thinking. And if I was going to do research at Steele Cottage then I had better prove my worth.

Therefore, as a white woman who kept coming back to Steele Cottage to study life there, it was important that we dig really deep into racial inequality, white supremacy, and the lived realities of being a Black man in America. It is argued that intimate interracial relationships are difficult in the United States because of the vastly different belief systems and experiences of racism.[31] I believe intimate interracial *research* relationships are also very difficult, due to the historical medical research exploitation of African Americans, and current racial inequalities that shape all kinds of institutions. Therefore, Arthur decided that my "intervention" was to talk at length and in depth about racism, color-blind ideology, and the chasms between white and Black Americans. Arthur named me "Lily White" during this stage of intense discussion and vetting. I had to prove that I was not going to be another white person coming in and taking from Black men. I had to prove that I could recognize my white privilege and listen to noncolor-blind and antiwhite conversations. I was observed for racist tendencies and micro-aggressions. The chasm between mainstream white, middle-class America and the young, poor, institutionalized Black boys of Steele and all youth at Havenwood was profound, I was told, and I needed to prove I could understand this. We had to talk openly about racism and its affects, and the unrealistic aspects of psychiatric ideology, because these things mattered in the lives of African Americans. As we talked my nickname eventually changed to "Li'l Bit."

Without this intervention, I never would have earned access into the intimate world of Steele Cottage or made the kinds of relationships I did there. These conversations about race in America have had profound reverberations in my life. Not only did they allow me access to the life that is revealed in this book, but they profoundly shaped my analytical understanding of some of the ways in which race operates in the United States. Without this intervention, the story presented here could not have been told, at least not by me.

Outline of the Book

Friendship, Love, and Hip Hop is organized into three parts. In Part I I focus on contexts. In chapter 1, "Histories and Social Contexts," I provide a general context and historical trajectory for children's institutions in the United States. I illustrate how institutionalizing youth shifted from religious and moral reform to psychiatry and mental illness rehabilitation. I discuss how psychoanalysis, milieu treatment, and residential treatment emerged in large part due to shifts in psychiatric knowledge. I also provide a historical and cultural context for how race, either explicitly or implicitly, informs incarceration, psychiatry, and psychiatric custody in the United States. Chapter 1 also introduces the history and context of hip hop as it is a cultural practice currently in conversation with psychiatric custody and treatment practice at Havenwood. I also include historical information about Havenwood using local texts, as it was a "junior municipality" established in 1897, and has weathered the historical shifts in institutions and therapeutic treatment in the United States.

Chapter 2, "The Ethnographic Setting," builds on this historical context and discussion of treatment paradigms by honing in on my ethnographic setting. In this chapter I describe the paradigms at Havenwood used to organize life and treatment there. These paradigms include psychiatric diagnosis and psychotropic medication use, therapeutic milieu logic, behavior modification practices, crisis intervention strategies, self-esteem cultivation, and religious traditions. I also use demographic information and case file social histories to give a general description of those who comes to live at Havenwood and also describe the professional roles of the adults who work there. I also distinguish between Havenwood and Steele Cottage, a living unit I chose to focus on during ethnographic research. Chapter 2 includes an ethnographic vignette from an Intake Meeting, to illustrate how youth are talked about as they are admitted to the treatment facility.

Part II is a description and analysis of life at Havenwood, often focusing on Steele Cottage. Chapter 3, "Institutional Living," describes the total institutional context of Havenwood. Using documents from Havenwood and ethnographic vignettes, I illustrate how life is organized under a grand plan and how minute behaviors are regulate to achieve the goal of the institution. I also discuss how staff members are trained as part of the total institutional setting, as they are cultivated to be technologies of government implementing the treatment paradigms. I conclude this chapter with a discussion of the "give" in the system and how hip hop is sampled into daily life at Havenwood.

In chapter 4, "*Crazy Shit*," I describe crisis events and the extremely unusual behavior that occurs at Havenwood. First, I situate the crisis events in context at Havenwood, specifically how they are defined, documented, and regulated. I then discuss how people make meaning of crisis and the extremely unusual behavior that occurs at Havenwood. I argue that empathy and compassion emerge as important ways in which people interacted in these circumstances. Compassion and empathy help to disarticulate the moral judgment often linked to extremely unusual behavior. This chapter illustrates how this unusual behavior both makes up and unmakes life at the psychiatric institution, and how the compassionate responses makes up life there as well. I conclude with a discussion of how this form of intimate violence is compared with other forms of violence found in the noninstitutional and "out-there" lives of the residents.

Chapter 5, "A Keepin' It Real Group," describes group therapy as a therapeutic ritual practice in psychiatric custody. I also discuss how group sessions become more spontaneous in many instances, what I describe as sincerity in psychiatric custody. In particular, I analyze the ways that young Black men relate to one another in these therapeutic events. This chapter illustrates how the youth use the group therapy session as a therapeutic device and a means by which important relationships can be established and nurtured. I also illustrate how racial sincerity is also part of the therapeutic practice of group therapy as young men integrate hip hop into formal treatment practice, by asking for "keepin' it real groups."

Chapter 6, "*Kickin' It*," investigates the role of friendship in psychiatric custody. During times of *kickin' it*, the men and woman of Steele build on the therapeutic relationships, adding elements of friendship and mentoring relationships. These kinds of relationships are contrary to other research and literature on young, urban, poor, Black men or in residential treatment cottage life. Friendships are relationships often missing from anthropological investigations but they were particularly important for the socially ajbected and disarticulated young men of Steele. It is within these friendships that love develops.

Chapter 7, "Becoming Good Men," focuses on how gender is significant in the how young men talk about and engage in therapeutic work to become what they identify as good men. The masculinities cultivated within intimate relationships among young and adult men include an integration of hip hop and therapeutic logic. These masculinities are cultivated as part of the transformation process within intimate relationships among the young and adult men of Steele Cottage. I offer a way of thinking about African American masculinities in ways that have often been neglected.

Part III is a two-part conclusion where I provide an analysis of the subjects and power at Havenwood. Chapter 8, "A Hip Hop-Therapeutic Subjectivity," is a discussion of the subjectivity that is cultivated and emerges through important relationships built and daily life lived in psychiatric custody. Rather than learning to only follow formal therapeutic models and frameworks of treatment success, the youth of Havenwood, particularly at Steele Cottage, integrate hip hop culture into their therapeutic process. I argue that a new subjectivity is formed through the work of treatment and the relationships among these African American men, which is neither hip hop nor therapeutic alone. This is the fragile healing or transformation cultivated at Steele and Havenwood.

Chapter 9, "Mad Love: Theorizing and Politicizing Transformation," is my concluding analysis of *how* young Black men come to change in psychiatric custody. I argue that love is more than just an emic framework for what happens in treatment. I argue that love is both a power and a politicized force. Love is what changes these young Black men; it is what cultivates the hip hop-therapeutic subjectivity. It is also a balm to racism, prejudice, and injustice that bear down on young Black men in America, particularly those who have been socially abjected and institutionalized.

Part I
Contexts

Chapter 1
Histories and Social Contexts

Havenwood was founded in 1897 as a summer camp for six poor urban white boys. In the early part of the twentieth century, Havenwood's population grew and it became "junior municipality for misfit and unwanted children,"[1] a permanent, residence for the founding couple and urban boys. At this time Havenwood was a "boys' home" and organized life using Christian doctrine. Over the course of the twentieth century, following trends in institutional living, and psychology and psychiatry in the United States, Havenwood shifted its focus from being a boys' home that taught discipline and obedience to a therapeutic milieu designed to meet the emotional, cognitive, and psychological needs of society's troubled youth. In this chapter, I provide a general context and historical trajectory for children's institutions in the United States, illustrating how and when frameworks shifted from religious and moral reform to psychiatry and mental illness rehabilitation. Havenwood has been in existence during these phases, reinventing itself along the way. I also provide a historical and cultural context for how race, either explicitly or implicitly, informs incarceration, psychiatry, and psychiatric custody in the United States. I also introduce a history and the context of hip hop, which emerged as a meaningful cultural practice at Havenwood. This chapter is organized thematically, rather than chronologically, as I braid these histories together to illustrate how they have come to shape psychiatric custody in the United States. These histories are not meant to be exhaustive, and I direct readers to the appropriate literature for further reading.

American Children's Institutions

The construction of institutions in the United States occurred in a very particular historical moment. Historian David Rothman states that, beginning in the 1820s, the United States "all at once erect[ed] penitentiaries for the criminal, asylums for the insane, almshouses for the poor, orphan asylums for homeless children, and reformatories for delinquents" (1971: xiii). Following the Revolutionary War, the United States quadrupled in size and the economy was rapidly developing. The United States was undergoing a time of great social change. Construction of institutions was a "vigorous attempt to promote the stability of the society at a moment when traditional ideas and practices appeared outmoded, constricted, and ineffective. The almshouse and the orphan asylum, the penitentiary, the reformatory, and the insane asylum all represented an effort to insure the cohesion of the community in new and changing circumstance" (Rothman 1971:xviii). Asylums, in particular, fulfilled two purposes: rehabilitate inmates and, by virtue of its successes with individuals, set an example of correct and right action for the broader society. This included children's asylums.

In the 1830s and 1840s, there were 50 private orphan asylums operating in New York, Boston, Philadelphia, Maine, Richmond Virginia, Mobile Alabama, Cincinnati, and Chicago (Rothman 1971:207). By the 1860s, there were 200 orphan asylums that housed young people in the United States (Hasci 1997). Reformatories, institutions to house juvenile delinquents rather than orphans, were also established during this time. However, while the distinction between the two kinds of institutions was made in name, in practice they housed similar populations. The children in these institutions were "the abject, the vagrant, the delinquent, the child of poverty-stricken or intemperate parents" (Rothman 1971:209). Institutions housing socially abjected Americans became part of the fabric of social life (Courtney and Hughes-Heuring 2009). Havenwood was established in these circumstances, as a "junior municipality for misfit and unwanted children."

An anticruelty movement in the United States helped support the construction and maintenance of institutions to house children (Hasci 1997). In the late 1800s, Henry Bergh, the leader of the American Society for the Prevention of Cruelty to Animals, led the movement to found the New York Society for the Prevention of Cruelty to Children. This society raised awareness of child abuse and neglect (Courtney and Hughes-Heuring 2009). The children found to be maltreated were removed from their homes and placed in institutions for refuge and care. These institutions received funds from city councils, state legislatures, and philanthropic charities.

In 1909, President Theodore Roosevelt convened the first White House Conference on the Care of Dependent Children (Hasci 1997).

The result of this conference was a commitment by the nation-state to intervene in the lives of abused and neglected children through a robust Child Welfare League of America. The state declared a commitment to keeping children in homes rather than in institutions. However, rather than being closed down, institutions reinvented themselves and created more "home-like" atmospheres. They began calling themselves "homes," or "schools," and "cottages" were erected as living quarters (Courtney and Hughes-Heuring 2009). The founders of Havenwood made every effort to recreate a home-like environment there. This included cottage living, where a "cottage mother" would care for the young men. This woman was responsible for mothering, counseling, disciplining, and mending clothes for the boys in her cottage.

During the nineteenth century and in early part of the twentieth, Christian doctrine and religious practice informed the work of children's institutions.[2] At the time, the goal of life in an institution was the cultivation of a healthy, moral constitution (Rothman 1971). Rothman states that the founders of orphanages and houses of refuge and reform feared "that anyone not carefully and diligently trained to cope with the open, free-wheeling, and disordered life of the community would fall victim to vice and crime" (1971:210). Because of these fears, the houses of refuge and reformatories not only provided shelter, they disciplined and reformed the youth therein. The establishment and enforcement of a rigorous and orderly daily routine would result in a healthy moral constitution and absolute respect for authority. This routine was thought to mold youth into decent, educated, God-fearing citizens (Courtney and Hughes-Heuring 2009; Rothman 1971). Institutions not only sheltered children, but they used Christian ideology as a framework of social control.

In the early part of the twentieth century, Havenwood focused on teaching obedience and discipline to the young boys who lived there. Young men were taken out of their immediate surroundings in the nearby city at the first warning of delinquent behavior. According to Havenwood's historical texts, obedience and discipline were instilled in four ways: prayer, work, exercise, and cottage living.

Havenwood was built on Christian doctrine. A chapel was constructed on site and religious services were held every morning. Bells rang every evening as a call to prayer. Obedience and discipline were also instilled through the rigorous farm work required at Havenwood. Havenwood had its own vegetable garden, hay fields, a chicken house, cows, and a pig farm. Young men raised and grew their own food. This work also provided unpaid community service, an important aspect of becoming a member of a community according to Havenwood's founder.

In addition to prayer and farm activity, calisthenics and physical activity were part of daily life at Havenwood. These activities were thought to build posture and discipline. It was argued that through physical coordination, a skill thought to be lacking in the young men before they arrived at Havenwood, a young man would learn confidence. This confidence would help him "on his way to becoming an important member of society." The young men would perform these calisthenics and "statuesque exercises" in front of audiences, visitors, and inspectors as "proof" of Havenwood's "good work."

Concurrently, laws were established that influenced the management of young American citizens. By 1919, there were 39 states that had some sort of mother pension law, which provided state funds allowing "deserving" mothers to be able to care for their children at home (Ashby 1997; Courtney and Hughes-Heuring 2009). Many child advocates at the time pushed for home foster care rather than institutional care. In 1935, the United States federal government created Aid to Dependent Children as Title IV of the Social Security Act. This Act meant that monetary aid was given directly to needy families rather than to institutions (Courtney and Hughes-Heuring 2009:180). By the 1940s and late 1950s, this Act shifted the trend away from institutional care as more children were sent to live in foster families than in institutions. With fewer children to live in them, the number of institutions dramatically declined.

Despite the decline some institutions survived. They shifted their focus from orphanages or "junior municipalities for misfit and unwanted children" to "residential treatment centers for children and youth with emotional, behavioral, or psychological disorders" (Courtney and Hughes-Heuring 2009:180). Psychological theories of child development and the treatment of psychopathology within therapeutic milieus coincided with these changes. I return to this phenomenon later in the chapter, here I just wish to flag how milieu therapy fits into the time frame of children's institutions in the United States. The only reference to Havenwood as an institution in the historical academic literature states that Havenwood was one of the children's institutions in the United States that redefined itself as an agency devoted to the mental health of children. This is obvious as Havenwood is still functioning as a child mental health center today.

The 1940s through to the 1960s saw the application of psychological theories into residential treatment centers (see later in the chapter). In 1935, August Aichhorn was recognized as the first to use psychoanalysis with delinquent youth living in state institutions. In the 1940s other institutions, including those in Pennsylvania, Ohio, Illinois, and New York, explicitly reorganized themselves, making explicit the psychiatric direction of the institution, specifically with the emphasis on individual psychotherapy (Robinson, Gardner, Greenwood, Hagan, and Richmond 1957). In the 1940s, the focus of child inpatient psychiatric care was the use of individual therapy for children with emotional disorders, who could not be treated in outpatient settings. It was in the 1940s that the relationship between institutional living and psychiatric treatment became solidified. In the 1950s and 1960s another shift occurred as individual therapy gave way to milieu therapy. During this time, much was written on the subject of inpatient psychiatric care for children. Not only were psychiatrists interested in the healing process of children due to the latest psychiatric practices (see e.g., Barker 1974; Bettelheim 1950; Greenwood 1955; Reid and Hagan 1952; Robinson et al. 1957), but sociologists were interested in the social phenomena of institutional living as well (see e.g., Goffman 1961; Polsky 1962/1977; Polsky, Claster, and Goldberg 1968; Polsky, Claster, and Goldberg 1970).

Despite the robust connection between the growing field of psychiatry and institutional living, the 1970s saw a dramatic decline in the number of children sent to live in institutions through what was known as the "permanency planning movement." The permanency planning movement asks "child welfare agencies [to make] every effort to assist families before placing children in out-of-home care and to actively plan to find children permanent homes as quickly as possible" (Courtney and Hughes-Heuring 2009:181). The goal of this movement was to try and find the least restrictive environment for children—a home rather than an institution. This drive for noninstitutional living was in tandem with the adult deinstitutionalization movement during the same time period (Brodwin 2013; Estroff 1981).

Despite the various movements, institutions for young people did not dissolve. The Adoption Assistance and Child Welfare Act of 1980 had a hand in keeping psychiatric institutions viable for the treatment of young people. This Act created a reimbursement program for states that removed poor children from their families and placed them in alternative forms of living. States were not reimbursed for home services. It was more cost effective for states to remove poor children from their homes, than to assist the family with services (Courtney and Hughes-Heuring 2009).

By the end of the 1970s and in the early 1980s, the Child Welfare League of America had established standards for residential treatment settings, specifically stating the kinds of therapeutic services that should be offered in institutionalized psychiatric treatment.[3] Today, residential treatment centers are supposed to include a mix of services for children and families, "including mental health services, health and nutritional care, recreation, education, independent living skills training, family reunification services, and after care" (Courtney and Hughes-Heuring 2009:183). As we will see in chapter 2, Havenwood provides these kinds of services.

In 2012, the United States Child Welfare System served 399,546 American youth, down over 60,000 from when I conducted my research in 2006–2008. According to the 2012 Adoption and Foster Care Analysis and Reporting System (AFCARS) 9 percent of these 400,000 youth lived in institutions, around 36,000 children (US Department of Health and Human Services 2013). In addition to foster care youth living in institutions, the juvenile justice system sends young people to residential treatment. According to a nationwide juvenile justice report 79,165 youth live in residential institutions (US Department of Justice 2013). This census does not include a tally of youth in facilities exclusive to substance abuse, mental health treatment, or abused and neglected youth (US Department of Justice 2013). Therefore, a conservative estimate of American children in residential treatment would be between 90,000 and 100,000 annually. Almost 200 youth lived at Havenwood in 2006.

With the shift to treatment, the work of reformatories, orphanages, and residential treatment centers became focused on the emotional, social, and cognitive development of children (Courtney and Hughes-Heuring 2009). Children could no longer just be housed in these institutions. Instead, their development—emotional, cognitive, and social—required attention and direction.

Psychoanalysis, Milieu Therapy, and Residential Treatment[4]

In the 1920s, the United States saw the direct application of psychological theories to residential institutions for children (Barker 1974). The earliest inpatient treatment programs for children were for the treatment of aftereffects of encephalitis. However, very quickly hospitals and children's institutions broadened their scope to apply the psychiatric theories of the day to institutionalized populations (Barker 1974). In the 1920s, psychiatric practice focused on individual psychotherapy, therefore, psychotherapy was implemented in the institutional setting. The individual therapy session was the designated space for "*therapeutic* treatment" within institutions (Cotton 1993:4). In addition to psychiatry's focus on psychotherapy, by the 1930s psychiatrists understood that children were different from adults, requiring different forms of treatment focusing on the developmental process (Robinson et al. 1957). Applying these principles to institutional living for children, August Aichhorn (1955) fundamentally altered the paradigmatic focus of children's institutions.

August Aichhorn was the first to use psychoanalysis in residential treatment (Hoffman 1982). Aichhorn (1955) argued that wayward youth, including those who were delinquent, dissocial, and those suffering from neurotic symptoms, should be removed from the home environment and placed in institutional treatment to rehabilitate their dissocial behavior. This was in contrast to simply requiring individual therapy for dissocial young people. As a director of an institution, Aichhorn observed interactions between nonpsychologically trained adults who worked in treatment and the institutionalized children. He wondered if psychoanalytic principles could be applied to other relationships besides the child/psychiatrist dyad. Aichhorn argued that wayward youth could benefit from peer relationships and emotional transference from staff members. The emotional connections or transference could be used therapeutically (Aichhorn 1955; see also Hoffman 1982). August Aichhorn (1955) thought that psychoanalytical principles established for patient/client individual therapy sessions could be applied to all relationships at the institution (e.g., between boys and "cottage mothers"), thereby initiating the first major implementation of psychiatric knowledge to institutional treatment.

Others, including Anna Freud (1969), Bruno Bettelheim (1950), Emmy Sylvester (with Bettelheim 1948), and Joseph Noshpitz (1962), also found that psychoanalytic principles could be applied to institutional treatment. Like Aichhorn, these researchers and clinicians questioned the separation of milieu and psychoanalytic treatment, arguing that management was not enough and that milieu living could be its own treatment.[5] Bettelheim and Sylvester argue that only benign interpersonal relationships among adults and children "can combat the impoverishment of the personalities of children who suffer from emotional institutionalism" (1948: 191). Therefore, by the late 1930s and early 1940s inpatient psychiatric treatment for children expanded psychiatric practice in institutions from individual therapy to milieu therapy.

"Milieu therapy," the term coined in Germany in 1900, was used to identify psychiatric environments that focused on compassion and humane treatment of patients (Hoffman 1982). Milieu treatment in institutions was an effort to make the children's living situation a comprehensive therapeutic intervention. Through this comprehensive therapeutic intervention, institutional living came to be seen as facilitating ego development and an effective treatment of child psychopathology. More contemporarily, a therapeutic milieu is defined as "a group living situation for children, specifically for children with emotional problems, children who must live away from home and whose lives are full of crisis" (Trieschman, Whittaker, and Brendtro 1969:2). Milieu treatment, like other forms of therapeutic community, focuses on group work, community building, and the cultivation of a "culture" of the milieu (Hoffman 1982:2). "What goes on daily between children and adults is seen as an opportunity for therapeutic education and re-education" (Trieschman, Whittaker, and Brendtro 1969:3). The 1956 American Psychiatric Association conference on psychiatric inpatient treatment for children in the United States found that child psychiatry concepts of the day were being and should be used in the development of residential services in inpatient child psychiatric care, especially milieu treatment (Robinson et al. 1957).

While psychiatrists and child care workers were interested in the treatment of psychiatric illness in milieu contexts, sociologists were interested in the social dynamics of institutional living (Goffman 1961; Polsky 1962/1977; Polsky, Claster, and Goldberg 1968; Polsky, Claster, and Goldberg 1970). Polsky and his colleagues were interested in investigating, through sociological methods, how young people actually made a life in residential treatment, and if milieu treatment actually worked in rehabilitative terms. He analyzed the social system of residential treatment, particularly of the cottage context, arguing that a delinquent peer culture prohibited effective psychiatric rehabilitation (Polsky 1962/1977). He also found that differences among the staff, psychologically trained professionals for individual therapy and nonprofessionally trained cottage personnel, limited the achievement of rehabilitation goals (Polsky, Claster, and Goldberg 1968). In an effort to remedy some of the shortcomings of residential treatment, Polsky, Claster, and Goldberg (1970) published an extensive edited volume that examined the social system of residential treatment, rather than the psychiatric mechanisms of milieu therapy.

Similarly, Erving Goffman analyzed the inner workings of total institutions and the moral career of mental patients in his classic study *Asylums: Essays on the Social Situation of Mental Patients and Other Inmates*. I will come back to Goffman's discussion of total institutions as a theoretical concept later. However, in terms of sociological analysis of institutional living, like Polsky, Goffman found that the social situation of life in inpatient centers profoundly shaped the therapeutic work therein. Residential treatment centers are founded on psychiatric principles and are structured to produce a particular kind of psychiatric outcome for the patient. However, what works, how it works, and what happens inside of these institutions in terms of social life and psychiatric rehabilitation have been the subject of much discussion and debate. Even clinicians at Havenwood identify residential treatment as a "black box," as what happens inside to change the resident is unknown. Despite these questions, residential treatment centers remain viable today, integrating institutional living with psychiatric treatment practices, such as individual, and milieu therapy, and psychotropic medication regimens for the youth who live there (I will come back to this in chapter 2).

Missing from the historical accounts of child institutions and ways to treat "wayward youth" is a discussion of how certain behaviors come to be identified as psychiatrically healthy (Gaines 1992), how psychology has been shaped by the ideology of white supremacy (Guthrie 2003), and how institutionalization practices reflect racial hierarchies (Alexander 2010; Metzl 2009).

Race, Psychiatry, and Custody

African American psychiatrists William Grier and Price Cobbs, Martinican psychiatrist Franz Fanon, and historian and psychiatrist Jonathon Metzl provide important examples of how racial identity and systems of racial oppression shape definitions and experiences of mental illness and psychiatric custody. Psychiatric custody at Havenwood cannot be disarticulated from the broader American context of how race shapes institutionalization practices, psychiatry, and mental health.

In the early nineteenth century, when institution construction was in its infancy, the system of chattel slavery kept Black children from entering orphanages or reformatories. In the late 1800s and the early twentieth century, when institution construction was robust, and when Havenwood was constructed, racial prejudice against African Americans meant that few institutions, including children's homes and health centers, would be integrated (Byrd and Clayton 2000; Courtney and Hughes-Heuring 2009). In the United States, slavery and the legacy of the ideology of white supremacy have resulted in differentiated health systems, including mental health, for African Americans and whites. In other words, "health systems" or "institutions" meant health systems and institutions that served white Americans. Throughout much of US history, the "culture of American medicine has mirrored the larger culture that encompassed enslavement, segregation, and less dramatic forms of inequality" that have adversely affected African Americans (Washington 2006:9).

Early reformatories and orphanages housed white children almost exclusively. If institutions did house Black children, they were segregated from the white populations and given inferior accommodations, especially in the South (Byrd and Clayton 2000). Otherwise, many of the needy African American children in the nineteenth and early twentieth centuries lived in kinship circles and did not receive any state-level assistance (Ashby 1997; Billingsley and Giovanni 1972; Courtney and Hughes-Heuring 2009). Havenwood, like most institutions, seems to have been home to only white boys throughout much of its history. (I will come back to demographics of current residents in the next chapter.) In 1965, Havenwood's graduation photo reveals that 1 African American boy graduated along with 12 white boys. However, prior to this 1965 graduation image, only white male children appear in the photos.[6] Residential treatment in the early part of the twentieth century, like other institutions of the time, reflected racial segregation in the United States at large. In the latter half of the century, however, institutionalization practices shifted; I come back to this in a moment.

Despite institutional segregation and health systems that focused on white populations, race has always been a significant factor in the domain of mental illness and psychiatry. In his book *The Protest Psychosis: How Schizophrenia Became a Black Disease*, historian Jonathon Metzl traces the relationship between race and mental illness that reaches far into American history. For example, he discusses how medical journals in the 1850s identify and describe mental illnesses such as *drapetomania* and *dysaethesia aethiopis*. Drapetomania was defined as a psychiatric disorder that caused slaves to run away from white masters. Dysaethesia aethiopis was identified as a mental illness that manifested through "rascality" and "disrespect for the master's property" and was cured by extensive whipping (Metzl 2009:ix). Even at the turn of the twentieth century, Metzl illustrates how leading academic psychiatrists claimed that "Negroes" were "psychologically unfit" for freedom (2009:ix). While these are no longer classified as mental disorders in the Diagnostic and Statistical Manual of Mental Disorder, Metzl argues that "anxieties about racial difference shape diagnostic criteria, health-care policies, medical and popular attitudes about mentally ill persons, the structures of treatment facilities, and ultimately, the conversations that take place there within" (2009:xi). In other words, racial difference and oppression in the United States has profoundly shaped the mental health system.

Racial segregation and Jim Crow laws following the Civil War continued to see that African Americans did not receive the same kinds of mental health treatments as their white counterparts. If African Americans sought private mental health treatment, fewer than 3 percent were accepted (Metzl 2009). In addition to patient care, in the early part of the twentieth century only 8 of the US's 4,432 psychiatrists were African American. During this time, research would be conducted with whites only, in white-only wards, or in northern areas of the United States allowing "Negro hospitals" to operate outside of the institutional research agenda (Metzl 2009). If research was done with African Americans, researchers reveal racist framings of mental illness (Guthrie 2004; Metzl 2009). The racist framings include using code words like "primitive" and "civilized" to index "black/insane" and "white/sane" (Metzl 2009:103).

During the Civil Rights Movement, however, African American men were no longer excluded from treatment but became the subject of psychiatric institutionalization. Metzl (2009) documents how anxieties about the Black Power movement and the integration of American society shifted the symptoms, diagnosis practices, and institutionalization rates for individuals suffering from schizophrenia. Before the 1960s, schizophrenia was associated with white women, a benign neurosis characterized by, among other things, by not wanting to perform housework. During the era of the Civil Rights and Black Power era, schizophrenia became a disease afflicting Black men; it became understood as a socially dangerous and violent psychotic disorder, the "protest psychosis." Whether exclusionary to African Americans or using psychiatric diagnosis to constrain African Americans, recognizing race as mattering in mental health research, theories of psychological distress, and institutionalization policies was rarely made explicit. This omission downplayed the significance of racial identity or systems of racial oppression as meaningful to psychiatry or psychological distress in American society.

Black psychiatrists, however, have long discussed the relationship between racial oppression, the ideology of white supremacy, and mental illness in the United States and colonial nations.[7] Martinican psychiatrist Franz Fanon (1952/2008; 1963/2004) illustrates how colonialism and racism shape individual life experiences in general and psychiatric distress in particular. Fanon (1963/2004) situates psychiatric distress (and other forms of subjectivity) within the context of colonialism, imperialism, and liberatory struggles. As a psychiatrist practicing in Algeria, he found that particular patients suffered mental distress due to the colonial regime, systems of disempowerment, oppression against nonwhite people, and the struggle for liberation from these structures. Mental symptoms, he states, are the consequences of colonial oppression, especially among colonized subjects (Fanon 1963/2004:182). Fanon also argues that colonial ideological systems, particularly the ideological system of white supremacy, perpetuate disenfranchising myths about people of African heritage. He illustrates how psychiatry—through psychiatrists and psychiatric hospitals—identifies and tries to "cure" colonial subjects who show resistance to oppression. Much like examples in the United States provided by Metzl, Fanon's work reveals how, as Metzl states it, "In unintended and often invisible ways psychiatric definitions of insanity continue to police racial hierarchies, tensions, and unspoken codes in addition to separating normal from abnormal behavior. Sometimes, the boundaries of sanity align closely with the perceived borders of the racial status quo" (2009: ix). Fanon's work is his effort to reveal the unspoken codes, to make visible the way psychiatry itself is an oppressive system, as well as to illustrate how these oppressive systems shape the experience of psychiatric distress. Fanon's work on psychiatry and decolonizing the minds of people in the Black diaspora has had significant influence on African American responses to white supremacy in the United States (Hall 1992).

African American psychiatrists William Grier and Price Cobbs (1969) also link psychiatric distress among African Americans to issues of racism and the system of white supremacy in American society. Grier and Cobbs sought to link individual psychiatric distress with environmental constraints on African Americans. They also discerned psychiatric illness from the healthy rage and grief that emerges due to racial oppression. They argue, like many psychiatrists and psychoanalysts at the time, that mental illness emerges from a conflict between the inner drives pushing for gratification and the group demands of the social environment. The conflict is pacified when the inner world, the outer world, or both worlds change. For Grier and Cobbs a focus on changing the inner world by adapting to an oppressive social world is psychologically unhealthy. "Black people cannot abide [adaptation to the social world] and thoughtful therapists know it. A black man's soul can live only if it is oriented toward a change of the social order" (Grier and Cobbs 1969:150–151). Where Metzl's work argues that psychiatry maintains racial hierarchies, Grier and Cobbs and Fanon illustrate how racial hierarchies actually contribute to the psychological distress of African Americans and oppressed peoples. If we take both perspectives—that psychiatry is a system by which racial hierarchies are policed and maintained *and* that such oppression causes psychiatric distress in oppressed populations—we see the connection between individual life experiences, racial ideologies, and understandings of mental health and illness in US society.

If we add to this complex web of psychiatry the myriad ways to examine the meaning of race in the lives of people—as a category of personal identity, a way to identify cultural practices, and a system of oppression through the ideology of white supremacy—we see how psychiatric health and race cannot be disarticulated in American society.

Race and racial discrimination do not just shape the American health system. The ideology of white supremacy has also had a profound effect on the legal system in the United States. The popular image of the criminal is of an urban Black male (Neal 2013). The ease with which the American public imaginary links Black men with criminality is well established (Neal 2013; Van Deburg 2004).[8] In slaveholding communities in the South, assumptions about Black criminality and subsequent laws to prohibit perceived dangerous behavior, such as the congregation of multiple Black men, were used to preserve the labor system and to solidify white hegemony (Van Deburg 2004). This system of oppression did not cease with the end of slavery, but was perpetuated with segregation until the Civil Rights Movement in the 1960s. Due to religious and pseudoscientific theories that supported the ideology of white supremacy, including the Great Chain of Being and biologically ordered taxonomies informed by ethnological studies, African Americans were seen and treated as dangerous criminals. Today, this stereotype of Black villainy and criminality remains, as does the fear of Black criminality.[9] Mark Anthony Neal (2013) argues that the most "legible" Black body is thought to be a criminal body and a body in need of policing and containment. In fact, this legibility and subsequent fear of assumed Black criminality results in high incarceration rates.

In her book, *The New Jim Crow: Mass Incarceration in the Age of Colorblindness*, Michelle Alexander (2010) finds African American men are being incarcerated at disproportional and exceedingly high rates in contemporary United States.[10] Using national statistics, Alexander illustrates how the "American penal system has emerged as a system of social control unparalleled in world history" (2010:8).

As the United States integrated Black and white populations in mainstream society, the US prison population skyrocketed from around 300,000 to 2 million (Alexander 2010:6). "The uncomfortable reality," Alexander states, "is that convictions for drug offenses—not violent crime—are the single most important cause of the prison boom in the United States, and people of color are convicted of drug offenses at rates out of proportion with their drug crimes" (2010:99). The prison boom, the focus on drug crime, and the conviction rates of people of color result in a stigmatized racial group being locked into a subordinate position, and in some cases, permanent social exclusion by law (Alexander 2010).

Juvenile justice research finds that young white men commit about 60 percent of all of the juvenile crimes reported (Puzzanchera, Adams, and Hockenberry 2012). However, young Black men are three times more likely to be incarcerated or institutionalized for any kind of criminal charge than their white counterparts (Puzzanchera, Adams, and Hockenberry 2012). Racial disparities prejudicing African Americans are evident in crime rates, criminal histories, prosecution and sentencing, responses to crime, and the criminal justice policy (Mauer 2006; see also Kennedy 1997). Young Black men are being locked in a subordinate position, as a caste of criminals.

According to US national statistics the likelihood of imprisonment for males born in 2001 is 32 percent for Blacks, 17 percent for Hispanics, and 6 percent for whites (US Department of Justice 2003). Alexander's most recent statistics reveal that one in three young African American men is currently under the control of the criminal justice system, either in prison or jail, or on probation or parole (2010:9). For adults, prison populations escalated in the United States, due to the deinstitutionalization of its mentally ill populations. Lorna Rhodes (2004) illustrates how psychiatry is integrated into the prison industrial complex. In the United States, many who might have been psychiatrically institutionalized are now in prison, swapping one manner of incarceration—treatment, for another—confinement and punishment.

The history is different for young people in need of treatment, however. Currently, the juvenile justice system and the child welfare system place youth in psychiatric custody as well as in detention facilities. Today many young Black men are housed and treated in psychiatric custody in an attempt to change their behavior before they reach adulthood. According to a 2013 Child Welfare System report, 42 percent of children in the foster care system were white, 26 percent were black, and 21 percent were Hispanic (of any race).[11]

Demographics on race within the different foster placements, into a foster home versus an institution for example, are not reported (US Department of Health and Human Services 2013). Juvenile justice reports, however, provide this information. The custody rate for Black youth, the placement of youth into residential treatment institutions, was more than 4.5 times the rate for white youth (US Department of Justice 2013). Across the United States, for every 100,000 Black youth, 606 were in residential treatment as compared to 228 Hispanic youth and 128 white youth (US Department of Justice 2013). These Black youth are feared to be at a very high risk for adult criminal behavior and incarceration; they are read as criminals.[12]

Due to this historical context: (1) the availability of institutions to house and treat youth identified as psychiatrically disordered; (2) the assumed criminality and danger of Black men, including the disproportionate numbers of children of color in the criminal justice system and institutionalized in psychiatric custody; and (3) the role of psychiatry in policing racial hierarchies—it is not difficult to understand the current social situation of African American boys being identified as dangerous and institutionalized into psychiatric custody.

However significant the structural forces are that confine Black youth, my research at Havenwood reveals a profound agency within psychiatric custody. Young Black men are not just the passive victims of racist ideologies. They direct their treatment process with meaningful African American cultural practices, namely, hip hop.

Hip Hop: Black Music and Culture

Hip hop has an interesting, complex history and contemporary social location. "Hip hop is a cultural form that attempts to negotiate the experiences of marginalization, brutally truncated opportunity, and oppression within the cultural imperatives of African-American and Caribbean history, identity, and community" (Rose 1994:21). As a music form it can be located along a social and historical trajectory among other African American musical genres including jazz, bebop, soul, gospel, funk, reggae, and rock (Neal 1999; Chang 2005). However, hip hop is also understood as *more* than rapping or music. In current scholarly literature on hip hop, it is referred to as *a way of life* that reflects a nation and a generation (Chang 2005; Forman and Neal 2012; Kitwana 2002; Perry 2004). To illustrate this way of life, I contextualize hip hop within the urban American context, specifically the deindustrialization of American city centers, New York in particular. This sets the stage for hip hop's emergence, which illustrates how the cultural form is related to other histories, power dynamics, and cultural shifts in the United States. Using an ethnographic example, I bring hip hop, as a cultural form, to the local context of Havenwood, psychiatric custody and healing processes.

The Urban Context[13]

It is impossible to understand hip hop outside of a variety of social forces, both local and national, that were underway in the United States in the 1970s. One of the most significant contexts of hip hop is urban deindustrialization. Urban centers in the United States were experiencing a rapid decline in industry and manufacturing plants and jobs. Major economic and social restructuring of cities left the poorest and least powerful groups, often those with a long history of racial discrimination, even more vulnerable. In New York City, the Bronx alone lost 600,000 manufacturing jobs, 40 percent of the sector (Chang 2005). Youth unemployment was between 60 and 80 percent, especially for youth of color (Chang 2005). Exacerbating this downward economic spiral, especially in poor neighborhoods, were "urban renewal" projects. In New York City, areas of the Bronx, Brooklyn, and Queens saw communities and neighborhoods destroyed in order to build new expressways, public works projects, and housing projects. In the 1970s, around 60,000 homes in the Bronx were razed for urban renewal projects, and 30,000 fires were set (Chang 2005; Rose 1994). The Jewish, Irish, Italian, and German residents relocated to new suburban communities, while the Black and Puerto Rican residents relocated to new consolidated housing projects in other poor parts of the city. In the 1970s, the South Bronx became the national symbol of ruin, isolation, and urban decay (Rose 1994).

Out of the fires and ruin, amid severe youth unemployment, and the need to refashion a community displaced by urban renewal, hip hop emerged. Hip hop and rap music are a "black cultural expression that prioritizes black voices from the margins of urban America" (Rose 1994:2). In an era of dramatic urban decay and restructuring urban renewal projects favoring white and wealthier constituents, hip hop became an African American response to this decay and disenfranchisement. Hip hop scholar Tricia Rose tells us hip hop is "*black* urban renewal" (1994:61, emphasis added).

The Origin Story[14]

Hip Hop's origin story begins in the very ruins of the South Bronx in the 1970s. The founding fathers include DJ Kool Herc with his powerful sound system, Afrikaa Bambaataa with his charismatic leadership and his Zulu Nation, and Grandmaster Flash with his wide musical interests. These young men, the young teenagers in New York City who with their block parties, their Zulu Nation as opposed to gang affiliation, and the scratching and beatboxing, launched one of the most dynamic and powerful African American, popular, and American cultures (Forman 2012; George 2012).

Before hip hop was named, a young Jamaican-born, aspiring DJ named Kool Herc was using his access to a powerful sound system to host parties in the South Bronx. According to the origin story, hip hop began in the rec room of 1520, Sedgwick Avenue, in the summer of 1973 during a party thrown to raise money for school clothes. With the decline in discos, the increased gang activity in the South Bronx, and the rampant poverty of deindustrialization the almost monthly parties Kool Herc deejayed provided pleasure, fun, and resources for the youth of the area.

Afrikaa Bambaataa, a former Black Spade gang member turned charismatic nation-builder, led youth from various parts of the Bronx to parties hosted by the likes of DJ Kool Herc. In addition to being music-savvy, Bambaataa also created the Universal Zulu Nation, the first hip hop institution and organization committed to raising consciousness and community development, rather than in promoting territorial rivalries (Chang 2005). In the context of urban decay and destruction, extremely high unemployment, and poverty, Bambaataa gave the youth of the Bronx something to believe in. It was through the Zulu Nation that Black Muslim, pan-African, and Black Panther ideas were shared and cultivated as part of hip hop's legacy. "Bambaataa took Herc's party and turned it into the ceremony of a new faith" (Chang 2005:107).

Grandmaster Flash, the third father of hip hop, was known for his style and his ability to "turn beat-making and crowd-rocking into a science" (Chang 2005:112). As the tides of hip hop turned, the power of the sound system was replaced by showmanship and style. Where Kool Herc made the break and encouraged the b-boys and b-girls to show their style, Grandmaster Flash led the way for the emcee and rapping.[15] The emcees told stories, shared ideas, and expressed important themes using versions of black cultural storytelling including toasting, or chanting over a rhyme common in Jamaica, freestyling or spontaneous riffs linked to jazz and blues, and call and response, part of African American oral tradition based on the relationship between artists, pieces of music, and artists and audience (Perry 2004; Rose 1994). Over time the emcee (MC) became known as the rapper.

In 1979 the party went national with the recording of "Rapper's Delight." With "Rapper's Delight," hip hop and rap broke through into Black radio. It made the American Top 40 and it crossed the globe. After this first record, hip hop would never be the same.

Along with the origin story of hip hop, and its location in the South Bronx with a few key figures and elements of the genre, hip hop as an important cultural force must be understood in relation to other histories and social contexts in the United States.

Politics, Power, and Music

African American music traditions cannot be divorced from all aspects of the African American experience (Neal 1999). Mark Anthony Neal illustrates how changes in the Black community—including migration patterns, political movements, public spaces, religious institutions, youth culture, crack cocaine, gender relations, class stratification, police brutality, and economic restructuring of urban spaces—affect Black popular music (1999:xi). Therefore, when the youth of Havenwood perform, identify with, or embody hip hop, they are indexing a whole set of important cultural, historical, and political ideologies, knowledges, and traditions.[16] Rather than detail the extensive history of hip hop, I want to focus on its gestational period. If hip hop emerged in the mid-1970s and 1980s, I want to hone in on how the 1960s gave rise to this important musical and ideological tradition.

After decades of segregation practices and Jim Crow laws, the American south was desegregating its schools, drinking fountains, lunch counters, and buses in the 1960s. Concurrently, northern American cities saw the push for the rejection of integration and assimilation, and the establishment of a pan-African nation and identity. These two movements, the former supported by Christianity and located in the South, and the latter supported by the Nation of Islam and the North, were radically different. However, Black public spaces such as the Apollo Theatre in New York and Chicago's Regal Theatre assisted in bridging the gaps between these two movements by hosting musical groups and performances from both the North and the South. These artists and performances were known as traveling along "the Chitlin' Circuit." The Chitlin' Circuit of Black popular music "represented a distinct link to a worldview predicated on the suppression, exploitation, and disenfranchisement of the black community" (Neal 1999:31).

The Chitlin' Circuit and African American musical forms such as jazz, blues, gospel, bebop, funk, and soul told the narratives of suppression, exploitation, and disenfranchisement. These narratives brought people together. African Americans in the North and the South could identify as a community based on suppression, exploitation, and disenfranchisement through this live music circuit. The Chitlin' Circuit narratives and community building can be contrasted with popular or mainstream African American music of the time.

Also in the 1960s, Motown with its rhythm and blues, upbeat Black pop, and soul artists gave voice to a rising African American middle class. However, Motown was "increasingly criticized for its inability to adequately address the totality of black life" (Neal 1999:46). Motown neglected Malcolm X, the Watts riots, the Black Panthers, and the abandonment of city centers, often the enclaves for poor, not middle class, African Americans. Hip hop was an response to this neglect.

Hip hop emerged from disenfranchised African Americans following the Civil Rights Movement, the Black Power movement and the Nation of Islam, the Black Panther movement, and in response to popular African American music that seemed distanced from the struggles of many Black Americans. As young hip hoppers were partying in the Bronx, they were also hearing their parents lament the unrealized dreams of the major social movements of the 1960s. By the 1970s, instead of equality and upward mobility, African American youth saw the failure of urban renewal projects, the crack cocaine epidemic, new drug laws disproportionately affecting African Americans, and the increasing separation of the African American middle class from the poor disenfranchised African Americans in the city centers. Hip hop became the mouthpiece of disenfranchised and increasingly politicized African American youth, emerging as an oppositional cultural force and as an activist musical tradition (Perry 2004). African American youth used hip hop to formally question and give voice to a displeasure with the social reality. "From the outset, rap music has articulated the pleasures and problems of black urban life in contemporary America" (Rose 1994:2).

More specifically, hip hop music and culture is driven by Black *youth*. Hip hop artists from Queens and Long Island including Public Enemy, Run DMC, and L.L. Cool J took to the studios to give voice to the struggles of African American youth in the 1980s.[17]

These young, politically minded, often college-educated young rappers saw the failings of the Civil Rights and Black Power movements and wanted to destabilize what had become the stereotypes of African Americans in the public imagination. "Therefore for African-American youth, hip hop music also allowed them to counter the iconography of fear, menace, and spectacle that dominated mass-mediated perceptions of contemporary black life by giving voice to the everyday realities of black life" (Neal 1999:138). While Public Enemy, Run DMC, and L.L. Cool J were centrally located in New York City, their hip hop articulated political narratives of police brutality, racism, and harassment gave voice to a common Black youth experience and thus gave rise to other local rap scenes across the country (Neal 1999; Rose 1994).

Los Angeles, South Central, and Compton specifically, saw the rise of another form of rap, gangsta rap. Gangsta rap, epitomized by NWA, shifted rap lyrics away from political narratives, like those of Public Enemy, and focused on a high-rolling drug dealer and forms of violence and destruction. Gangsta rap is a by-product of the crack epidemic, and explicitly expresses disdain for police brutality and poverty in the inner city (Perry 2004). "What South Bronx had been in the 1970s, South Central would be for the 1980s. It was the epitome of a growing number of inner-city nexuses where deindustrialization, devolution, Cold War adventurism, the drug trade, gang structures and rivalries, arms profiteering, and police brutality were combining to destabilize poor communities and alienate massive numbers of youth" (Chang 2005:315). Beyond the East Coast/West Coast divide, hip hop was diversifying and expanding. Cities across the country saw their own hip hop artists emerge and give voice to specific locales. Hip hop gave youth a way to identify with a specific locale, as well as echo a national experience of African American oppression.

Hip hop's popular culture influence did not stop with music. In the 1990s, hip hop was the subject of television shows, especially on the new Music Television channels (*MTV*) with *Yo! MTV Raps*, movies, such as *Do the Right Thing* from the streets of Brooklyn and *Boyz-N-the-Hood* from South Central, and magazines, such as *The Source* and *Vibe*. Hip hop was even used to sell clothing, soft drinks, alcohol, and athletic shoes. Hip hop became a lifestyle of a generation, its own "nation" to echo contemporary scholars of the subject (Alim 2006; Forman 2002).

Hip hop is currently more popular than ever with its commercial and mainstream successes. For example, vernacular phrases associated with hip hop, such as "keepin' it real," are ubiquitous in American culture. And rappers have political and social influence, as exemplified by Jay-Z, who was a guest of the president of the United States during his inauguration. However with popularity has come controversy. With gangsta rap's commercial success, rap is now a popular "playground for caricatures of black gangstas, pimps, and hoes" (Rose 2008:1; see also Perry 2004) rather than a venue for young Black Americans to counter such dehumanizing stereotypes and the powers that reinforce them as its origins desired (Rose 1994). I will come back to these stereotypes in chapter 2. But hip hop, despite its mainstream popularity and use of African American caricatures, remains meaningful for Black youth across the United States, from New York to LA, Atlanta to Chicago.

In terms of local context, hip hop is meaningful to the African American youth of Havenwood in very profound ways. Many of the Black boys of Havenwood and adult Black men who worked with them, use hip hop culture, language, style, and music to do the therapeutic work required in psychiatric custody. In addition, hip hop was part of the culture the young men brought with them to treatment.

As I have explained earlier, hip hop is a method by which young African Americans give voice to Black experience. In some cases, Havenwood youth used rap in particular to give voice to their experiences as young Black men in psychiatric custody and struggling to make sense of their circumstances. Much like famous rappers, these young men use the medium of rap to express their experiences and to link themselves into an important African American history and culture. For the young men of Havenwood born in the 1990s, after almost two decades of recorded rap and the explosion of hip hop culture, rap has always been available to give voice to struggles or desires, and as part of their African American existence. These young men are not professionals and their raps do not enter the public sphere nor are they engaging audiences and producing culture in more public ways. Nonetheless, they rapped because they enjoyed it and it was a meaningful cultural practice that helped them express identity, longings, desires, and knowledge within the context of psychiatric custody. Let me use an example from one of the rap sessions recorded at Havenwood to illustrate what I mean.

I would loan my digital recorder to the youth so that they could record their raps and I could then burn a CD of the session for them. They would set up a boom box and play the latest beats. Sometimes individually, sometimes in groups, and always after extensive lyrical construction and practice they would play the beats and rap into the recording device. During the session presented here, three young men from Steele Cottage explicitly discuss what rap means to them. The album begins with an interview between RastaMan and two rappers, SlowMo and D-Man Strong. These young men integrate hip hop's Caribbean roots, with RastaMan's name and Jamaican accent, with contemporary debates about the commercialization of gangsta rap as they discuss why they rap. These boys give local voice to the scholarly texts that provide the historical and cultural narrative of the music genre and cultural form:

> *RastaMan*: Waz up man. This is RastaMan. Live, right here, right now with D-Man Strong and SlowMo. They call themselves Sick Boyz, you know.
> *D-Man Strong*: [City] represents!
> *RastaMan*: So D-Man Strong, where are you from, man?
> *D-Man Strong*: I'm from [number of building], where that would be is at, you know, [city]. Shout out! Big shout out to Katie, you know what I'm saying, making this possible. Big shout out to all my fans, all the people keep listening to my CDs. And shout out to [city], you know how we do it, baby.
> *SlowMo*: I wanna give a shout out to my family, you know, I want to thank the Man above, mostly. I want to thank my moms, my pops, my gramma, grampa. I wanna thank my boy Allen, my boy Jim, Steve, you know, they made this thang possible too [all staff members].
> *D-Man Strong*: Big shout out to staff!
> *RastaMan*: I mean, what you guys get outta rapping?
> *D-Man Strong*: I get a lot of stuff outta rappin', man. I let 'em know how *I* feel [emphasis in original]. You know what I'm sayin'? 'Cause some people rap just for the money, man. We rap to let people know how we feel, man. We grew up in the gutter. Born in the gutter, might as well as say we born in the dumpster how bad it is out there. But we made it, baby. We gonna let this, you know…ya niggas need to get ya'lls hustle up.
> *SlowMo*: On the real. You know what I'm sayin? Life out there, ya'll need to get on your grind. Niggas gettin' popped everyday, you know what I'm saying. That's why a lot of people, you know, need to get they hustle up.

In the recording, someone presses a button and the beat begins, SlowMo and D-Man Strong begin their track "Hustle Up!"

Much like rap outside of psychiatric custody, D-Man Strong and SlowMo are quick to give "shout outs" or thanks and recognition to their local neighborhoods and their "crew" or friends and loved ones. In psychiatric custody this includes "staff" and the anthropologist who loans out technology. There is also a focus on the "real," authentic feelings and knowledge about rising up and getting oneself together. D-Man Strong engages the hip hop debate regarding commercialization of rap and he sides with authenticity rather than money. Also, D-Man Strong and SlowMo use the rap to teach others how to rise up, to not get shot like other young Black men they know, and do what they need to do. These young men see themselves as having "made it" and D-Man Strong states this explicitly. It might seem counterintuitive that a young man confined in psychiatric custody would claim he "made it." However, as I will illustrate, the young men see themselves transformed, changed, and improved. They see themselves integrating various treatment practices and hip hop culture as they do the work they need to do to "make it." As we will see hip hop is not just about rapping or music but about ways to understand treatment practice and success. We will see how hip hop and psychiatric forms are woven together to tell a unique tale from the voices of African American men inside psychiatric custody.

Conclusion

The institutional situation and treatment paradigms at Havenwood are the outgrowth of historical changes that have occurred in the child welfare system, in child psychology and psychiatry, and with the institutionalization of children. Children are still institutionalized in the United States and their treatment in these institutions is based on a long history of understanding human development and treating psychopathology. What is missing from detailed historical accounts is an analysis of how race shapes psychiatric institutionalization and experiences of mental illness. Furthermore, what is missing is how African American cultural practices and forms might influence treatment, albeit in unofficial ways. Havenwood has survived the historical shifts over the course of its 120-year history. Presently, Havenwood is home to mostly African American youth, members of the hip hop nation. I turn now to how psychiatric treatment is organized, officially and unofficially, at Havenwood.

Chapter 2
The Ethnographic Setting

"Dwayne came last week; he is tough like the other Steele [Cottage] kids," Tricia informs us.[1] Tricia is an intake specialist. As an intake specialist she meets with the youth seeking admittance at Havenwood, and she screens them to assess fit with the psychiatric institution. Havenwood does not treat sex offenders, nor does it specialize in treatment for drug abuse. Dwayne is not seeking treatment for either of these issues. Tricia passes out the ten-page document she created from Dwayne's two-inch thick foster care file: Dwayne's Mental Health Assessment and Social History (MHA/SH).[2]

Havenwood's week begins with Intake Meetings: Monday morning, 9 a.m.[3] The individuals tasked with deciding who is to be admitted and what their initial treatment plan will be include the director of intake, a handful of clinical directors who are also trained therapists, a consulting psychiatrist, the director of residential education, the director of family services, intake specialists who present the information, and case workers who represent the cottages where the youth might eventually come to live. I look around the room and most people are looking through Dwayne's MHA/SH.

Dwayne is a 15-year-old African American male, whose guardian is the state foster care system. I turn the page of Dwayne's MHA/SH as Tricia begins to share with us her impression of Dwayne and the vital information the group needs to make a decision about his admittance. Havenwood has a long waiting list, I am told; evidently more children and youth need psychiatric custody than there are places for them.

"He has been [psychiatrically] hospitalized and in foster care. He was moved [from the foster home] because of his behaviors. He was non-compliant and aggressive. His aggression becomes very volatile and the judge is referring him to residential treatment [as opposed to juvenile detention]. He is diagnosed with Conduct Disorder, Oppositional Defiant Disorder, and a mood disorder. The M.D. thought he was really Bipolar and that medication could improve his behavior. He has cyclical behaviors per the M.D." No wonder, I think, she likens him to all the "other Steele kids." Steele Cottage is known around Havenwood as the "little juvie home" because most of the young men who live there are African American teenage boys with histories like Dwayne: noncompliant; aggressive; and having experience with the criminal justice, psychiatric, and foster care systems. However, rather than having Conduct Disorder, the psychiatrist thinks that Dwayne suffers with Bipolar Disorder and will adjust his medication when he arrives.[4]

"I liked the kid," Tricia continues. "He tried to be tough but a piece of him felt bad about being tough. He tried to be oppositional but he had a nice piece to him. He has had some legal involvement but no drugs or alcohol."

"Do we know much about his early childhood? His mom was using [drugs], right?" Sarah, who is Steele Cottage's director and a director of residential services at Havenwood more broadly, asks.

"Yeah until he was about 4." I hear pages being flipped as people look through the MHA/SH for this important information.

"Then we need to mark 'neglect' in his file," Sarah tells her. Tricia makes a note in her document. I am told that the files need to be up-to-date and accurate as the youth move through the system. Sometimes, I am told, the only "available" stories of the children's lives are the case files (I come back to this in chapter 3).

"Dwayne was resistant. He said, 'There is no point in locking people up because they are not going to change.' But after we went to Steele and he saw that the kids were going to the movie and to the mall and then when we walked past the school he said, 'This is pretty sweet.' But he was very argumentative, I couldn't convince him." Tricia continues telling the group about her experience and assessment of Dwayne. This information is not in his official file.

"What is his goal?" Sarah asks.

"To return home," Tricia states. The goals vary little. Most residents either have a goal of returning home, or of living on their own at the age of 18.

A pause fills the room. Cindy, the director of intake, asks, "Any thoughts?" She looks around the large round table where we all sit. No one says anything. "Ok." Dwayne is admitted to Havenwood and will stay at Steele. "Next?"

* * *

In this chapter, I provide a general outline of the official treatment paradigms at Havenwood to help define the context of life there, and a description of those who live and work in this institution.

Havenwood Treatment Paradigms

Havenwood is a private, nonprofit, residential treatment center, where children with psychiatric disorders live and receive 24-hour treatment.

Psychiatric Disorders

Upon entry to Havenwood, youth, like Dwayne, are diagnosed with a psychiatric disorder and prescribed a psychotropic medication schedule. Psychiatrists screen the youth at intake and reevaluate them every three months. Dwayne's diagnosis is changed, at his admittance to Havenwood. Dwayne went from suffering with Conduct Disorder to being diagnosed with and receiving psychotropic medication for Bipolar Disorder. Figure 2.1 is an emblematic example of the differential diagnosis and medication regimen as documented in the case files.

DIAGNOSIS:		M.D. 11/05/07			
Axis I	296.45	Bipolar Disorder Last Phrase Manic in Partial Remission			
	305.20	Cannabis Abuse in recent Remission			
	314.01	Attention Deficit Hyperactivity Disorder			
Axis II		None			
Axis III		None			
Axis IV		Severe: H/O physical abuse, educational, legal, social, and primary care group			
Axis V		GAF = 45/45			
MEDICATION:	Refer to 11/05/07 Psychiatric Evaluation for current comments/concerns.				
Current Medication	Dosage	Dr./Date Ordered	Date Started	Last Change	Related prob. area
Seroquel 300 mg	2 at 8 p.m.	On Adm.	On Adm.	Time Change 12/20/06	Danger to Others
Lithium Carb. 600 mg	1 at 3 p.m. 1 at 8 a.m. 1 at 8 p.m.	On Adm. 9/19/06	On Adm.	Increased 2/01/07	Attention/ Impulse Depression
Focalin XR 10 mg	1 at 8a.m.	/ 07/02/07	7/19/07	Increased	Attention/ Impulse

Figure 2.1 Diagnoses and Medication in File

The resident whose psychiatric diagnosis is depicted in Figure 2.1 is diagnosed with three disorders requiring clinical attention (Axis I diagnoses): Bipolar Disorder Last Phase Manic in Partial Remission, Cannabis Abuse in Recent Remission, and Attention Deficit and Hyperactivity Disorder (ADHD). He takes Seroquel, Lithium Carb, and Focalin XR to address these disorders or more specifically "to address problems related to: danger to others, attention and impulse, and depression." He takes medication at 8 a.m., 3 p.m., and 8 p.m., during the scheduled medication dispensing times (see Figure 3.3 for the daily schedule and medication dispensing times). This diagnosis and medication regimen is located in the child's file. I come back to this information later. For now, I use it to illustrate how young people are framed by the institution. I was told that state law required a differential diagnosis from the American Psychiatric Association's Diagnostic and Statistical Manual (DSM-IV) (2000) for funding allocation.[5]

In addition to individual diagnoses and medication regimens, Havenwood organizes its living units or cottages into psychiatric categories based on the DSM. At Intake Meetings, it is decided what cottage is most appropriate for each youth's treatment trajectory. For example, Dwayne is placed in Steele Cottage.[6] Specifically, the cottages are grouped into three main diagnostic categories: severely emotionally disturbed, severely mentally ill, and severely behaviorally disordered. Within these broader categories, each cottage is also known to treat specific diagnoses. According to the official Havenwood document titled "Terms and Definitions to Know in Your 1st 90 Days," staff members learn the official ways Havenwood identifies its cottages and the psychiatric issues of those who live there include:

> **Severely Emotionally Disturbed: Shelby South (female) and Bradley North (male).** General diagnostic categories include Post-Traumatic Stress Disorder and Other Anxiety Disorders; Bipolar Disorder and other Mood Disorders; Borderline Personality Disorder, Narcissistic Personality Disorder and other Personality Disorders. These youth often are extremely anxious and depressed, engaging in severe acting out. They may have difficulty controlling anger and can be interpersonally exploitative.
>
> **Severely Mentally Ill: Shelby North (female), Bradley South (male), and Kerry (became female in 2007).** General diagnostic categories include Pervasive Developmental Disorder, Schizophrenia, Post-Traumatic Stress Disorder (Severe), Personality Disorder (low functioning) and Mentally Ill with low IQ. These youth exhibit severe levels of disorganized behavior, poor reality testing and poor self-care.

Severe Behavior Disorder: Steele (male), Roger (male), Terrance (male), Evelyn's (female). General diagnostic categories include Disruptive Behavior Disorder, Post-Traumatic Stress Disorder, Bipolar, and other Mood Disorders. These youth exhibit severe levels of agitated, aggressive, assaultive externalizing behaviors.

Once the resident is living in a particular cottage based on his psychiatric diagnosis and he has an appropriate medication regimen, it is common knowledge at Havenwood that he can now participate in the therapeutic practices that cultivate self-change.

Therapy and the Therapeutic Milieu

Each youth participates in individual therapy one or more times a week. As part of a psychiatric institution all youth have to participate in individual therapy. As part of the broader residential treatment, therapists present information regarding individual therapy during meetings, such as Team and Staffings, and in seminars where the youth's treatment progress is discussed (I will provide transcript data in later chapters). I observed these meetings and the brief interactions between therapists and residents. However, when I asked about individual therapy in the 20 life history interviews, not one resident freely talked about individual therapy as a meaningful practice at Havenwood. Common responses to my question, "What about individual therapy?" were, "Oh yeah, individual therapy," "Yeah, I guess therapy is good," and "You get to say whatever you want in there." So while individual therapy was part of everyday life, the youth I formally interviewed did not remember it as meaningful without my prompting.

In addition to individual therapy, every day each cottage runs a number of group therapy sessions. For example, the morning would include a Goal Group where youth identified their treatment focus of the day. In the evening another Goal Group would be held where the youth would recount how they achieved or failed to achieve their morning goal (see also chapter 3). Throughout the rest of the day other groups were held, depending on the day. Formal groups included Anger Management, Needs and Issues, Goals, Community, Healthy Choices, and Therapeutic Recreation. Groups are scheduled into the daily structure as well as used for spontaneous conflict or decision making. I will come back to group therapy in chapter 5.

As I mentioned in chapter 1, milieu treatment logic argues that in residential treatment the living environment should be used as a treatment intervention itself, extending therapeutic intervention from the one hour of therapy to the "other 23 hours" of care (Trieschman, Whittaker, and Brendtro 1969). Youth live in cottages, or the milieu, with the same youth with whom they share group therapy. Therefore, the milieu and group sharing practices are used in tandem to facilitate emotional awareness and proper expression. It is during group therapy and in daily life in the cottage (milieu treatment) that the youth of Havenwood participate in constant therapeutic practice and cultivate their State-mandated transformation. It will become apparent how milieu treatment and group therapy make up the daily lives of the youth at Havenwood and how these formal sessions and therapeutic practices are modified, hip hopified.

The Level System

At Havenwood, the primary way of assessing transformation on a day-to-day basis is by measuring behavioral change. The way of measuring residents' behavior change is through an institutional behavior modification system or the "Level System." The Level System is an official paradigm that values some behavior over others in a hierarchical system. If the resident's behavior is good, he earns higher Levels. The higher the Level, the better one is doing in the psychiatric treatment process. Points reflect behavior; much like other scoring or judging systems, the better the behavior, the higher the points. Movement up or down Levels indicates treatment progress or regression. Each week, residents' Levels are determined and the resident is "on" that Level for a week. Discussion of Levels are ubiquitous in the conversations at Havenwood. In addition to indexing official treatment progress, Levels also determine daily activities, including the kinds of snacks one can have, bed times, and how freely one can move around campus. I'll come back to how the Level System and other institutional regimens are put into practice in chapter 3.

Levels result from the aggregation of point scores accumulated over the course of a day and week. At Steele Cottage, per the official Cottage Program, Levels are an average of points earned in the following areas[7]: "(1) cottage daily activities, (2) recreation, (3) school, (4) allowance points, (5) resident's evaluation of their daily goals, and (6) any serious negative behavior which was documented by staff." The weekly tally sheet is provided in Figure 2.2 that follows (I will also reference this tally sheet in chapter 4 as it is used in group therapy sessions).

PROGRAM - WEEKLY SUMMARY Date: 10/30/07

NAME	ITP AVG	REC AVG	SCH AVG	ALLOWANCE POINTS	DAILY GOALS	MAJORS	MINORS	LAST LEVEL	CURRENT LEVEL
	4 / (3)	4 / (3)	3.7 / (2+)	600			1	8	3w
	4 / (3)	4 / (3)	5 / (3)	600				8	8
	2.97 / (2)	3.16 / (2)	3 / (2)	150			4	2	2w
	3.71 / (2+)	3.64 / (2+)	3.2 / (2)	425		1		2	2
	3.66 / (2+)	3.4 / (2)	3.18 / (2)	675			1	2	2
	3.21 / (2)	3.33 / (2)	na /	50				2	2w
	3.09 / (2)	3.59 / (2+)	4.4 / (3)	200		1		2	2w
	4 / (3)	4 / (3)	5 / (3)	550				T	T
	4 / (3)	3.95 / (3)	4.6 / (3)	700				3(3)	8
	3.63 / (2+)	3.78 / (3)	3.88 / (3)	475				2w	2
	4 / (3)	3.94 / (3)	3.7 / (2+)	675			1	3(2)	3w
	3.25 / (2)	3.21 / (2)	2.4 / (1)	450				2w	1
	3.16 / (2)	3.4 / (2)	1.8 / (1)	300			1	2w	1
	/	/	/	350				2E	2E
	/	/	/						

LEVEL 1	1.00-2.44	1.00-2.44		0-399 PTS
LEVEL 2	2.45-3.54	2.45-3.54		400+ PTS
LEVEL 2+	3.55-3.74	3.55-3.74		500+ PTS
LEVEL 3	3.75-4.20	3.75-4.20		600+ PTS

Figure 2.2 Weekly Level Tally Sheet

Scores are based on formal treatment goals and objectives. Each resident has an "Individual Treatment Plan" or ITP. Each ITP has specific goals. For example, one of the resident's ITP goals are:

1. Will eliminate dangerous behaviors that place others at risk of harm.
2. Will reduce hyperactivity to a level that does not interfere with daily activities.
3. Will comply with the rules and expectations at home, school, placement, and in the community, and eliminate noncompliant behavior patterns.
4. Will comply with all court recommendations and stipulations of his probation.
5. Will reduce depression to a level that does not interfere with daily functioning and relationships.

Twice a day residents are scored on how well they are achieving their ITP goals. These scores are averaged into a weekly ITP score (see Figure 2.2). Residents also have goals for school (SCH) and therapeutic recreation (REC) and they earn points during these activities (see Figure 2.2).

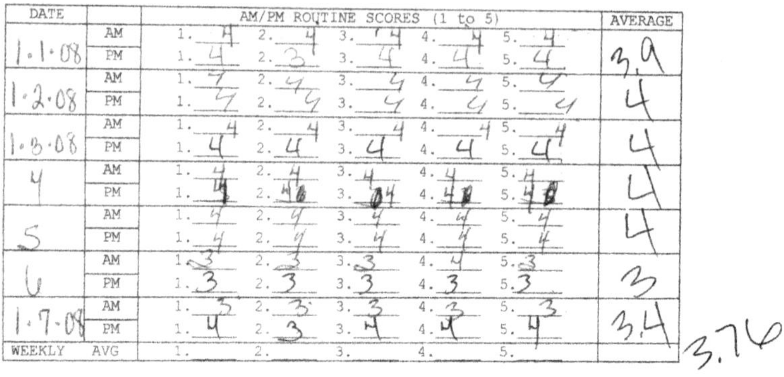

DATE		AM/PM ROUTINE SCORES (1 to 5)					AVERAGE
1.1.08	AM	1. 4	2. 4	3. 4	4. 4	5. 4	3.9
	PM	1. 4	2. 3	3. 4	4. 4	5. 4	
1.2.08	AM	1. 4	2. 4	3. 4	4. 4	5. 4	4
	PM	1. 4	2. 4	3. 4	4. 4	5. 4	
1.3.08	AM	1. 4	2. 4	3. 4	4. 4	5. 4	4
	PM	1. 4	2. 4	3. 4	4. 4	5. 4	
4	AM	1. 4	2. 4	3. 4	4. 4	5. 4	4
	PM	1. 4	2. 4	3. 4	4. 4	5. 4	
5	AM	1. 4	2. 4	3. 4	4. 4	5. 4	4
	PM	1. 4	2. 4	3. 4	4. 4	5. 4	
6	AM	1. 3	2. 3	3. 3	4. 4	5. 3	3
	PM	1. 3	2. 3	3. 3	4. 3	5. 3	
1.7.08	AM	1. 3	2. 3	3. 3	4. 3	5. 3	3.4
	PM	1. 4	2. 3	3. 4	4. 4	5. 4	
WEEKLY	AVG	1.	2.	3.	4.	5.	3.76

Figure 2.3 Points for Daily Work toward Individual Treatment Plan Goals

In Figure 2.3, the document has typed numbers 1 to 5. These numbers corresponds to the individuals ITP goals (listed earlier). Twice a day, during the morning and evening, a resident's behavior is scored using a scale of 1 to 5. The higher the score, the better one is doing. Those scores are averaged each day. For example, in Figure 2.3 we see how a young man earns daily averages of 3, 3.4, 3.9, and 4 points for a particular week.[8] These daily averages are then averaged for a week. The resident earns 3.76 points this particular week. This weekly averages is part of the overall Level, aggregated with other scores as seen on the form in Figure 2.2.

In addition to points for achieving one's therapeutic goals, allowance points, which are monies earned by doing chores and by earning "bonuses" (which are small monetary amounts for good behaviors above and beyond expectations) or being "fined"(which are small monetary amounts for bad behaviors such as cursing or walking out of single file lines) are part of the Level System. In addition to weekly averages and allowance points, "serious negative behavior documented by staff" is also considered when figuring Levels. These are listed as "Majors" and "Minors" in Figure 2.2. The term Major (or Minor) is the shorthand term used to index a "major dangerous behavior incident." Majors require a significant treatment intervention, often a restraint or seclusion. All of the information aggregated on this tally sheet is calculated into a Level. The resident is then "on" this Level for a week.

Each cottage has its own Level System. Steele Cottage's Levels range from 1 to 3, Gratis (G) and Transition (T). Also included are Level modifiers, such as the "w" or 3 with a number, for example 3^2

(see Figure 2.2). The "w" means "warning" that not all of the points reflect the Level and that a lower Level could be earned next week (no one wanted to earn a lower Level). The small number, or the two in 3^2, reflects the number of weeks one has been on Level 3.

The Level also informs institutional life. At Steele Cottage Level 3 is understood as doing well, not getting in trouble, and doing what one is asked of him in terms of treatment goals. Figure 2.4 provides an example of what one gets to do, if one has earned a Level 3 score; this definition of Level 3 comes also from the Steele Cottage Program.

Let me translate what Level 3 means. If a resident earns a score of 3 or above by achieving his goals (i.e., reduce hyperactivity to a level that does not interfere with daily activities) at school, in the cottage, during group therapy, and during recreational therapy, doing his chores, and refraining from any major or minor infractions he will earn and be on Level 3. While on Level 3, the youth has many privileges. For example, he can go to the basketball courts without needing or waiting for a staff member to accompany him; staff can watch him from the cottage ("eyesight"). He can play video games, watch television, or listen to the radio during free time. If the cottage goes to the movies or mall as a planned activity, he is able to go along (off-campus privileges). He can use a "pass" or walk around campus without a staff escort or supervision, even out of the viewing range of staff members. Rather than spending Quiet Time (defined in chapter 3) in his room like those not on Level 3 or above, he can continue to hang out in the living

<u>Level 3</u>

- AM/PM, recreation, and school weekly averages of 3.75 to 5.00
- Allowance points of 600 to 1500
- Eyesight per resident treatment plan.
- All radio, TV, and video game privileges per program.
- Off-campus privileges.
- Passes per program
- Quiet Time maybe served in living room.
- Two personal food and drink snacks per snack period.
- Bedtime is 10:00pm.
- May have $5.00 on person.

Figure 2.4 Definition of Level 3

room during this half hour in the evening. He can use his allowance, the $5.00 on his person, to purchase and eat his own snacks (i.e., his favorite candy or chips) rather than the snacks provided by Havenwood (e.g., an apple). And his bedtime is much later than that of youth not on Level 3. Being on Level 3 has many perks and privileges and the residents feel good about themselves, when they are able to carry on without the close supervision of staff members, when they can eat nondining hall snacks, and when they can have more freedom around the cottage.

Crisis Intervention

Youth are placed in psychiatric custody because they are identified as having serious mental health needs and significant behavior issues. Havenwood has two official crisis intervention philosophies that inform how staff members intervene with youth in crisis. These include: Life Space Crisis Intervention (LSCI) and Therapeutic Crisis Intervention (TCI). Staff members are trained in these paradigms.

LSCI is a nationally recognized therapeutic intervention strategy used by a variety of residential treatment centers, alternative schools, and other institutions focusing on behavior change (Long, Wood, and Fecser 2001). The goal of LSCI is for young people to understand the connection between their thoughts, feelings, and behaviors. Once a youth can understand the dysfunctional connections, which are identified as a "Conflict Cycle," changing these connections can occur. For example, youth can learn to identify their own negative emotions, such as anger, before these emotions cause behavioral issues, such as aggression.

LSCI focuses on crisis events, which include anything that might trigger what LSCI identifies as a youth's irrational beliefs or a negative self-perception. A crisis event and negative self-perception leads to negative feelings, which are oftentimes acted out by the youth in the form of observable behaviors. These observable behaviors elicit a response from others in the youth's life, particularly adults or authority figures. All of these—negative self-perception, negative feelings, observable behaviors, and reaction from adults—reveal the youth's pattern of crisis or his "Conflict Cycle." A poster of the Conflict Cycle hangs in every classroom and cottage, and in administrative and therapy offices at Havenwood depicting the following example: a youth gets a bad grade on a test (crisis event) and this reinforces some of his self-perception, such as "I'm dumb" (irrational belief or negative self-perception). The youth then feels shame or anger (negative feelings), which he acts out by cursing at his teacher (observable behaviors). The teacher gets upset and then punishes the student by giving him detention (adult response). In addition to a poster hanging in every building, meetings are organized around this cycle and each youth has his or her own conflict cycle mapped out, see Figure 2.5. Each bubble is marked and the cycle progresses from the youth's view of [1] self/others and a [2] stressful event to the youth's [3] feelings, [4] behavior, and then the [5] adult response. This cycle informs crisis intervention procedures and the ways staff members relate to the youth while in crisis. This mapping of the youth's Conflict Cycle was part of his or her file.[9]

A main focus of official clinical treatment was to identify each youth's Conflict Cycle and to help him or her understand it. LSCI tells us that once one knows one's Conflict Cycle, he or she can make positive changes.[10] However, sometimes serious crises erupt at Havenwood and knowledge about how to deal with these events is critical for the overall functioning of the institution.

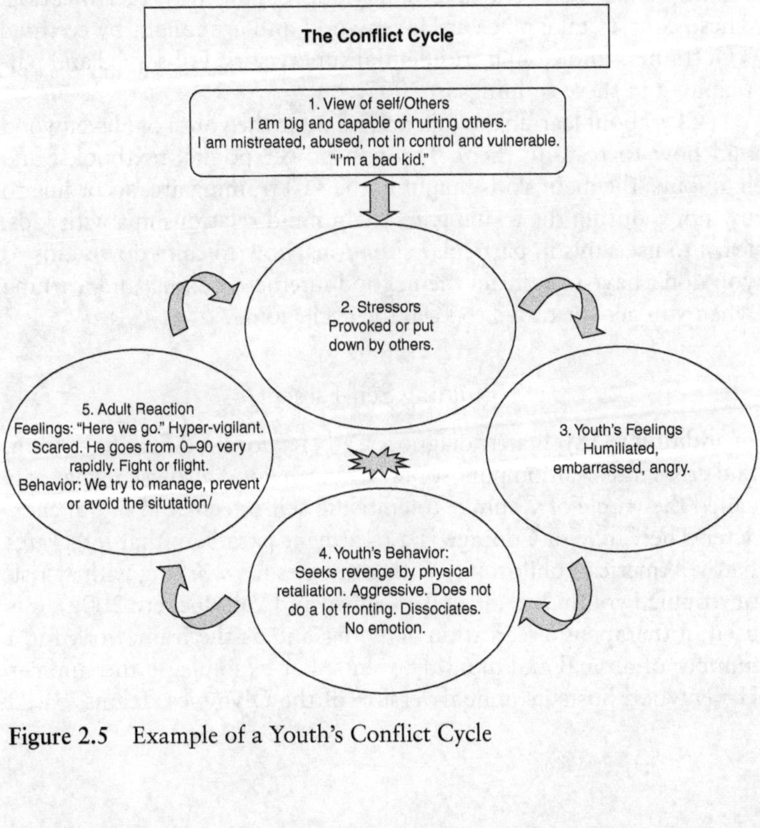

Figure 2.5 Example of a Youth's Conflict Cycle

TCI is a "restrictive behavior intervention model" developed by the Family Life Development Center of Cornell University. TCI also includes concepts from LSCI that together provide a "comprehensive practice structure that has common values and language to facilitate communication" (Havenwood document). LSCI and TCI are used strategically together at Havenwood to understand and change the crisis behavior of residents.

What makes TCI unique is that it is the intervention model for physical restraints, specifically those that result in young people being held down in the prone position by adults (I discuss restraints in chapter 4). Like LSCI and Counter Response, TCI is part of the training curriculum at Havenwood (I will come back to this in chapter 3). However, whereas LSCI, through the Conflict Cycle, is put into practice in agency-wide meetings, only line staff—those who work in the cottages—are formally mandated to attend the TCI trainings.[11] Each line staff member is required to get certified and maintain that certification. This certification is obtained through participation in a four-day course and passing an exam. Every six months staff members take a daylong course for recertification. These courses take place at Havenwood and are taught by certified TCI trainers and campus residential supervisors. I observed and participated in these trainings in 2007.

TCI is about learning to talk and relate to the youth of Havenwood and how to restrain them. Through power points, textbooks, and handouts, the main skills taught in the TCI training are, according to my notes during the training, to "help build relationships with kids, learn to use skills in particular situations, how to calm down kids so you don't have to restrain them, good interactive skills, and learning when you get frustrated to keep the cycle going."

Building Self-Esteem

In addition to psychiatric diagnoses, a behavior modification system, and crisis intervention philosophies, Havenwood also used what was called the Circle of Courage to cultivate self-esteem and moral character. The Circle of Courage is a treatment paradigm that integrates Native American philosophy with strategies for working with at-risk or troubled youth (Brendtro, Brokenleg, and Van Bockern 2002). It is used in therapeutic recreation activities and as the framework for a number of annual and monthly events. For example, in the summer Havenwood hosts its annual version of the Olympics. Teams, based on the cottage or living units, participate in athletic events and team-building activities, including relay races, a whiffle ball tournament, and thematic chalk drawings on the sidewalks. Key concepts in the Circle of Courage philosophy—Belonging, Mastery, Independence, and Generosity—are linked to the activities as well as in the build up to the event. Following each activity, youth are asked to identify and discuss which concept was most meaningful to them as part of the therapeutic aspect of the activity.

The Circle of Courage core concepts were put into practice in other events throughout the year including an annual Generosity Festival. The Generosity Festival modeled one of the four pillars of the Circle of Courage—Generosity—by having a few hours of free carnival-type play and games, food, and conversation among youth and staff members. However, the Circle of Courage seemed less important a treatment paradigm than psychiatry, behavior modification techniques, or crisis intervention because it was not integrated as well into the institutional structure. Rather than the Circle of Courage, youth identified with hip hop ideology as a self-esteem building philosophy. I will come back to this later.

Religious Services

As mentioned earlier, Havenwood was first constructed as a Christian institution, where moral character would be instilled through prayer and discipline. In fact, one of the oldest and most beautiful buildings on campus is the chapel. The chapel had dark wood pews, an original pipe organ, stained glass, and an ornate pulpit. Every Wednesday night the on-campus director of religious services and ordained minister holds religious services. Chapel services are the only activities that are voluntary. In addition to weekly services, which are facilitated by a different cottage each week, the director of religious services interviews each new resident about his or her religious needs and made sure these needs were met.[12] She also participated in treatment meetings and staffings. However, like the Circle of Courage, the religious services are secondary to psychiatric frameworks. In fact, the director of religious services proposed to run a group on grief and she was denied the opportunity. She told me she was informed that she did not have the adequate training to do so. She quipped that religion has "cornered the market" on grief for thousands of years. The director of religious services felt fully qualified to discuss loss and grief with residents, despite not being a trained psychotherapist. The clinical administration disagreed.

* * *

Havenwood has survived over 120 years and numerous paradigm shifts and is currently recognized as a psychiatric institution that uses the latest psychotropic medications, behavior modification techniques, and crisis intervention strategies to promote emotional and psychological stability. These official treatment paradigms and strategies are the therapeutic context in which the young people live. However, as we will see throughout this text, young people are suspended in the web of these organizing paradigms. These paradigms shape their lives—young people are restrained when in crisis and they organize their understandings of self via the Level System. However, young people challenge the constraining aspect of these paradigms almost constantly and create a "give" in the system. I come back to this throughout the book.

Havenwood Residents

Official Demographics

I was fortunate to conduct research in an agency that, as part of the Department of Family and Children Services, is required to document and track demographic information on its residents. I relied on Havenwood's bimonthly lists, year-end demographic data, and case files to understand the demographic make up of the residents of Havenwood.

About 100 young people live at Havenwood at any one particular time. Another 50 live in off-campus group homes or individual apartments as part of their treatment process. If one was doing well on Havenwood's main campus, he could transition to living in a group home. I will come back to transitions into group homes in chapter 8. I visited every group home and the independent living apartments, however, my main ethnographic focus was on Havenwood's main campus and on Steele Cottage in particular.

Table 2.1 shows the number of total clients and the number of clients per funding source over the course of my research. Funders, including the Department of Family and Children Services, Department of Health Services, Juvenile Probation, State Board of

Table 2.1 Number of Clients Per Funding Source

Funding Source	Number of Clients	Percentage of Clients
Department of Family and Children Services (DFCS)	88 (August 2006)	61%
	87 (May 2007)	60%
	90 (December 2007)	60%
Department of Health Services/ Individual Care Grants (DHS/ICG)	42	29%
	40	28%
	36	24%
Juvenile Probation	0	0%
	0	0%
	3	3%
State School Board of Education	14	10%
	17	12%
	20	13%
Private	1	1%
	0	0%
	0	0%
Total Number of Clients	145	
	144	
	149	

Education, and private insurance, cover room and board as well as educational and therapeutic costs for each child. The Department of Family and Children Services has guardianship over those they fund. The Department of Health funds children whose parents apply for funding for severe mental illness treatment resulting in Individual Care Grants. Juvenile Probation funds one month of treatment, and then the State School Board of Education usually funds the remaining treatment for juvenile offenders not sent to detention. Almost no one has private insurance. This information came from lists aggregated twice per month. The average stay for the residents is 18 months, with some leaving after a month or two and others staying for years. In Table 2.1, I provide the number of clients from my first, tenth, and eighteenth months of fieldwork to show how little the numbers of residents and funding sources fluctuated during my research period.

Havenwood also collected demographic information: 62 percent of Havenwood clients are male; 38 percent female. Of this, 50 percent are 13–16 years old, 42 percent are 17 and above, and 8 percent are 12 and under. While 61 percent of Havenwood youth are African American, 30 percent are white, 4 percent are Hispanic, and

5 percent are others. In other words, the majority of youth who live at Havenwood are African American, male, and 13 to 16 years old.

Social Histories: Mental Health Assessment/Social History Narratives

As with Dwayne mentioned earlier, residents almost always come to Havenwood after many other placements along the continuum of foster care and mental health services found in American psychiatry and the foster care system. Most of the residents have been to psychiatric hospitals or lived in group homes, foster families, and other residential treatment centers. The case files chronicle when and where the youth moved in narrative form, telling the youth's neglect and abuse histories. While each resident has a unique story, common themes emerged in the narratives as I read through hundreds of case files. I will describe Havenwood youth in broad strokes using these themes. I also do this for four reasons. First, young people who find themselves in psychiatric custody have had a difficult childhood. Not all young people with difficult childhoods live in residential treatment. However those who do, have been seriously injured by guardians or family members. It is important to acknowledge that the young people at Havenwood are a particular population, one congregated into a community based on traumatic and violent childhoods. Second, the MHA/SH documents are narrative accounts of critical junctures in the life of the youth, such as significant instances of neglect or abuse, rather than quantified incidents or the frequency of abuse, neglect, drug use, and other issues. Therefore, the point of MHA/SH data is not how many times a youth was abused or hospitalized but that they were, that their young lives include such events. Third, during my review of the data I juxtaposed life history interviews with case files to compare incidents and stories.[13] A similar story of neglect, abuse, hospitalization, and so on does emerge but in broad strokes, not in details. Therefore, counting frequencies might be more misleading than accurate. Finally, I do not want to reduce the young people to quantitative incidents of abuse or to exoticize them through excessive description of abuse histories. Therefore, I provide a general, common social history of the *official institutional accounts* of why youth are at Havenwood.[14] To do this I use the terms such as "most" or "often" to illustrate that not every child is exactly the same but that similarities exist. These official accounts inform the treatment interventions, objectives, and goals for the resident while at Havenwood.

Most of the residents had suffered prolonged episodes of abuse and/or neglect. Cigarette burns on appendages, being whipped with extension cords, being locked in closets for hours or days, and being "unattended" by guardians due to incarceration or drug abuse are common childhood experiences of the Havenwood residents. Many of the residents have also been sexually abused in addition to suffering emotional and physical abuse. This abuse comes to the attention of state authorities—either police, hospital workers, or the Department of Family and Children Services—when the residents are between 4 and 10 years old. The residents are often removed from their families and guardians at this time.

Once a resident reaches age 10, the reasons for removal shift from the guardian's problems—drug raids or substance abuse—to the *resident's* problems—suicidal ideation, fighting at school, or drug use. For example, even if a foster mother is documented as or accused of abusing the resident, by the time the child is 10 years old, the reason for his placement in psychiatric custody is primarily identified as the resident's "emotional or behavioral needs." Many residents have multiple psychiatric hospitalizations, lasting from a few days to months. Also many residents have been incarcerated in juvenile detention facilities. These hospitalizations or incarcerations are the result of behaviors labeled as "aggressive" or "self-harming." At about age 10, youth are removed and placed in either hospital psychiatric wards or detentions centers for "psychiatric evaluation," rather than being removed from their homes due to parental abuse.

Following psychiatric evaluations, the youth are diagnosed with mental illnesses and prescribed psychotropic medication. Diagnoses shift over time and depend on the diagnosing physician, as we see with Dwayne mentioned earlier. Therefore, the case files are comprised of diagnosis shifts and medication changes. Many of Havenwood residents have been on psychotropic medications for years, some starting from as young as age 9.

In addition to the history of disrupted primary residences, abuse, and neglect, school expulsions or behavioral difficulties in school are significant aspects of Havenwood youths' lives. Most of the residents, upon their intake at Havenwood, test well below grade level in math, reading, and writing. They have sparse records of school attendance. Often their home lives have been so fragmented that the resident cannot remember the names of schools he attended, and primary caregivers are no longer in contact with the Department of Family and Children Services. Many of the residents have been expelled from schools for fighting. Truancy is listed as a common legal offense.

Other interactions with the juvenile justice system are also common. Many Havenwood residents have burglary or drug charges. Most have written documentation of substance use, including alcohol and marijuana. In addition to this, some of the files include gang involvement or affiliation. Many of the young women at Havenwood have a long record of what is identified as "inappropriate sexual behaviors," either at the hands of their caregivers or when they were runaways. Often many of the legal issues noted in residents' files are related to "peer interactions." Therefore, in addition to primary home instability, the residents are often seen to have problematic peer relationships that result in the young men and women getting into trouble at school and with the law.

The case files include an account of a resident's history of trauma exposure and traumatic experiences. Common traumatic experiences include witnessing criminal activity, significant family and/or community violence, physical, emotional, and sexual abuse, and traumatic grief or separation.[15] Abuse and criminal activity is sometimes framed using a trauma narrative. For example, a child is said to have experienced what is officially called "interpersonal trauma" if he or she is abused, or "social trauma" if he or she is involved in or a witness to a police raid at home.

In addition to all of the difficulties the residents experience, a small section of the file and intake discussion involves soliciting what the young man or woman does well or enjoys. This is often a short list, but includes rapping, basketball, coloring, drawing, and listening to music.

According to case files and demographic information Havenwood is a large campus that houses about one hundred young people who are predominantly African American, male, 14–18 years old, behaviorally disordered, with histories of abuse or neglect, disrupted schooling, criminal behavior, traumatic experiences, time in juvenile detention, and stays in psychiatric hospitals.

Havenwood Staff

In addition to the one hundred residents who live in nine cottages, I also spent considerable time in meetings and talking with adults who worked in various professional roles across Havenwood. Havenwood employs psychiatrists, nurses, teachers, teacher aids, school administrators, clinical administrators, residential administrators, intake specialists, family therapists, individual therapists, recreational therapists, social workers, line or cottage staff, campus-wide crisis supervisors, custodians, and clerical staff. We meet individuals from a variety of these roles. For example, Sarah, mentioned earlier, has a doctorate in psychology and has been a therapist and clinical director at Havenwood. She oversees the clinical programs at Steele, Roger, and Terrace cottages. We meet Derrick's teacher Ernest, his case worker Craig, and his individual therapist Paige in chapter 7. Intake specialists like Tricia and Cindy were introduced earlier. Carter, a campus-wide evening crisis supervisor, and Sophie, a clinical consultant, and line staff members Tina, Robert, and Tom appear in chapter 4. However, most staff members are not featured in this book, other than those who live and work at Steele Cottage.[16] I provide ethnographic accounts from Havenwood at-large. However, my in-depth ethnographic research focused on Steele Cottage and the men and women who lived and worked there.

Steele Cottage—"The Little Juvie Home"

Steele Cottage was home to 35 residents during my time at Havenwood. Demographically the numbers break down to 30 African American, 3 white, and 2 Hispanic boys. The Steele Cottage percentage of African American youth of 85 percent is higher than Havenwood's 61 percent. However, even this percentage is misleading. Two of the three white youth bookended my research, one left soon after I arrived and one arrived just before I left. The third white youth ran away shortly after arriving, in the middle of my research project. The two Hispanic youth were there at different times. Therefore, Steele Cottage is often exclusively home to Black boys aged 14 to 17 years old. Steele Cottage is known as a behavioral cottage and the young men are identified as oppositionally defiant troublemakers.

My ethnographic experience and the data that emerged from 18 months of participant observation in the living unit Steele do not support this identification or total institutional implementation of the treatment paradigms discussed earlier. Rather, I hope to illustrate the very complex humanity, lives filled with violence, precariousness, friendships, and love, of the African American youth in Steele and Havenwood more broadly. The data I collected does not support the identification of Steele youth as simply troublemakers.[17] Instead, by examining the everyday lives, feelings, fears, relationships, hopes, and transformations of William, Lamar, Derrick, Dwayne, Chris, Jonathon, Marlon, Wesley, Manny, Mark, Kyle, and Andy at Steele Cottage, I ask the reader to think about some of the negative stereotypes that bind and constrain the lives of young Black men in America, and to perhaps see these often stereotyped "troublemakers" as sons, friends, children, victims, and emergent good men trying to make it in life, despite considerable challenges.

Other anthropologists may not feel compelled to ask readers to suspend judgment or to be open to alternative ways of thinking about the people they work with and write about. However, considering the dominant negative narratives about African American young men (Neal 2013; Van Deburg 2004), I find it necessary to do so. At the turn of the twentieth century, W. E. B. Du Bois (1903/2005) identified that African Americans were "a problem" in American society. Over one hundred years and many social shifts later, African American men continue to be considered problems, to be perceived as threatening to the mainstream established social order, and to be stereotyped as "an undifferentiated cohort of villains" (Van Deburg 2004). Cultural theorist Mark Anthony Neal (2013) identifies the Black villain as the most legible Black male body and this contemporary Black villain is one either associated with prison, gangs, or rap music. The African American boys of Steele Cottage can be read to fit into all three of these categories—most were identified as gang related, as hip hop aficionados in style, dress, and comportment, and they are all contained in State custody (although in psychiatric custody rather than prison). However, the ethnographic evidence I provide challenges these stereotyped caricatures and asks us to think about the young men of Steele Cottage in alternative ways.

Each cottage has a "Team." The Team, and they identify as a team, is largely comprised of people identified as line staff members. I will use "staff" in many cases rather than "staff members." "Staff" refers to the plural. These staff work with the youth after school and over night. They work on the weekends, take the residents off campus on home visits, and are tasked with implementing the bulk of each resident's treatment. Other official Team members include cottage clinical directors, like Sarah mentioned earlier, who consult each week on the functioning of the cottage and the progression of each resident's treatment.

Steele Cottage has a Team of seven line staff: Steve, Allen, James, Jim, Zac, Pete, Arthur, and Angie. Pete and Zac are white; everyone else is African American. Therefore, Steele Cottage is home and workplace to mostly African American individuals. We will get to know these men and woman throughout this book. However, a few details here are important. Steve is the supervisor of Steele Cottage and he has worked at Havenwood for 25 years. He is an athletically built, gregarious man. He hails from the same city the youth do and went to college in the area. Allen is a mid-twenties college graduate who was considered exceptionally "cool" by the residents. He was raised in the same neighborhood as some of the youth who live at Steele Cottage. Allen is witty and quick to laugh. Jim is a young, thirties African American man from the American South. He is the biggest man at Steele Cottage at about 6'4" and 260 pounds. He is quiet and reserved in speech. James is a strong, athletic, and sharp-tongued man. He tries his best to cultivate the athletic gifts and talents of the Steele Cottage youth. Arthur self-identifies as a "40-year-old thug" through his embodiment of East Coast hip hop attitude and style. He is also known for his strict adherence to rules and his fairness and for teaching at the local community college. Pete is a mid-twenties white male who enjoys a good laugh; he has roots in mechanics, and was seen working on his truck with the help of residents. Zac is a quiet white male with a strong athletic bent. He is happy to supervise hours of basketball scrimmages. Both Pete and Zac are from the suburbs or rural area where Havenwood is located and are also very large men. Angie, the lone woman of the group, is known as the matriarch of the cottage. She is a mid-forties African American woman from the African American suburbs of the city. Angie spends a lot of time teaching the young men to do their laundry and to cook. I spent many evenings with Steele Cottage youth and Angie off-campus at the local mall or laundromat.

Three to four staff members work during the evening hours, 3 p.m.–11p.m. Two are on duty for the overnight shift, 11 p.m.–7 a.m. Therefore, the adults and youth of Havenwood come to spend a considerable amount of time together. It is within this setting that important relationships are cultivated and love emerges. It is within this setting with these individuals, the predominantly African American boys and men at Steele Cottage, use Black cultural practices, particularly hip hop, in psychiatric treatment.

* * *

On my way to the Intake Meeting where we heard about Dwayne, I emerged from my building at the time that residents walk to school. On a typical Monday morning I would see residents from all of the cottages walking in single file lines to the school located 20 yards from my front door. I was never sure if everyone was quiet because they were tired, their medications had kicked in, or they knew the rules of not talking while walking in the single file lines.

This Monday morning I see a handful of the young Steele men I have come to know quite well. I exchange head nods with Mark, Andy, William, and Wesley. I notice Jonathon brushing his hair forward, enhancing his "waves." I make eye contact with Derrick. I notice he looks particularly well put together this morning in his hip hop inspired fashion. His XXL black T-shirt matches his new black Nike Air Force One sneakers, better known as "Ones," and his jeans are neatly pressed. Derrick moves closer to me on the sidewalk and he gives me a fist bump. I tell him to "have a good day at school." He nods in response. I watch him and the other single file lines disappear into the school building. I turn in the next chapter to how the institutional structure of Havenwood shapes life there and how hip hop also finds space to be meaningful.

Part II

Life at Havenwood

Chapter 3
Institutional Living

"Step to the back?" Marlon asks, as he stands where the living room meets the hallway, which runs perpendicular to the back of the cottage.

"Yep," Jim answers, as he follows Marlon into the back hallway. Marlon is not allowed to be in the back hallway without supervision, he is not on a high Level.

"Get on the game?" Derrick asks, as he stands in front of the video game console.

Allen nods.

"Step to the kitchen?" Wesley asks, standing at the doorway to the kitchen, near the small dining room table where Arthur is playing a game of Spades.

"What do you need?" Arthur asks.

"Drink of water."

Arthur nods his head, and Wesley enters the kitchen.

"TRANSITION," Allen shouts, so everyone can hear his directive.

All at once everyone begins putting away the cards at the Spades table and shutting off the video games. It is 4:50 p.m. and it is time to Transition to dinner. The boys of Steele have to walk to the dining hall for their meals. The dining hall is about one hundred yards away, across a big field, past the chapel, gym, and outdoor basketball hoops. The boys move to the couches in the living room and the staff members retreat toward the staff desk, directly behind the couches. No one is talking. Once everyone is seated and quiet for about a minute, Allen, standing behind Steve's supervisor desk, states, "Levels."

Derrick, Wesley, Jonathon, Chris, and Lamar stand up and walk out of the door. I watch them walk across the field toward the dining hall. "Levels" indicates that those youth who have earned the privilege can walk to dinner without being in a single file line.

After the cottage is quiet again, following the clang of the heavy front door shutting, Allen continues. "Level 2." Allen is in charge of the unit this evening; therefore, he is the staff member calling out directives. Mark, Kyle, Dwayne, and Andy move toward the door, and stand in a single file line. The cottage is quiet.

"Level 1."

William, Tye, and Marlon get in line behind Andy. Allen holds the boys in formation for about 30 seconds before he states, "Okay." At this command, Mark pushes through the front door and leads the boys in a single file line to the dining hall. Jim, Allen, and Arthur follow the young men. I look behind me and see the young boys from Roger Cottage, the cottage for 7 to 13-year-old males adjacent to Steele Cottage, walking to the dining hall in a single file line as well. It is dinnertime at Havenwood.

Once Mark and the rest of the line reach the front door to the dining hall, the youth stop and wait for direction. Allen waits about 15 seconds and then says, "Okay." As long as everyone is following the rules, the transition from outside to inside dining hall is short. It is when people are talking, not paying attention, not standing still, or in some other way not following the rules of single file line behavior that transitions take longer than a quick few seconds. Today the boys are following the Program. The boys on Levels 1 and 2 enter the dining hall and sit at the table on the north side of the serving area. Derrick, Wesley, Jonathon, Chris, and Lamar, the boys on Level 3 or higher, are already sitting at the south-side table. After all of the boys are sitting quietly, and Allen gets a head nod, the "go-ahead," from the head cook, he says, "Line up." The young men stand up in unison and get in line for dinner. The line for food begins near the south-side table, privileging the youth on Level 3 or higher. Each boy grabs a plastic tray, plastic cup, and silverware and waits to pass the tray to the cooks behind the counter. Today's meal is pollack and tarter sauce, mac and cheese, green beans, salad bar, and milk. The menu has a four-week cycle; it will be a month before the fish is served for dinner again. I stand in line behind William, as I eat the vast majority of my meals at the dining hall.[1]

"How was school today?" I ask him. Boys are allowed to talk while in line, as long as they remain relatively quiet.

"Good. I didn't get any Minors." William has been struggling for a few months, so for him to not have received a Minor Behavior Incident (see chapter 2 for a discussion of Minors and Majors) is good news. It took me a while to learn how the Level System was also a register for well-being. It was common for youth to respond, "I'm on Level" to my "How are you?" I learned that this meant, "I'm on a Level that earns me privileges and to be on this Level I am not doing anything to get into trouble such as earn Minors or Majors."

Of course, one has to learn the Level system and the definition of Majors and Minors to be able to communicate in this register. The residents are allowed 30 days to get acclimated to life at Havenwood, the Cottage Program (see the rule book that follows), and the new way of communicating about daily functioning and behavior.

"Awesome," I respond. This is no small feat for William.

Behind us the young boys from Roger Cottage line up, also following a similar line up protocol.

After the Steele boys have finished dinner, which lasts about 15 minutes, and ends with the boys having bussed their dishes and returned to their seats to wait to go back to the cottage, Allen states, "Transition." Everyone but Derrick goes quiet. Derrick is caught rapping out loud as everyone else goes silent.

"Derrick," Jim calls out.

"My bad." Derrick apologizes for his verbal infraction, a loud comment in the quiet time of Transition.

After about 15 seconds, "Levels."

Once again, Derrick, Chris, Jonathon, Lamar, and Wesley stand up and walk out of the dining hall. About 30 more seconds pass.

"Level 2."

Mark, Kyle, Dwayne, and Andy get up and stand in line at the dining hall door.

After they quietened down and became still, "Level 1."

William, Tye, and Marlon line up behind Andy. After another 30 seconds, Allen states, "Okay." Mark pushes out of the front door and leads the single file line back to Steele Cottage.

Derrick, Chris, Jonathon, Lamar, and Wesley are standing in line against the brick wall perpendicular to the front door. Steele Cottage is locked when no one is inside. Mark, Kyle, Dwayne, Andy, William, Tye, and Marlon line up behind them and wait. Allen walks up to the door to unlock it. Everyone is quiet. Arthur and Jim are standing behind Marlon and off to one side. Allen unlocks the door and says, "Okay." The boys file inside. Allen brings up the rear. Once he is inside, Allen shouts, "QUIET TIME!" The boys know that after dinner they have to go to their rooms for 30 minutes of officially sanctioned and regularly scheduled "Quiet Time." Those on Level 3 can play video games; and this is also the time to make phone calls to relatives. Arthur follows the boys back into the bedroom area of the cottage. He sits at the chair placed in front of the confinement room, where the small hallway from the living room meets the long hallway of bedrooms and two bathrooms, next to the phone the residents can use. From here he supervises "Quiet Time" in the back hallway.

"We have Rec tonight," Arthur reminds Allen once everyone is in their rooms or quiet in the living room. Allen nods. It is Wednesday and Steele Cottage has a Therapeutic Recreation Group on Wednesday nights after dinner, Quiet Time, and Chores.

* * *

As mentioned in chapter 2, Havenwood has a variety of frameworks that organize the treatment process. The frameworks shape life in this total institution; however, they are secondary to the grand plan of the project of total institutional living. In this chapter, I illustrate how Havenwood is organized to operate as a total institution, following Goffman's definition. This grand plan is put into practice as youth, for example, must ask to go to the bathroom or to get a drink of water. They must be quiet during transition periods, walk in single file lines, and behave properly during Transition, Quiet Time, and while walking across campus. However, as I have mentioned previously, Havenwood is not just about structure, there is considerable "give" in the total institution. It is this "give" in the system that allows for some of the healing dramas to take place, the sampling of hip hop into an otherwise totally structured psychiatric institution. Therefore, I discuss how this "give" emerges at the level of the institution's grand plan.

The Grand Plan: Life in a Total Institution

In his classic *Asylums: Essays on the Social Situation of Mental Patients and Other Inmates*, Erving Goffman tells us that the central features of total institutions are:

> First, all aspects of life are conducted in the same place and under the same single authority. Second, each phase of the member's daily activity is carried on in the immediate company of a large batch of others, all of whom are treated alike and required to do the same thing together. Third, all phases of the day's activities are tightly scheduled, with one activity leading at a prearranged time into the next, the whole sequence of activities being imposed from above by a system of explicit formal rulings and a body of officials. Finally, the various enforced activities are brought together into a single rational plan purportedly designed to fulfill the official aims of the institution (1961:6).

It is the goal of total institutions to organize all aspects of life, all of the people who live there, and all activities to reform, treat, or change the individuals into a tightly organized grand "single rational" plan (see also Barker 1974; Polsky, Claster, and Goldberg 1968; Robinson, Gardner, Greenwood, Hagan, and Richmond 1957).

At Havenwood the official aim, as mentioned in the "Introduction" (to take troubled youth and make them good citizens) is organized in a variety of ways. I mentioned in chapter 2 all of the frameworks for the therapeutic process, including psychiatric diagnosis and cottage living, medication regimens, the Level System, crisis intervention strategies, and even esteem building programs. Here I want to discuss how these frameworks are themselves organized into an institutional plan.

The ethnographic vignette just mentioned demonstrates how young men of Steele are organized into this grand plan. First, they live and eat at Havenwood and they do so together. Their time is tightly scheduled, even into periods of time identified as "Transition" or "Quiet Time." And they follow a system of explicit formal rules such as asking for permission to move around the cottage. The young men of Steele, and all residents of Havenwood, follow what is called a Cottage Program. Steele's Cottage Program is 26 pages of formal rules, schedules, and definitions. Each resident is given this document when he arrives at the cottage. At Steele, the Program is stapled to the living room cork-board, one of the first places visible on entering the cottage. In practice, however, Steve designates a boy to teach the new resident the Program, because many of the young men cannot read very well.[2]

Important terms such as Transition and Quiet Time are stated by Allen as we have just seen. In Steele Cottage's Program, these terms are defined:

Transition:

- Residents are to be sitting down QUIETLY on the couches awaiting the next directive.
- Residents are to keep their hands and feet to themselves.

Quiet Time:

- Residents are to complete quiet time after meals back in the unit in their rooms.
- Residents on level 3 and Gratis may choose to serve quiet time in the living room.
- During quiet time residents may relax, read, do homework, or quietly listen to their radio (if off restrictions)
- Personal requests or needs will be honored by staff on a case by case basis

Residents are expected to know these definitions and how to perform these tasks (as well as all tasks defined in the Cottage Program). Staff members are also supposed to know and enforce how residents perform these tasks. As illustrated in the vignette just mentioned, they do. The Steele Cottage Program consists of 11 pages of definitions (including Aggression, Line Up, and How to Perform Cottage Chores), the definition of Levels (see Figure 2.4), and the daily schedules (see Figure 3.1 and 3.2 later).

The daily schedules inform youth and staff how each day will be organized. Take Wednesday, for example. Figure 3.1 illustrates

WEDNESDAY	
3:00p–3:15p	Transition back from school. Dispense medication
3:15p–3:30p	Afternoon snacks, if available.
3:30p–4:50p	Cottage Clean-up or Recreation.
4:50p–5:00p	Transition.
5:00p–5:30p	Dinner.
5:30p–6:00p	Quiet Time.
6:00p–6:20p	Chores.
6:20p–6:30p	Transition to evening.
6:30p–7:50p	Recreation.
7:50p–8:00p	Transition.
8:00p–8:15p	Evening Goals Group.
8:15p–8:30p	Evening snacks. Dispense medications.
8:30p–10:00p	Evening routine and bedtime

Figure 3.1 Steele Cottage Program's Wednesday Schedule

WEEKDAY OR NONHOLIDAY MORNINGS-DURING FALL/WINTER SCHOOL SESSIONS	
7:30a	Wake-up call for all residents.
7:30a–8:00a	Morning hygiene and room clean-up.
8:00a–8:30a	Breakfast.
8:30a–8:50a	Chores.
8:50a–9:00a	Mornings Goals Group.
9:00a	School.

Figure 3.2 Steele Cottage Program's Weekday Morning Schedule

how Wednesday is organized. Each day is similar, only altering what happens from 3:30 p.m.–4:50 p.m. and 6:30 p.m.–7:50 p.m. Otherwise, everyday after school is Transition, snacks, and medication dispensing. Quiet Time always follows Dinner, and Chores are always performed after Quiet Time. On Wednesday, the 3:30 p.m.–4:50 p.m. time frame is used to do a deep cleaning of the cottage. On Monday, for example, youth participate in Process Group, and on Tuesday they have Community Group. Such variation is the same for the 6:30 p.m.–7:50 p.m. time slot. On Monday and Wednesday, Therapeutic Recreation is in the evening. Both staff and youth of Steele Cottage have a Living Skills Group on Tuesday evening and Healthy Choices/Young Men's Group on Thursdays. Transitions are official parts of the Schedule; the young men of Steele Cottage Transition four times every evening. The mornings are also tightly scheduled. Morning routines only differ depending on whether it is a holiday, weekend, or summer school session. Figure 3.2 is Steele Cottage Program's morning schedule for weekday nonholiday fall/winter school session. As mentioned in chapter 2, the morning goal a young person chooses is discussed during the Morning Goals Group and then revisited in the Evening Goals Group. Figure 3.3

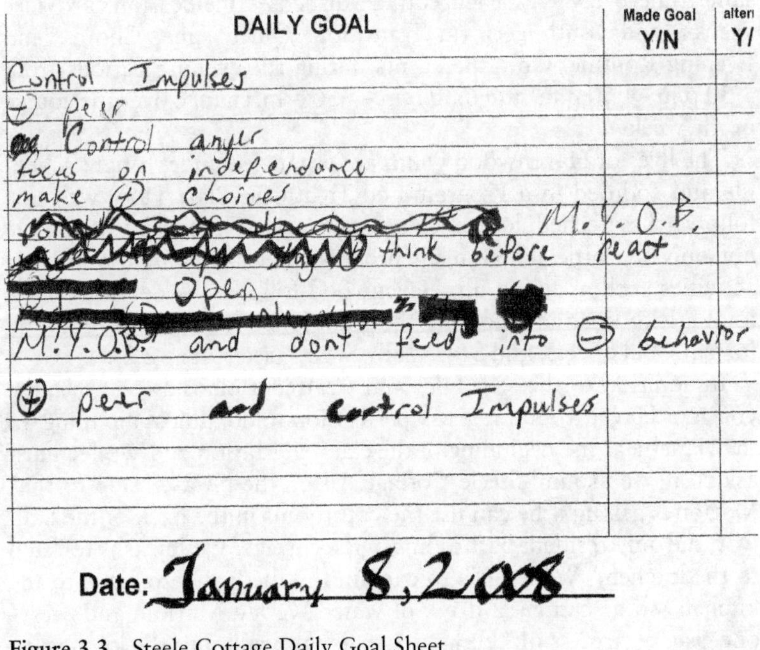
DAILY GOAL | Made Goal Y/N | alten Y/

Control Impulses
(+) peer
Control anger
focus on independance
make (+) choices
M.Y.O.B.
think before react
Open
M.Y.O.B. and dont feed into (−) behavior
(+) peer and control Impulses

Date: January 8, 2008

Figure 3.3 Steele Cottage Daily Goal Sheet

is an example of how these goals are written down to ensure that residents remember and try to achieve them each day. These goals include "control anger," "positive (+) peer", and "M.Y.O.B." or "Mind Your Own Business." One resident is identified as the note-taker for the Morning Goals Group and this person then leads the Evening Goals Group. The Goal Sheets, like the files, are stored in a desk in the staff office.

These images illustrate how life at Steele Cottage, and Havenwood more generally, is scheduled and codified into a particular official plan. Even the goals are officially written down and the document saved. Daily goals such as "control impulses" are linked to the resident's Individual Treatment Plan (ITP) Goals, mentioned in chapter 2 such as "Will comply with the rules and expectations at home, school, placement, and in the community, and eliminate noncompliant behavior patterns." Achieving daily goals and ITP goals are linked to daily scores and daily scores are linked to the resident's Level. As is shown in the ethnographic vignette mentioned and in Figure 2.4 depicting Level 3 in chapter 2, Levels determine privileges or whether one has to "line up" to walk in a single file over to the dining hall for dinner.

Other cottages followed similar programs and schedules. At the same time every day, each cottage dispenses medication, provides snacks, and youth perform Transition, Quiet Time, Chores, and Evening Routine. Only the events during the evening periods from 3:30 p.m.–4:50 p.m. and 6:30 p.m.–7:50 p.m. change over the course of the week.

The lives of Havenwood youth are organized under a tight schedule and codified in a Program and Treatment Plan. How well one follows these schedules and plans and acts in activities determine not only the official treatment progress, but also simple quotidian activities such as lining up. Havenwood follows the definition of a total institution and it codifies the grand plan in a Cottage Program, formal Goal Sheets, and Score Tally Sheets (see Figure 2.2).

In addition to the schedules and treatment plans and Levels, the youth of Havenwood must ask permission to do almost anything. In the vignette at the beginning of the chapter, Marlon and Wesley must ask to move around Steele Cottage. Using the phrase "step to the" Marlon is asking if he can use the bathrooms in the back of the hallway, the only resident bathrooms in the cottage. Wesley asks to "step to the kitchen." Wesley has to explain that he wants to "step to the kitchen" so he can get a drink of water. Wesley, Marlon, and everyone else, regardless of Level, have to ask to walk into the kitchen, to get a drink of water, to go to the bathroom, to use video games, to go to one's room, to go outside, to play Spades, and to do pretty much anything. A staff member always has to give explicit permission, and in cases with the back hallway example, has to follow the youth in order to supervise.

Goffman states that life in total institutions is formally administered (1961:xiii). This formal administering disrupts actions that in civil society lead individuals to believe they have some control over the world, autonomy, and freedom of action. It is difficult to imagine many American teenagers having to ask to go to the bathroom or to get a drink of water at home. However, at Steele and Havenwood, if youth do not ask to "step to the" they can be penalized, "fined" to use the Level System register, and their treatment progress and privileges are affected. As new residents move into Steele, it is common to see residents almost walk into the kitchen (or the back hallway) but dramatically catch themselves by the doorway, so that their feet do not break the invisible barriers. They also dramatically turn to make eye contact with any staff member around and ask for permission. The question is almost always: "Step to the…?"

My presence disrupted this formal administration of daily life in many ways. After I had been at Havenwood for a while and new residents would come to live at Steele, they would ask me for permission to move around. My answer to, "Katie, step to the back?" was "I don't give permission." The resident would then have to find a staff member to ask. These exchanges with new boys revealed the rigid system of movement regulation, as well as my very different role in this system. I was considered the only adult on campus who did not regulate behavior, fine residents, or "tell on" youth when they did something they knew would get them penalized (the most common thing was to curse in front of me without fear of punishment). Any adult, working in any capacity can give a Minor, Major, fine, or give permission to a youth who lives there. After observing life at Steele for a number of months, I asked Steve how he felt about having me around. He said that at first it was difficult because *I*, not the residents, didn't follow the Program. Lamar states it nicely when I asked him about the Program: "I like it when they stick to the Program. 'Cause I know the Program. It's nuthin' major, you know? You [learn] the Program and just maintain. Program's easy."

Like the residents of Havenwood, the staff members of the institution are also highly regulated to follow and make others follow the grand plan.

Training Staff

Goffman (1961) and Polsky, Claster, and Goldberg (1968) differentiate the staff world from the inmate or resident world. Both sociological texts argue that staff members and inmates are largely antagonistic toward one another, and that the boundary between the worlds is important and distinct. While I found an important hierarchy between staff and residents, I also quickly learned that the adults who worked at Havenwood are as tightly organized as the youth who live there. In his analysis of the residential treatment center he supervised (he calls it a "School"), Bruno Bettelheim found that, "just as the children have to cope with the tasks that are set by the particular world of the School, so staff members, too, have to integrate themselves in this cosmos before they can make any attempt to help children to do so" (1950:30). At Havenwood, this integration takes the form of official trainings and on-site learning.

Staff members have to learn the Cottage Program well enough to enforce it. They have to know each resident's goals and discern if they are achieving them. And they have to know all of the official treatment paradigms in order to regulate behavior, process difficult feelings, dispense medication, and run group therapy sessions. Therefore, Havenwood staff members have to integrate themselves into the "cosmos" before they can ask the children to do so. They are helped along in this integration process by their own institutional schedule, which includes initial trainings, follow-up trainings, supervision, support groups to ease the transition, and weekly meetings.

When I first arrived at Havenwood I participated in the two-week orientation required of all new staff (except therapists and others associated with the clinical portion of Havenwood; they had their own orientation and in-services. I also attended the in-services). During these two weeks, I accumulated over three inches of paperwork that detailed such things as Havenwood's organizational hierarchy, mission statement, and emergency plans. I received handouts specifying driving guidelines, documentation methods for Medicaid insurance, and licensing standards for child welfare agencies. I also received a manual for mandated reporting of child abuse. During these two weeks I participated in formal trainings in Behavioral Management, Behavioral Management Training II, Life Space Crisis Intervention (LSCI), Milieu Therapy, The Helping Relationship, Adolescent Developmental Behavior, Milieu Therapy II, Counter Response, Professional Boundaries, and the Art of Setting Limits. I collected handouts, outlines, and PowerPoint Slides from these trainings.

In the Behavior Management Training, staff members learn that "clear rules and predictability" are key factors in regulating behavior. New staff members are also taught to identify programmatic rule violations (Minors and Majors) and to document these infractions in the official institutional forms. The Milieu Therapy trainings stress that the milieu is "a place that is strong and able to contain violent behavior but not hostile," as well as a place "that issues consequences" but "listens to concerns." Staff learn that the "bottom line goal for every kid" is to teach youth "ways to get [their] needs met in a socially acceptable manner." The Helping Relationship training focuses on "boundaries" between staff and youth, "limit setting" strategies to help regulate relationships, and "boundary violations" that psychiatrically disordered youth make. New staff members also learn how to maintain a "helping relationship" by "utilizing the support and staff within the agency, being open to feedback, monitoring our own feelings, and following policy and procedures." All staff members who work in the cottages are required to participate in these trainings before they can work with the residents in the cottages or at school.

Following this two-week orientation, every other Wednesday morning all new staff members attend additional trainings. These two-hour trainings include Introduction to Psychotropic Medications in Children and Adolescents, Sexualized Problematic Behavior in Children and Youth, AWOL (Absent WithOut Leave) Precaution, and Learning Disabilities.

In the Introduction to Psychotropic Medications in Children and Adolescents, medications to treat depression, anxiety, mood disorders, schizophrenia, and Attention Deficit Hyperactivity Disorder are reviewed. Staff members learn that mood disorders, specifically Bipolar Disorder, can be effectively treated by atypical antipsychotics such as Seroquel (see Figure 2.1). However, for other disorders, specifically Conduct Disorder and Oppositional Defiant Disorder (one of the common diagnoses for Havenwood youth), "no medications can treat such problems successfully." Rather "for the most part the individual can only find help by participating in a structured program where he can learn new values in a setting which rewards them." In the AWOL Precautions training, reasons given for youth running away from residential care include "discomfort with growth and change." They experience "fear of intimacy, rejection of individual responsibilities, a lot of anxiety about external control, inability to undergo change, and peer and staff pressure or conflict." Staff members are taught to know which residents have patterns of running away, and to be on the lookout for youth displaying behavior that shows that they may be at risk for running away. Every staff member who works in the cottages must attend these trainings.

In addition to the Wednesday trainings, each line staff member has to be trained in Therapeutic Crisis Intervention (TCI), which is a four-day training (I return to this in chapter 4). At the end of the training, staff members must pass an exam. If they pass the test, they become certified in TCI, a requirement at Havenwood for all staff. Following the initial certification of TCI, every cottage staff member has to renew his or her certification every six months.

In addition to the trainings, staff members are "supervised" on the job by the cottage supervisor. For example, Steve, the Steele Cottage supervisor, not only had to supervise all of the residents at Steele Cottage, he also has to mentor and to provide feedback on job performance for the staff members who work there. In addition to this formal kind of "supervision," two Cottage supervisors lead a biweekly New Staff Support Group. In this group session, new staff members talk about working at Havenwood and problem-solve difficult scenarios. For example, in one New Staff Support Group session, a new staff member brings up an incident of being hit by a resident. The supervisor asked the group, "What is our first reaction when you are hit? To hit back, right? [*Heads nod all around the room.*] But you can't, I know you want to. I'm keepin' it real. We are human, we get angry and we want to defend ourselves. But you can't." The supervisor continues giving advice about how to go about interacting with children who attack you: "You have to observe them and you have got to be consistent. I tell my Team that they can't do their own thing. Talk about it in Team [Meeting] today; ask your team about it. But observe [the resident] and figure out how to [interact with her]." Staff members use New Staff Support Group to discuss the reality of being attacked by the youth, teach how to interact with the youth, instruct how to work with a team to be consistent and supportive in future interactions with the resident, and to encourage staff members to observe and "figure out" how to work with each individual resident.

Line staff members are rigorously trained by Havenwood to know the correct procedures and reasoning behind behavior management, psychiatric diagnoses, mediation regimens, mental health issues, crisis interventions, and building positive relationships in the cottage or milieu. They are taught to work in teams and to get support and feedback from one another in order to "be on the same page," or to be consistent in implementing the Cottage Programs and rules. In other words, the staff, like the residents, are organized under the grand plan of the total institution, they to must integrate into the "cosmos" of the institution. They are trained to see the youth in particular ways, and to understand how to relate to them in institutionally recognized methods.

My purpose in illustrating the system here (without much analysis) is to show how rigidly the lives of Havenwood youth are regulated, as it allows the reader to understand some of the nuances in later ethnographic vignettes. For example, in chapter 4 it will make more sense why Zac asks about the correct procedure for dealing with William when he is in crisis, and how Steve's response creates a procedure for consistent responses from all staff members. Chapter 7 ethnographic vignettes will be clearer, in particular why Derrick asks to use my recorder, why I have to ask Steve, and why I follow Steve to the back hallway when permission is granted. When I first arrived at Havenwood, I honed in on the rigor by which everyone was regulated. I was fascinated by the organization of the total institution and the power with which it molded residents and staff. However, the longer I stayed, the more I realized that the "give" in the system and the spontaneity of life in this total institution was as or more meaningful than the structural system. Therefore, in addition to understanding how the rules are followed, knowing the rules also allows the reader to understand how significant and important deviation from the institutional rules or grand plan really is. Throughout the book, I will illustrate the rigid institutional rules, but also the considerable and meaningful "give" in this rigid, formal, and codified system. And that it was in this "give" that love emerged.

The "Give" in the System

In her book on maximum security prisons, Lorna Rhodes (2004) finds that those live and work in such environments "struggle out" ways to resolve issues raised by forms of confinement. Struggling it out is not a framework or plan but a "pragmatic and fracture work of local change" (2004:194), where hope can emerge within the confines of a prison. This struggling it out unsettles the terrain of total institutional business as usual. In her ethnography, simple conversations between administrators and inmates unsettles the terrain of prison life. At Havenwood, subtle ways of humanizing the boys who live there, as well as the integration of hip hop into the structured therapeutic life illustrate the positions and voices that occupy such formally organized places. These positions and voices, which will become clearer in later chapters, unsettled Havenwood's psychiatric terrain and allowed for hip hop and forms of counterhegemonic practices to create a "give" in the psychiatric custodial system.

Steele and the File: Challenging the Hegemony of the Documents and Formal Structure

The day after observing the Intake Meeting I discussed in chapter 2 I saw that a large brown envelope had been delivered to the cottage. I knew it held Dwayne's MHA/SH. During my nightly hangout at Steele, I asked Steve what he thought of the young man about to come live there. Steve shrugged, "I don't read the kids' files."

I looked down at his command-center table to be sure I saw the envelop correctly. I looked back at Steve. Steve had watched me gaze down and then up. He does not say anything.

"Really?!" I am shocked. So much effort is put into consolidating information into the Mental Health Assessments. I think of the all the hours I have spent sitting in the Intake Meeting and how much importance this meeting puts (as well other meetings and other professionals put) on the files. I think of all the meeting time that directors fill their days with, thinking this time is shaping unit life and milieu treatment and the implementation of the treatment paradigms in the cottages. "You don't read any of the files?" I ask incredulously.

Steve makes one of his faces; he raises his eyebrows and curls his lips. He slowly shakes his head. He explains, "I get the files but I don't read them. I let the kid tell me who he is. Gives him an opportunity to start over, do his thing." Steve statement is in direct contrast with the official perspective that the file is the "only" version of the youth's childhood that is available.

"I don't either," Allen adds. I turn to Allen who is organizing paperwork. It seems so contradictory that he would be meticulously organizing paperwork only to disregard it as important.

"Then how do you know what their goals are, medications they are supposed to take, their diagnoses..."

"Come on, Kate," Allen teasingly chastises me. "We get the meds from nursing and we give them out. We know their goals. We fill out the paperwork for Medicaid. But you been here long enough to know how we do."

I nod; I had been. I observed how the flow of Steele Cottage life was officially framed by therapeutic practice and how, when required, the staff members of Steele would use therapeutic and psychiatric registers to communicate the treatment of the youth who lived there. However, in practice, when not under official scrutiny or overtly surveilled, life at Steele had an informality, a flavor, and a do-its-own-thing about it. Sure the Team worked together and therapeutic interventions were the order of the day. However, at Steele, people didn't talk about psychiatric diagnosis or conflict cycles despite the requirement that every resident be diagnosed with a mental disorder.[3] This will become clearer to the reader throughout this text, as psychiatric diagnosis and conflict cycle registers are all but absent from what transpired on a quotidian basis in Steele Cottage. And yet, I was shocked that Steve didn't read the files, to know the histories of the kids he and his staff worked with. He was the primary professional tasked to work with residents in psychiatric custody and others worked laboriously to construct the file. But Allen was correct, I had been around long enough to see how this do-your-own-thing often overrode the formal treatment paradigms. I look at Steve, confused.

"If he wants to tell me, he tells me. And they always tell me. But I let them do it." He says of his residents. He then gets up and takes the brown envelope into the staff office. I follow him. Steve opens a desk drawer and adds it to a pile of large brown envelopes. He closes the drawer, turns, and shrugs. I follow him back out to the living room. I interpreted Steve's (and others') decision to not read the files as a counterhegemonic move that rejected the power of the case file and psychiatric framings in favor of personal lived experience (do his thing) and narratives (he'll tell me). This move was less active resistance to the total psychiatric institution, the codification of these young men into bureaucratic files, and various power dynamics at Havenwood and more a simple everyday buffering, a shrugging off of Havenwood's paradigms if you will, of the young men of Steele and the relationships these men built from the structural forces that constrained them. As we will see, this buffering happened all of the time, in group therapy, in the milieu, or in transitional going away parties. I do not think the directors, therapists, and others in authority knew that Steve did not read the files. But the young men did. And this buffering opened up space, a "give," for nonpsychiatric framings to permeate psychiatric custody.

The Uniform

In Goffman's description of a total institution he finds that inmates are stripped of their possessions and required to wear uniforms. In most cases they are groomed to look the same, for example, with their heads shaved. Goffman argues that this loss of identity markers—clothing and individual style—"can prevent the individual from presenting his usual image of himself to others" (1961:21). With these sorts of disruptions and losses, the "territories of the self" are violated (Goffman 1961:23). He argues that a main goal of total institutions is to strip inmates of their prior identities in order to reinforce a new self.

At Havenwood, residents do not lose their possessions or wear an institutional uniform. Instead, at the beginning of their stay, Havenwood provides $200 for each child to have new clothes and a pair of shoes.[4] For example, when Dwayne, whom we met in the previous chapter, first arrived at Steele, Manny, Andy, and I went with Angie to buy him some new clothes. After school one day, we all piled into Angie's van and went to a mall about 20 minutes away. This was one of my first trips to buy clothing. Once in the store, Angie told Manny to look for pants and a few shirts, and Andy to go pick out some shoes. Angie asked me to go with Andy, while she helped Manny. I followed Andy, who went directly to the Nike Air Force One shoes to see if they carried Dwayne's size. We asked someone to check in back as the size was not on the floor. While we waited, I walked over to some Vans and picked one of the shoes to show Andy. He replied, "No, those are skater shoes." Andy, and the other young Black men of Steele, don't wear "skater shoes." While Andy and I failed to find hip hop related shoes, Angie and Manny found three pairs of jeans, two shirts, and a hoodie, all hip hop related brands including Akademics and Ecko Unltd. Dwayne was pleased that Andy and Manny made sure he had some style when it came to his new clothes. Not only are Havenwood youth not forced to wear a uniform, as they do in detention, but they are allowed to pick out the style of clothing they want to wear. In addition to buying hip hop clothing, Allen, Steve, and others often bring in their hand-me-downs for the boys. These items include Air Force Ones, Timberland Boots, and hip hop brands of jeans and T-shirts. The adult men of Steele also wear hip hop related clothing. Therefore, the uniform worn by the boys and many of the adult men of Havenwood and Steele is a hip hop uniform. For the most part, the boys of Steele choose and are allowed to wear hip hop clothing.

Returning to Goffman's argument that stripping the inmates of individual clothing is a method of violating the sense of self and of disrupting a usual self presentation, Steele youth and staff actually allowed for and spent money to reinforce the hip hop styled self that most youth brought with them. Rather than a uniform stripping the inmate of his former self, Havenwood purchases clothing that reinforce an external to the total-institution-self, one that would rarely, if ever, be interpreted as a uniform of psychiatric custody. I found it somewhat contradictory and yet profoundly enlightening that within the highly structured single file lines that moved almost silently across Havenwood's campus, youth would be wearing highly stylish outfits, almost universally (including the white youth) hip hop related. Instances such as this, individual clothing choices that reflect counterhegemonic and oppositional ideologies, revealed some "give" in the otherwise total institutional structure of Havenwood.

In addition to clothing style, hip hop finds its way into the less constrained and structured aspects of total institutional life. For example, during scheduled free time, youth rap, practice dance moves to new hip hop songs, or sit and listen to hip hop music, sometimes on Mark's large, booming sound system that he carried outside. As I watched Mark bring his large speaker outside, I thought of DJ Kool Herc and the early days of hip hop, when the sound system allowed for a public party. I spent many afternoons, especially in the spring and summer when Mark would play music outside, watching Steele Cottage and Roger Cottage boys practice dance moves on the sidewalks. I watched older boys, namely Chris, known for his smooth moves, physically move younger boys into correct dance-move positions. The older boys would holler and clap when the younger ones performed the moves correctly. While Mark, Chris, and others are dancing, Derrick, Jonathon, and Wesley are often rapping or writing lyrics. As I would sit and watch the dancing, Derrick would sit next to me and share his lyrics. Derrick was particularly nuanced in his hand gestures and lyrics, often changing speeds and breaking, common elements in hip hop music. The dance moves and songs were almost always hip hop, sometimes R&B songs were mixed in too. As we will see in later chapters, hip hop in the form of language and practice is prevalent in group therapy, evening life, and even frameworks of success.

This integration of hip hop into therapeutic work and the flexibility of allowing youth to "tell their story" is not ubiquitous at Havenwood. In fact, rapping as a method of expression comes up as problematic as part of individual therapy, during the weekly psychoanalytic seminar I observed. The idea of this seminar is to have therapists discuss residents in a group supervision format. Every four weeks a therapist chooses a particularly challenging resident and he or she tape records individual therapy sessions with this individual and brings in these recording to the seminar.[5] During one seminar,

Paige brings in a recording of Derrick rapping as his way of expressing himself during the session. Paige and the other therapists comment on the value (or lack thereof) of rap in therapy. Various comments about the rap include: "He is being representational in the rap versus talking it out in therapy," "Instead of talking about his feelings he is just repeating things over and over like a wheel," and "I think the rapping is a vehicle for stardom not a tool for exploration." Other therapists were concerned that Paige was manipulated and used by Derrick, stating, "Rap is about money and he might be using you to write down the lyrics," and "He wants you to validate the credibility of the rap." Only one therapist comments that rap could be a "meaningful way," by which Derrick is communicating his feelings to Paige. The session ends with the supervising psychiatrist asking Paige to remind Derrick that he needs to share his feelings, "not just to get rich and famous but because it is the right thing to do." I use this example to illustrate how problematic hip hop is in individual therapy, despite it being a meaningful venue for the expression of feelings (see the rap interview in chapter 1). It is important to understand that hip hop was not encouraged in these settings to see how being able to wear hip hop uniforms and tell one's own story, for example, in other contexts at Havenwood might be very significant for the young Black men who live there.

Conclusion

My point in this chapter is to illustrate how the psychiatric institution constrains the lives of the youth of Havenwood. It does this by having a rigid schedule, codified definitions of behaviors, and regulating youth through scoring systems. In the ethnographic vignette that began this chapter, the youth must not only line up to walk around campus and to enter buildings, but they must ask to move around the cottage, get drinks of water, and even to go to the bathroom. Staff members are trained to enforce these schedules and rules. Havenwood is a total institution in the Goffman sense.

However, there is considerable "give" in the system. Staff members open up space for this "give" by not conforming to the total institutional-ness of Havenwood. Rather than read the files to understand who the youth being placed in Steele are, Allen and Steve allow for the young men to "start over" and tell their own stories. By allowing young men to tell their own stories, Havenwood, through Steve and Allen, does not strip the resident of his former self. In addition to telling their own stories, this "give" is often articulated, expressed, and experienced through a "uniform" that is distinctly not one commonly associated with psychiatric custody. Havenwood, in general, does not try to actively remove hip hop cultural practice from the youth. In fact, Havenwood purchases hip hop clothing for them. In addition to that, line staff members allow for hip hop to be mobilized in a variety of therapeutic ways (I will come to this in later chapters). It is in these moments and practices of "give," or agency in an otherwise highly structured environment, hip hop and psychiatry are integrated in the cultural practice of and self transformation in psychiatric custody.

Chapter 4
Crazy Shit

It is the stench of feces. I had just opened the door to Bradley North Cottage when the smell assaults me. Before I can grimace or cover my nose, I see Mike and Jason, two African American teens, sitting on the couches in the living room, watching television. They both greet me with a head nod; I manage a quiet "Hi."

"Fuck. You!!"

My attention turns to the sound of Travis shouting. I had been summoned by a text message to Bradley. I walk through the living room, around the staff station—the round windowed enclosed space in the middle of the building that separates the shared living spaces from the residents' rooms. Every time I walk into Bradley North, and Bradley South for that matter as they were constructed as mirror images, I think of Jeremy Bentham's panopticon or inspection house.

In the late eighteen century, English philosopher Jeremy Bentham believed that people could be changed through architecture, so he designed a prison based on disciplinary change rather than physical punishment. To serve his end, he created the "inspection house" or panopticon prison. In Bentham's prison, the inspection house is located in the center of a large circular room filled with prison cells, which faced the center of the room and the inspection house. The architectural design was such that the inspection house allowed for an inspector to gaze upon the prisoners at all times, usually without being seen. Bentham argued that the prisoners would internalize this gaze, regardless of whether or not they could see themselves being watched, instilling a new form of discipline.[1] There in the center of the cottage is a windowed room, an inspection house, where anyone in this room can gaze upon most of the cottage.

Unlike one of Bentham's prisons, however, Bradley North and Bradley South are constructed to afford the young residents a modicum of privacy. The bedrooms have doors, rather than bars, and these rooms face out into a hallway, outside the gaze of the inspector.

A watcher in the inspection room, or the staff office, cannot see inside the bedrooms. But if a resident leaves his room or sticks his head out for a moment, he is visible. Their privacy goes only so far. The view of the hallway is to instill a fear of running away. Today, the panopticon seems rather impotent and misplaced, with the stench of feces and Travis's suffering wails. I see staff members huddled together on the other side of the windowed room.

Carter, Robert, and Tina are standing outside the confinement room. Robert is holding down the red button on the wall just to the side of the confinement room doorknob. Holding the red button locks the room. Carter has his hands on his hips with his back to me; he is shaking his head.

"FUCK YOU!!!!"

Tina, a midthirties African American woman, sees me and I am unable tell if she smiles or grimaces. Probably both. I return the look.

Carter, a man of Asian heritage, turns around to see who Tina is looking at. He sees me and smiles/grimaces and extends his left arm to me. I slip into his side-hug and put my arm around his back.

"Travis," he tells me.

We drop our side-hug, I reach out and touch Robert, an African American man, on his left arm and make eye contact. He shakes his head.

I nod. "What happened?"

"Take a look," Carter tells me.

For a moment I pause. I know that something is terribly wrong, even though I am now accustomed to the stench. I am not sure if I want to see Travis like this. I do not know if Travis would want me to see him like this. I look in.

Through the 6-inch by 6-inch window to the confinement room I see Travis, naked, but his white gym socks and his eyeglasses. His clothes are in the corner of the small room. Brown stuff is all over the white walls and white floor. Travis is pacing, turning around as he reaches the limits of the 8-by-8 foot space. His pasty-white 5'4", 130-pound body reminds me of the underbelly of a fish, soft and vulnerable. He turns around in his pacing and looks at the door. We make eye contact.

"FUCK YOU!!!!"

I recoil from the window. My view into Travis's world is cut short by his rejection of my gaze. He is enraged. I feel a little relief to see his rage; at least he is not hurting himself. I had seen youth knock their heads against the wall, one inserted a pencil into his penis before staff knew he had "a weapon," and another dug a hole in his body, with foreign objects and with fingers. Travis, thank goodness, is not hurting himself. Then the image of Travis naked and his environment covered in his own excrement returns, and my gratitude fades.

I turn to Robert. He raises his eyebrows and nods.

"His dad came to visit today," Carter answers my earlier question.

"What!?" I am taken aback by the fact that Travis's father came to visit.

"Right?" Robert echoes my astonishment.

"I want to strangle him every time I see him," Carter admits. "Travis goes crazy every time he visits."

"Why isn't he in prison?" I ask. Travis's dad had abused him. He would starve him, lock him in dog cages or in the basement, and neglect him for days at a time. However, many abusive parents are not prosecuted, let alone made to serve jail time. The focus for the state is to help the child, rather than to punish the parent. Travis's father served no jail time and had been encouraged to visit Travis at Havenwood, to work on their relationship and maybe participate in family therapy. Few people who work directly with Travis think this is a good idea, and no one wants to work on the days that his dad visits.

Carter shrugs in answer.

I shake my head. I am not sure what to say. It seems the grimaces worn by Robert and Tina are more apt than words.

I notice a figure in a doorway and I immediately wonder about Mike and Jason in the front living room and the rest of the young men who live in the cottage. I imagine the boys are in their rooms. This is what often happens when a resident is in crisis or does what the staff call "crazy shit." If one resident is "in crisis," which means the staff members have to physically intervene in some way, usually a restraint or an escort to confinement, the rest of the residents are "shut down" and they have to wait out the crisis, usually in their rooms. Mike and Jason had returned from therapy before Travis was in the confinement room but not before he was acting out and in crisis, I was told later. Therefore, they were told to stay in the front, away from the confinement room.

The other Bradley North residents wait for Travis to calm down so they can resume their normal daily routine. I wonder if they are angry with Travis for upsetting their routine or causing their "shut down."

I look over at the figure in the doorway and see Garrett, an African American teen who has been at Havenwood for a few years. Seeing

Garrett is different for me than making eye contact with Robert, Carter, or Tina. Robert, Carter, and Tina work at Bradley North and there is an intimate distance in our eye contact. We nod knowingly, we have all chosen to work with "these kids," and we experience their crisis in profound ways. But we are not one of them; we are not counted among the people who do *crazy shit*. We also do not share living space with Travis; we get to go home when we want. We have professional, albeit intimate, distance.

I force myself to meet Garrett's gaze. He quietly maintains eye contact for a few seconds and then states, "We all have issues."

I am moved by his comment. His response to Travis's crisis is empathy and compassion. His world is disrupted by Travis's behavior. He may not have looked in the confinement room but he hears Travis's screams, smells the stench, hears Carter, watches Robert and Tina, and participates in Travis's crisis as a roommate, a cottage-mate, and as a fellow resident. During the crisis, Garrett empathizes with Travis and responds with understanding and acceptance: we all have issues. We will see later (in chapter 5), outside of crisis, how Garrett tries to get Travis to deal with his issues, which is the resident's mandate in psychiatric custody. However, during Travis's pain, Garrett is compassionate.

I soften my gaze and nod. He turns his head and stares off into the distance.

I look down the long hallway, every few feet another door announces a bedroom that opens out into the hallway. No one besides Garrett, Mike, and Jason are outside of their rooms. The ten other young men are sitting behind these doors, hearing the noises, smelling the smells, and being shut down. I see Tom, a white male staff member, sitting in the office chair at the end of the very long hallway. His job, evinced by his post, is to supervise the residents who must be in their rooms. I manage a weak wave.

"Hey Katie."

I walk down to ask him how he is doing. Before I can talk, Terrell, a 15 year old African American youth, sticks his head out of his door located about five feet from Tom, one of the last doors at the end of the hallway, "What's happening? Can I come out now? I have to go to the bathroom."

Tom sighs. "Terrell, go back in your room. I will let you know when you can come out. Play your game." Tom hopes a video game will occupy Terrell's mind during the crisis.

"Hey Katie, what's happening?" Terrell greets me and ignores Tom.

"Terrell!"

"Hi Terrell," I say.

"Fine," Terrell disappears and the door closes.

"He is really agitated. He gets anxious when other kids are in crisis. I don't want him to go off," Tom tells me. I have seen it happen a number of times. The intensity of an initial restraint or crisis sometimes results in other restraints (see later). The emotional charge in a room in the midst of the *crazy shit* can be too much for the young men and women of Havenwood to stand. I am told that sometimes a crisis reminds the residents of violence at home, something they witnessed, or something they endured. With all of the screaming or wrestling to control a youth in crisis, sometimes other residents not involved in the crisis "go off." This "going off" is understood as a form of dissociation, these residents mix up past and present, home and Havenwood, a violent beating with a choreographed restraint. They then react in ways that they used to—they hurt themselves, attack another, or pretend nothing is happening. The dissociation and behavioral reaction, I am told, are common defense mechanisms and psychological responses for individuals who have been abused and traumatized.[2] I am not sure about the psychological mechanisms that operate to help people deal with past or present interpersonal violence. My observations during, conversations after, and experiences in crisis lead me to believe that these events are difficult to endure, even if you do not have a history of abuse or have not been traumatized. The shouting, the smells, the grunts and groans of people wrestling, the slap sounds that bodies make when they hit each other, and the wailing, crying, and sobbing that usually accompanies the crisis make these events extremely intense, painful, and intimate. In an effort to limit the suffering, the units get "shut down."

"I have to go to the bathroom," Terrell is back.

"You just went."

Terrell frowns and disappears again.

Tom gives me a see-what-I-mean look.

"Katie, what are you doing here?" Terrell returns.

"TERRELL!"

"What? I was just trying to talk to Katie."

I look at Tom. I am expecting his you're-disrupting-the-current-situation look. It is time for me to move on, my presence is making his job—to keep the other residents calm—more difficult. I walk back up to where Carter, Tina, and Robert are.

Carter is looking in the window. He turns around and tells us, "He is lying down." Carter looks at Tina, "Let's get a sheet to wrap him in, get him into the shower." Tina grabs a bed sheet from the inspection office.

"I'll watch you get him into the shower, but then I have to go to Evelyn's, Janelle is threatening to go AWOL. Be sure you clean up using that new disinfectant. Even if his clothes aren't wet put them in the red bag so Laundry will know. I'll come back in a bit to sign the paperwork." Carter is directing the line staff to use proper institutional hygiene and documenting protocols as they tend to Travis's needs.

Robert releases the red button and slowly opens the door. He sticks his head in, "Travis?" he whispers. Travis sits up, but it seems to take a bit of effort to do so. He looks spent, exhausted from the fight he waged in the confinement room. Robert takes the bed sheet, walks into the room, and holds open the sheet like a robe. Travis stands up and lets Robert drape the sheet around him so he does not have to further expose himself on the way to the bathroom. Tina opens the door wide and lets Robert, with his hand on Travis's upper back, guide Travis out of the confinement room. They walk across the cottage together toward the bathroom. Tina follows silently.

Robert and Travis enter the bathroom. Within seconds, we hear water running. Tina nods to Carter.

I look at Carter and he nods his head toward the front door. I follow him.

"Bye guys," I tell Mike and Jason.

"Bye Katie."

Carter extends his fist to Mike and then Jason. They return the fist bump.

As we walk out the door Carter raises his eyebrows and breaths out heavily, "Never a dull moment."

"Are you heading over to Evelyn's?" I ask him. Evelyn's is a Behavior Disorder cottage for girls, located on the other side of campus, past the school, chapel, gym, and dining hall. He checks his phone; text messages are important ways in which cottage staff communicate with campus wide supervisors.

"Yes, Janelle is in support. She's calmed down but I'll go over to see what's up, see if they need anything. You know Evelyn's, one girl goes, they all go." "Support" is another term used for the confinement room. Carter spent a great deal of his time talking to, watching, and dealing with youth in these rooms.

I left Carter at the sidewalk that runs perpendicular to the one that leads to Evelyn's, at the entrance of the chapel and main administration buildings. I am heading to Steele Cottage, to see what is happening over there.

I walk in to Steele just as Allen hangs up the phone. He looks at Steve who is sitting at his command-center table located in the center of the cottage, "It's quiet now. We're good. We're going to take these guys to the court."

Steve nods.

"Come on ya'll, let's go." Allen says to the ten young men sitting on the couches with their coats on. He does not even line them up or Transition, they have been waiting so long and so quietly already, sitting on the couches with their coats on waiting to go to the gym to play basketball during the open evening hour. Zac and Allen follow the young men as they leave the cottage.

"Evelyn's?" I ask Steve. He nods. Word about crises spreads fast across campus, especially to Steele. Steve and Allen, and other staff members at Steele Cottage, are routinely called in to help when youth are doing *crazy shit*. In this case, Allen, Zac, and Steve had been on alert, in case they had to go to Bradley North or Evelyn's. However, both Travis and Janelle are no longer in crisis and a phone call to Steele freed up Allen and Zac to take the waiting Steele residents to the gym. Much like Bradley North, Steele had been in a sort of shutdown state. The *crazy shit* youth did in other cottages influences life for residents and staff members across campus. Because I spent so much time at Steele, I often saw them learn of across-campus restraints and the sudden shut down of cottage life. Sometimes I would hear a frustrated scoff or "come on man" as privileges, activities, and daily life are limited by someone somewhere else. Sometimes I hear a relieved, "Can I get back on the [video] game?" In this case, the young men had been sitting quietly with their winter coats on in the living room, waiting for the crisis to pass so they could go play basketball. The young men finally went to go play some hoops.

"Where've you been?" Steve asks me.

"Bradley North."

"I heard. Travis ok?" In addition to being on call to offer assistance in restraints, Steve and others know most of the kids across campus and are genuinely concerned about crisis events and their aftermath. Steve knows all about Travis and the *crazy shit* he does. He also cares enough about him to inquire about his well-being.

I groan and shrug. I think of poor Travis, the kinds of things done to him, what he does to himself, his dad, and the incident I have just witnessed. He nods and then shakes his head. "We think William's bad, stickin' screws into his leg."

I am not sure what to say. It is in moments like this, an offhanded comment about the hierarchy of behavior that determines that stripping naked and wiping one's own feces on the walls of a small room is worse than using a screw to dig an inch deep hole into the meat of one's calf, which exposes some of the bizarre aspects of life in psychiatric custody. William was among the young men waiting with his coat on; this time the crisis is not his. It is moments like this when we, Steve and I, pause silently, and I, perhaps he does as well, reflect on the fact that we have chosen to work in a place where these kinds of actions can and do happen, and, most importantly, we come to know and care about the youth who enact them. While we did not verbalize our reflections in this instance, Steve and I frequently talk about the work of treatment, what it means to have to restrain kids, to see them naked, and to know, so intimately, their bodies and souls. I spend countless hours sitting next to Steve as he sits in the back hallway of Steele supervising Quiet Time or allowing youth to rap in their bedrooms during the evening free hour. During these conversations Steve tells me he could only do this work "because of the kids." He tells me that witnessing them change helps him deal with the *crazy shit*. He would say, "When you see them working, it's a beautiful thing," and then he would smile his full, light-up-the-room smile. However, there are days when the *crazy shit* wins out. On those days, the pain of the crisis unmakes the world as Elaine Scarry (1985) tells us, and a little bit of salvaging fragments is all that is left. On other days, you feel as if you go right up to the edge of the unmaking, but you somehow avert total disaster. On days when the crisis happens at Bradley North and Evelyn's but not at Steele and he is not needed to help out, Steve averts unmaking. On those days Steve grounds life in the mundane.

Steve grabs his keys and jumps up, "Come on, let's go to the gym."

On many of those days we went to the gym.

Crisis: Restraints, Seclusions, and Dangerous Behavior

In chapter 2 I described the number of treatment models used at Havenwood. Two of these models focus specifically on crisis management. While "crisis" in not clearly defined by Life Space Crisis Intervention (LSCI) or Therapeutic Crisis Intervention (TCI), the TCI workbook states that "the majority of crises that young people in care [residential treatment] experience are a result of the young person running out of coping skills and being emotionally overwhelmed" (Residential Child Care Project 2001:6). Havenwood finds that TCI provides a way for line staff to "help children and young people when they are at their most destructive" (Terms and Definitions to Know in Your 1st 90 Days). At Havenwood, crises are times and events when young people's behavior require some sort of adult intervention.

Crisis interventions used at Havenwood are manual restraints and seclusions. According to the Terms and Definitions to Know in Your 1st 90 Days, manual restraints are officially defined as:

> "**Manual Restraint**" means a behavior management technique involving the use of physical contact or force, characterized by measures such as arm or body holds, subject to the provision of Section 384.50.[3] **At Havenwood all manual restraint is administered by appropriately trained staff in compliance with TCI standards and requirements. A manual restraint may be used to prevent run away only when the youth presents a threat of physical harm to self or others or as specified in the Individual Treatment Plan.** (Bold in original)

In the same document **Seclusions** are defined as:

> the contingent withdrawal of reinforcing stimuli by removing the child from an area to a specifically designated room from which egress (departure) is restricted. This procedure is considered a behavioral management technique and as such must be used only as a therapeutic response to dangerous behavior.

There are two types of seclusion:

1) Staff Assisted Seclusion: means the room is secured by a locking mechanism that engages only when a key, button, or handle is being held by a staff member. When that staff member takes his or her hand off the device the door unlocks and the child is able to easily and readily open the door from the inside. The door to such a room may not/does not remain locked when unattended.
2) Key-locked Seclusion: is prohibited.

Travis in the crisis mentioned is "in seclusion." Robert is holding the button, which secures the door. Once Robert is no longer pressing the button, the door is unlocked.

Both restraints and seclusions are a behavioral management technique when youth become dangerous. Dangerous behavior is defined as "behavior that is likely to result or has resulted in harm to self or others, if not immediately contained" (Terms and Definitions to Know in Your 1st 90 Days).

Restraints and seclusions are significant events at Havenwood. Not only does the institution explicitly define them, but whenever they occur, staff members must document them using official forms. These documents then go into the young person's case file. As Carter mentioned earlier, he will be back to sign the paperwork after he returns from Evelyn's Cottage. Robert or Tina must write up the "dangerous behavior incident" using the Dangerous Behavior Incident Report. Residents like Travis (and William later) accrue these documents in their file as part of the life in treatment.

Havenwood tracks restraints and seclusions as a main indicator of treatment quality. Havenwood investigates when restraints and seclusions happen, why they happen, the number of young people involved in a restraint or seclusion, the number of staff members involved in restraints, the individual residents involved in the most restraints and seclusions, if gender mattered in the type of crisis intervention, and the percentage and kinds of injuries that result from restraints or seclusions. This data is aggregated each year into Havenwood's Restrictive Behavior Intervention Outcome Data. I use reports from 2006 and 2007 (some of the data is not present in both reports).

In 2006 and 2007 the majority of restraints occurred at 9 a.m., 3 p.m., and 8 p.m. These hours of the day are considered "Transition times" between cottage and school (9 a.m.), school and cottage (3 p.m.), and bed times (8 p.m.) (Havenwood Annual FY 2007 Restraint and Seclusion Data document). Around 26 percent of all restraints occurred on Wednesday. The reasons proposed to explain this peak in midweek include: "(1) because kids receive their Levels on Wednesdays, that this is the primary catalyst for kids getting upset; (2) Wednesday is also the day that many home visit 'deadlines' occur (i.e., if it hasn't been set up with the family by that point, it was likely not going to occur). This may be a stressor for some kids, albeit a smaller percentage of the kids, but it could stir the pot nonetheless; and (3) it is the one day that the most staff seem to be present on the units (for that time after 3 p.m.)" (Havenwood Annual FY 2007 Restraint and Seclusion Data document). According to both reports, more restraints occur during transition months, such as going back to school, or holiday months, including September, December, and July.

In 2006, out of the 194 Havenwood residents, 125 had been restrained, but most only once. The majority of restraints occurred with 14 residents. These 14 residents accounted for 46 percent (247) of the restraints for the year. These clients had 10 or more documented restraints (Havenwood Restrictive Behavior Intervention Outcome Data document, FY06). In 2007, about 53 percent of the line staff were involved in a restraint. However, as with the youth, 10 staff members were involved in more than 20 restraints (Havenwood Annual FY 2007 Restraint and Seclusion Data document).

In 2007, around 472 restraints and 398 seclusions occurred. In 2006, around 57 percent of the restraints at Havenwood occurred because a client was aggressive toward a staff member as opposed to self-harming (6%), property damage (2%), runaway (9%), aggression toward a peer (15%), weapon possession (2%), or other issues which included pulling fire alarms, interfering in crisis situations, and other threatening incidents (11%) (Havenwood Restrictive Behavior Intervention Outcome Data document, FY06). In 2007, about 63 percent of Havenwood's population was male. Male residents were involved in 68 percent of the restraints and 85 percent of the seclusions. Females, 38 percent of the population, were involved in 32 percent of the restraints and 15 percent of the seclusions. About 30 percent of restraints ended with an injury to either a resident or a staff member. In 2007, about 31 percent of these resident injuries were "cuts or scratches," 7 percent were rug burns, 24 percent were identified as "pain in wrists, legs, knees, or shoulder" (Havenwood Annual FY 2007 Restraint and Seclusion Data document).

Restraints, seclusions, and dangerous behavior are significant aspects of Havenwood life. Not only are they codified into official forms and data, but they also shape what it means to live and work at Havenwood. In fact, dangerous behavior that leads to restraints and seclusions is often identified as *crazy shit,* and as we see in the ethnographic vignette earlier, the definitions and numbers, while important, do not accurately account for what it means to be involved in crises.

Crazy Shit: Disgust and Love

It is difficult to make sense of the bizarre behavior that occurs at Havenwood. In fact, I have struggled with the how to most accurately describe the situations mentioned earlier without coming off as judgmental or exoticizing. I want to communicate how some of the acts and events at Havenwood would be considered strange in daily life pretty much anywhere. If anything, such out-of-the-ordinary behavior resembles behavior of liminal stages in rites of passage, or rituals of inversion. In the betwixt and between time of life transitions or during rituals, otherwise bizarre behavior can be normalized, allowed, and encouraged as part of the ritual process. Similar are the rules for rituals of inversions, such as the Carnival. However, the crisis described earlier was not enacted in a liminal stage, nor is it part of a ritual of inversion.[4] In fact, it was considered in direct contradiction to desired behavior in the cottage, and often times identified as irrational or dissociative. How do we make sense of this behavior?

I find William Miller's (1997) work on disgust is useful in this context. Miller (1997) argues that "disgust" is at once a visceral, sensorial reaction, and a moral judgment. "Disgust," as a term, communicates sensorial reaction, and it is also "a moral and social sentiment.... It ranks people and things in a kind of cosmic ordering" (Miller 1997:2). Disgust lexically includes the terms such as "repulsive," "revolting," or "abhorrence," because all of these terms "convey a strong sense of aversion to something perceived as dangerous because of its power to contaminate, infect, or pollute by proximity, contact, or ingestion" (1997:2). Travis's behavior is, by definition, "disgusting" because he uses a polluting substance, his excrement, to contaminate the room he is locked in. Even before I saw what he did with it, I smelled the "offensive" smell of human waste. As a sensorial reaction, the first part of disgust for Miller, Travis's behavior does elicit disgust.

However, Travis's behavior is not called disgusting during the crisis, nor are people outwardly repulsed by his polluting substance. The moral sentiment of disgust seems removed from the event. It is because of this lack of moral judgment regarding Travis and his behavior that I use *crazy shit* to describe and define the otherwise disgusting or bizarre actions during crises. I use *crazy shit* because it is a local term used by staff members as a catchall phrase and concept for things that would happen to precipitate restraints or seclusions, for things residents would do to themselves in or out of crisis, and for things that would happen in crises that made these particular crises even more "crazy" than expected. When staff used *crazy shit*, it was said in a rather offhanded tone. For this reason, *crazy shit* seems to me less judgmental. It at once speaks to the bizarre and sometimes disgusting behavior, without the moral judgment toward the youth who enacted it.

In the crisis just described, people are not repulsed by Travis; rather, people are sympathetic and empathic toward him. Robert, Tina, Carter, and even Steve in another cottage sympathize with him. Carter even wants to lash out at Travis's father for what he has done to his son. Garrett empathizes with Travis: "We all have issues." When it is time to clean Travis up, Robert wraps a sheet around him, walks him to the shower, and does not, through any comment or facial expression, express disgust. It is not as if Garrett, Robert, Carter, Tina, and Steve think what Travis did is not disgusting, in the polluting sense of the word. They do. We can see this because of Steve's offhanded comment—"And we think William is bad." It is "bad" to have to witness and deal with *crazy shit*. However, why do most people, although not everyone of course, suspend the moral judgment of disgust, especially in the moment?

Miller argues, "Love bears a complex and possible necessary relation to disgust. Doesn't love (sexual and nonsexual) involve a notable and nontrivial suspension of some, if not all, rules of disgust? Disgust rules mark boundaries of self; the relaxing of them marks privilege, intimacy, duty, and caring" (Miller 1997:xi). Love allows for a "tolerance for bodies and a willingness to excuse their foibles as well as to indulge their dangerous and disturbing qualities"(Miller 1997:132).

Miller (1997) uses two examples of how love operates in the face of disgust. The first example, changing diapers, I find useful for understanding how staff at Havenwood engage with the presence of human waste, and yet continue to work there or be compassionate. He argues that it takes a humbling of oneself and an unconditional quality of parental love that allows for a "self-overcoming" an "overcoming of powerful aversions" placing the purity of self subordinate to the well-being of the child (Miller 1997:134). This makes sense; parents subordinate their purity of being for their offspring. While they are not Travis's parents, Robert, Tina, Carter, and even Steve understand their role in the lives of residents as "parental." It was ubiquitous to hear about the kinship-like relationship between residents and staff members. Staff members are "trained" to view the youth at Havenwood as their "little brothers and sisters," or to see themselves as "reparenting them." In the TCI four-day training, I noted the following ways in which staff are taught to view the youth:

- This job is very challenging [because we] work with these kinds of kids [whose] parents either were not there or abused them if they were there.
- The kids here are just like any other kid; they just want to belong, to be cared about.
- How do we not hurt them like their former abusers? We process with the kid, validate his feelings, check in with the kid. Staff members need to go the extra step and ask the kid if he is OK instead of just explaining why they restrained him.
- Lifting the fog for these kids, reparenting them, being their older brothers and sisters, this is our job here at Havenwood.

The job of these quasi-kin includes loving the youth, overcoming powerful aversions, and placing the "purity of self subordinate to the well-being of child." Robert, Carter, and Tina clean up Travis and his mess in ways that push even the limits of diaper changing. Travis could clean himself in the shower, however, someone had to clean the feces off of the walls of the confinement room and pick up Travis's soiled clothes from the corner. Was it love that allowed Robert or Tina to perform this act, or simply just part of the job?

Miller anticipates this question, and his work distinguishes the intimacy of love and the suspension of moral judgment of disgusting acts from proximity or cohabitation, in which we simply become habituated to disgusting habits that burden and end in contempt. Of course, some people simply tolerate the *crazy shit*, often warding off contempt by adjusting their work schedules so that they do not have to work as closely with the residents. Others simply quit. The turnover rate of cottage staff is high. On an average, staff members work in the cottage for 18 months. When I asked people why they were leaving many said, "It's just too hard to work with these kids" or "I'm tired of coming to work not knowing if I am going to be attacked or have to clean up shit or whatever." This is in direct contrast to Steve, a 25-year veteran of Havenwood, who comes to work "because of the kids." People either quit or continued to work at Havenwood "because of the kids." One day I asked Steve explicitly, "You love these kids, don't you?" He looked me squarely and nodded slowly, closing his eyes as he does so. People like Carter, Robert, Tina, Tom, Allen, and Steve suspended their aversions and put the well-being of the child above their own purity. Miller argues that it takes love to make this sacrifice.

How are we to make sense of Garrett and his empathic reaction toward Travis? The other reason to help us understand how Garrett, not a parental figure, mobilizes love in response to Travis's disgusting behavior is empathy and friendship (I explicitly discuss friendship in chapter 6). Miller (1997) argues that friends in need demand that we view them with love rather than aversion. Unlike a hierarchical parental–child relationship, the youth who live together must also learn ways of dealing with *crazy shit* and viewing those who enact it. I believe that Garrett sees Travis not only as a friend in need of his empathy and love, but he also sees himself in Travis; Garrett too demands empathy from the other men he lives with. "We all have issues," he tells me. He does not say "Travis has issues" or "I have issues," but rather, he mobilizes a collective framework, "we."

This "we" is critical for understanding how such *crazy shit* and the dealing with *crazy shit* is a cultural framework and a significant component of social life at Havenwood. Not only do "we all have issues" but Garrett tells Travis later, in a group session, that these issues are "why we are all here." The *crazy shit* makes up the world of residential treatment, rather than simply unmaking it.

As it makes up the world, so does the love that emerges in the midst of it. Following Miller's argument that love is the antidote to disgust, I think that the relationships established between people helped them make sense of the *crazy shit* and curbed their repulsion or moral righteousness. By living and working at Havenwood, you see people naked, you smell their feces, and you know that they have just wiped it on the walls. Travis's disgusting behavior does not breed contempt but the love-as-antidote-to-disgust framework emerges here because Garrett, Steve, Carter, Robert, and Tina respond with care, compassion, empathy, and love. This love, compassion, and empathy make up the world of treatment as much as the *crazy shit* that precipitates it.

Tough Love: Touch, Violence, and Care

> *The idea of physical restraint, in many ways, is a distasteful one to care professionals. Many see it as a use of force or punitive act toward a young person, a sign of failure on our part, or as unprofessional, anti-therapeutic, or even abusive behavior. But not to intervene, to allow a young person to be harmed through our lack of intervention, is just as problematic. Failing to protect a young person is a form of neglect.... Whenever possible, restraint should take place in the context of an ongoing relationship with the young person. The message behind restraint should be, "I care enough about you not to let you hurt yourself or others."*
>
> ~*Therapeutic Crisis Intervention Student Workbook*
> (Residential Child Care Project 2001:83).[5]

Over the course of my TCI training, 35 other staff members and I, learned about therapeutically intervening in a crisis. We were taught how to observe young people for signs of distress and impending crisis. We were instructed in ways to prevent crises through early detection. We learned about the amygdala, our "reptilian brain" which is responsible for our "fight or flight" reflexes. Using a clip from the movie *Antwone Fisher* to show how kids know how to talk to psychiatrists and to throw around labels, we discussed how kids come to test us and, then, if we are sincere in our care and honest in our responses, to trust us. We had workbooks, the source of the quotation at the beginning of this section, and we took quizzes and viewed diagrams in the text. We were taught how to "process" with young people after a crisis, to help them "drain off" the charged emotion and to return to the milieu fully able to participate in daily life. On the final day and a half, we practiced physical restraints on one-inch mats. TCI training was one of the foundational trainings for working at Havenwood, especially during crisis. Despite the formal training, we were also informed repeatedly: "What happens in [the training] is nothing like what happens in a real crisis."

Throughout all of these professional and scientific frameworks for understanding, warding off, and intervening in crisis, we were continually reminded that the most important thing was the "ongoing relationship" between staff and youth. Youth need to know that you care about them. As the passage from the student workbook states, "*Whenever possible, restraint should take place in the context of an ongoing relationship with the young person. The message behind restraint should be, 'I care enough about you not to let you hurt yourself or others'.*" Earlier, I listed the ways in which staff members are taught to see the youth (e.g., as little brothers and sisters). TCI trainings taught staff members to intimately engage with the youth, to cultivate an intersubjective relationship, and to bond with youth. It was the caring relationship, and viewing the young person as vulnerable, which would come to bear in real life crises, when the choreographed restraints we practiced proved useless.

To illustrate how this happened at Havenwood, I use two ethnographic vignettes regarding William's crisis. In the first vignette, William is being talked about in a Team Meeting. Staff members are trying to figure out how best to deal with him when he does *crazy shit*, and Steve reminds them all that William is "struggling." By commenting on William's struggle, Steve evokes some empathy. In the second vignette, William is restrained and we see not only the intimacy of physical touch, but the emotional recognition of William as a struggling kid who needs to be cared about. Touch, as intimate intersubjective interaction, plays a significant role in crises. Youth are either removed from touch, like Travis, or staff are physically intimate, they "put their hands on" residents. At the end of crisis, however, gentle touch is also used. Travis to gently guided to the shower. Steve is more forthright with William about his need for and Steve's willingness to provide intimate, caring touch.

William's *Crazy Shit*

Team Meeting

"So I'm tryin to understand, do we put our hands on William or not? I mean, the last meeting we had, you told us not to let him self-harm. So now when he's jamming his finger into the hole, are we supposed to just let him do it?" Zac asks at a weekly Team Meeting. The question resonates off the walls of Steele Cottage. The cottage is quiet. It is 11 a.m. on a Tuesday morning and the young men are at school. Sitting around the dining room table are Steve, Pete, Zac, Angie, Allen, Jim, and James—all cottage workers. They have to deal with the *crazy shit*. Sarah, and Sophie are also in attendance. Sarah is a trained psychologist and serves as the cottage clinical director. Everyone besides Sophie meets once a week to talk about how residents continue to present their illness, the progress they are making, and the need for additional clinical analysis. Team Meetings are where staff members of each cottage get together to discuss their collective work of changing the residents.

Sophie is a new face; she is what Havenwood calls a "clinical consultant." Her main job is to listen in meetings and to try to elicit emotional experiences from the staff members. She asks questions such as, "How does it make you feel to be attacked? Does it make you angry that he came at you with a broom and a trophy? Are you angry?" She reminds the staff to not let their emotional reactions to the residents get in the way of the residents' treatment.[6]

Sophie responds to Zac questions, "Don't get sucked in, he is trying to provoke you into restraining him. That is the last thing we want to do."

Zac looks at Steve for guidance. There is an unusually long pause in the meeting. I look around the table to study facial expressions. Allen and Jim have furrowed their brows in confusion. Pete lowers his head and shakes it almost imperceptibly. Angie picks a piece of lint off of her pants then straightens the fabric. James's eyebrows are raised and he blinks hard a few times. I interpret the reactions to Sophie, in this instance, as misunderstandings between the various treatment protocols used at Havenwood. Line staff members are trained in TCI and learn that physical restraints are sometimes necessary as a treatment intervention. Sophie has been hired to implement a treatment protocol based on individual therapy logic that viewed restraints as occurring when staff members are "sucked in" to them.[7] Often clinicians and clinical consultants interpret restraints as line staff members' inability to control their own emotional responses to residents (Hejtmanek 2014).

Steve told us earlier, "We think William is bad, when he sticks screws in his leg." William is a difficult case. When I first arrived at Havenwood, William was restrained and in confinement a lot. When in confinement, he sometimes self-harms. In his latest confinement episode, William has dug his finger into a deep wound in the meat of his calf. This wound was created in his previous confinement episode, when he used a screw to carve the original hole. If a staff member sees William, or any resident, inflicting self-harm that resident has to be restrained. TCI tells the staff, per the workbook: sometimes it is distasteful work, but so is neglecting the child who is going to self-harm. Zac wants to know what the latest clinical mandate is for William when he is self-harming. After the initial wound was created, the clinical order was for staff to remove all weapons and objects from William while he is in confinement, so he cannot self-harm and there could be no reason to restrain him. No one had anticipated that William would improvise with his finger. Now Zac wants to know if they are still "hands-off," or what he should do when he sees William "jamming his finger into the hole."

No one finds it particularly helpful that Sophie's response to Zac's question is "don't get sucked in" to restraining him. Zac and others do not get sucked into restraining. They do it as part of their job. Havenwood trains them to do it. And they are trained to perform restraints because they "care enough" about the residents to do so.

Steve breaks the pause. He leans back in his chair, having been sitting leaning forward, resting his elbows on his thighs. He adjusts the Ecko Unlimited sweatshirt as it gets caught on his broad shoulders. He looks around the table and makes eye contact with the team: "You all been working with William a long time. You know how he is. Right now he's strugglin'. [Staff members nod.] His mom missed the last visit. We will not let him self-harm. But we are hands-off 'til then."

Zac, Allen, Jim, James, Angela, and Pete nod and relax in their seats.

* * *

Steve and Sophie provide almost opposing perspectives on how staff members should engage with a struggling William. Sophie provides the new clinical perspectives for understanding how the reaction of Zac might influence William's behavior. Sophie's advice for Zac on how to deal with William in crisis is to "not get sucked in." She is indexing psychoanalytic perspectives that ask therapists to be aware of the emotions evoked by clients, countertransference, and to not let these emotions dictate one's behavior (see Hejtmanek 2014). In other words, Zac should not let William provoke him into acting on any of his feelings toward him.

Steve, on the other hand, not only gives an explicit directive, but he also mobilizes the TCI logic that indexes emotional responses to the residents. Steve states the obvious using a phrase that is more colloquial than clinical: William is struggling. Everyone sees him struggling. His mom has missed a few visits and staff members can sympathize with what it is like to be rejected from a loved one (this point comes up again in later chapters). The line staff also know that TCI encourages them to "care enough" about the residents to not let them hurt themselves. Therefore, the point of Steve's commentary is not just to share information but to remind staff members to follow the TCI protocol, which seeks to elicit a caring response from staff members, who might just view the behavior as *crazy shit*. By mobilizing care and love through empathy evoked by the sharing of William's intimate struggles, Zac, Allen, and others know how to intervene when William does *crazy shit*. Sometimes this intervention is a restraint.

William's Restraint[8]

It is an afternoon in February. Steve, Allen, Pete, Zac (all of whom are over 6' tall, at least 200 pounds, and athletically built), and I are sitting in Steele cottage. Steve looks out the wall of windows facing the school. Steve nods to the window and we all look to see William, a 300-pound, 6'3" tall 16-year-old, storming along the path from school toward Steele. We see school staff members trailing him at a distance. Steve makes eye contact with Zac, Allen, and Pete and nods to indicate "get ready." This eye contact means he has made the decision to be ready to restrain William because of his behavior. We all know from past experience that William will probably attack Steve or Allen, William's favorite staff members. Therefore, Pete and Zac step out front, toward the front door, and Steve and Allen hang back. The atmosphere in the cottage changes palpably—a calm milieu, where the residents were playing video games or talking, changes into one of hypervigilance and intensity. It is charged. The residents also watch William storm toward the cottage. Steve tells them, "Go to the back and do what you do." Using hip hop framing (do what you do), the young men of Steele are being shut down. All of the young men hop up and follow this direction immediately.

I sit on a chair near the dining room table, 15 feet from where Allen and Steve stand. I have just completed the TCI week-long training course so I know what to expect. However, I have never watched a restraint unfold in this way. Usually they are more spontaneous. My heart beats very fast and my stomach drops. I turn to face the front door because that is where Pete and Zac stand. William momentarily leaves our view as the windows end just before the door.

William throws open the cottage front door, "FUCK YOU!!"

Silence.

William kicks the mop bucket located near the front door. Restraints can be justified, via paperwork, for dangerous behavior. The rules of Havenwood state that restraints are justified to limit dangerous behavior to self and others. However, destroying property, kicking a mop bucket, is not a justifiable reason to restrain. I see Allen standing near the staff desk, 15 feet from the front door, with his head down. He appears to not pay attention, but I have observed Allen and talked with him enough to know that he has every fiber attending to the situation with William. Pete and Zac stand between William and Allen. They have their hands up, palms forward. This is the "TCI protective stance" and it is supposed, per the workbook and training, to communicate nonaggression. Steve, with his hands up, palms forward, stands five feet to the left of Pete and Zac, and Allen. No one says anything.

William, his eyes wide and wild, looks at Steve and screams, "FUCKING TOUCH ME! I KNOW YOU WANT TO! FUCKING DO IT!"

Steve silently stands still with his hands up, palms forward and says nothing.

William grabs coats off of the wall rack and throws them to floor. He kicks the door. However, this behavior does not elicit a restraint.

William spins around and in the blink of an eye moves between Zac and Pete and tries to kick Allen. Allen blocks as much of the size-13-Timberland-boot-kick as he can with his arm and he bends at the waist to protect himself. William's behavior has just turned dangerous.

Steve, Pete, and Zac lunge on William. Allen quickly recovers and helps them struggle to put William on the ground. They try to take him down to the ground using the TCI procedure for team restraints. However William fights hard. I do not see Steve, Pete, and Zac grab William's wrists, lift his arms, and lean him back to the ground as per TCI protocol. Instead, I see William fight. He swings his arms, grunts, curses, and thrashes. The four men and William—over 1,100 pounds of sweat, muscle, and force—bounce off walls, hit the front door with a slam, grunt, and curse. The restraint is choreographed and restrained ferocity.

The goal of restraints is not to beat William up—that might be much easier, quicker, and less intimate. The goal is to restrain William from hurting himself or others and then, once restrained, to allow him to calm down. Steve, Allen, Zac, and Pete finally get William to the ground, but not without William losing his pants and underwear. William keeps trying to get up; he shifts his weight and struggles to stand. Steve, Allen, Pete, and Zac lean on him so that he cannot.

On the ground, William is held face down as per TCI protocol. Steve and Zac hold his legs and Allen and Pete hold his arms and chest. According to TCI, this physical position is imperative because then the residents cannot swing their arms or kick their legs, yet it does not restrict their breathing.[9] Zac's shirt is ripped all of the way up to the neck ribbing and his back will bruise the size of a soccer ball in the days to come. Allen is dripping with sweat as he tries to hold William still. His forehead is swollen and bloody from where it has been slammed against the wall. Allen will find out later that a bone in his wrist, from the blocked kick, is fractured. Pete's pants fall, exposing his behind as he wrestles to keep William from getting out of his grip. He cannot let go of William to pull them up. William wails and pants during his remaining exhausted attempts to wrestle free from the restraint. Allen, Pete, James, and Steve grunt as they hold him down.

The pile of men is located 10 feet from the front door and right near the hallway that leads to the back bedrooms, bathrooms, and confinement room. I sit 20 feet away in my chair, transfixed by what is happening.

An evening supervisor and a couple of other line staff members run into the cottage. A resident had run over to a neighboring cottage to tell other line staff that the restraint was occurring. I believe these line staff had called or texted the evening supervisor, as we saw in Travis's case. The neighboring staff run to the staff office and get bed sheets. They hold them ready for when William calms down enough to cover him. They know better than to put anything on a resident in the middle of a restraint.

Two staff members walk up the short hallway toward the back hallway where the confinement room is. One staff member opens the door. Another moves the rest of the residents from their rooms into the living room. The residents sidestep the restraint, as they make their way to the living room. They are told to sit in the living room quietly. I observe them sit quietly. I notice that most wear a blank stare and sit very still, as they remain attuned to the restraint happening less than 15 feet from them.

William is quiet and no longer physically struggling to get up. Therefore, after the other residents are all in the living room, I hear talk I cannot make out from the pile of men on the floor. Standing around the pile are four other men. I do not know how it happens, but the pile shifts and soon the other men grab hold of William's arms and drag his 300 pound, 6'3" dead-weight body to the confinement room, 15 feet from the restraint site. Pete, Zac, Allen, and Steve, along with the other men, manage to get William into the confinement room. I see them from my seat but am unable to make out what is being said.

I look over at the residents sitting in the living room. I notice their calm but intense vigilance. The charge in the room is unmistakable. You can cut the air with a knife. I return my focus on what is happening and being said in the confinement room. I did not, in my focus on the restraint, think about what it must be like for these young men to experience what was happening, especially if they had been restrained before, or if the restraint elicited flashbacks of their abuse.

All of a sudden, my attention is forced back to the living room by loud grunts, cursing, and struggle of what looked like to me a mass of teenage boys fighting each other. I jump to my feet and think, "I cannot get involved in any restraints."[10]

"Help!!" I shriek.

From the confinement room area, the evening supervisor and Zac sprint into the living room. I frantically waved my hand and point at the group of boys.

The evening supervisor and Zac grab Kyle. The rest of the group had dispersed somehow and many of the young men are holding Mark. Zac, the supervisor, and Kyle topple over the coffee table in the living room. The supervisor and Zac wrestle Kyle to the floor. The other boys keep out of the way of the restraint as they hold Mark and tell him, "It isn't worth it." I would learn later that Kyle attacked Mark. The rest of the young men had been trying to break up the fight.

Lying face down on the floor with Zac holding his arms down and the evening supervisor holding his legs, Kyle calls Zac and the evening supervisor "bitches" and tells them he is "gonna fuck them up" once they let him up. His comments go unanswered. More staff members appear and Mark is led away. The rest of the boys are ushered outside and supervised by other cottage staff. Like Allen during Travis and Janelle's crises, these staff members have been on call to come help and their help has been needed. Kyle continues to curse.

William is curled up in a fetal position on the floor of the confinement room. He is sobbing. Steve has pulled up a chair in front of the half open door, he straddles the back of it, and waits for William to recover and "process" what has happened. After about 10 minutes, Kyle is calm and he is being let up and escorted to a chair in the living room. He continues to scowl, squint, move his lips, and shake his head emphatically; he is watched by Zac.

The restraints are over.

The on-campus nurse enters the building and walks directly to William. She checks him out as he sits in the confinement room. Pete is in the back staff office cleaning up. Allen is standing in the hallway watching Steve to be sure that things are okay. After the nurse finishes with William, she visits with Kyle. After she visits with Kyle, she looks at Allen's forehead, which has been cleaned of blood, and his wrist. His wrist is likely fractured, and he needs a brace.

"Kate, can you run get me a brace for my right wrist? And some ice?" Allen asks me.

When I return about 20 minutes later, the cottage milieu has returned to "normal." The young men are outside hanging out or inside playing video games. William is sitting in the confinement room alert, his eyes dry, and in conversation with Steve. Within a few minutes of my return, William is being sent to his room to rest. As he walks out of the confinement room, Steve tells him, "If you want a hug, ask for a hug. I'll give you a hug."

Kyle is sitting at the dining room table; his punishment for attacking Mark.

Pete, Zac, and Allen sit, supervise the residents, write up the incident, and try not to cringe when they move. Steve has ordered pizza for the residents and staff because dinnertime at the dining hall had passed. Steve sits at his table and watches the residents. Periodically, he purses his lips and shakes his head.

I choose not to ask any questions this evening. I am not only overwhelmed by the experience, but I know that my presence is disturbing. I would come to be teased and laughed at for the rest of my time at Havenwood for "not doing anything" during the restraint and for "shrieking for help." I was even used as an example in future training sessions of what cowardice looks like during a restraint, when other staff members need you. I did not like that the supervisors laughed at me for what they perceived as my inability to act, but I understood it. I still believe that my choice to not get involved in restraints was the right one.

After William's restraint we did not go to the gym. There was no grounding in the mundane but rather, an attempt to return to some semblance of everyday life until bedtime. As the residents readied themselves for bed, I returned to my room, in the building across the field. The next day, I see Steve. He shakes his head when he sees me.

"How are you today?"

"Sore. But we're good." He is physically sore from the restraint, as are Zac, Pete, and Allen, and William. Kyle remains at the table; he does not want to talk about the events.

* * *

"Touch is our most social sense. Unlike seeing, hearing, smelling, and tasting, which can generally be done alone, touching typically implies an interaction with another person" (Field 2003:19). Touch is also a method of communication; it "is not a private act. It is a fundamental medium for expression, experience, and contestation of social values and hierarchies" (Classen 2005a:8; see also Finnegan 2005 and Montagu 1971). Touch happens *between people*; it is intersubjective.

Touch is also an *intimate* intersubjective experience as it both permeates and establishes the boundaries of self and others. Merleau-Ponty argues that touch is an immediate experience, where people intersect and "engage each other like gears" establishing one's own subjectivity and an intersubjectivity in a phenomenological world (1945/2003: xxii). Tactile interaction is a process of living through the world phenomenologically with others. It is the "social sense" that establishes a network of relationships based on the immediacy of touching and being touched. Through touch, we establish an experience of the world that grounds us in our connection with others and at the same time reminds us of our own separateness, our own physical boundaries. Touch, then, is a way for us to feel ourselves into existence, through others, especially when touch includes another subject rather than an object.

During restraints, bodies touch. Unlike what we know about prisons (Rhodes 2004) and the physical interactions that occur there, no riot gear is worn to distance the individuals involved in the restraint. As an informal uniform, staff members wear what is identified as "restraint ready clothing," which included sweat pants, no jewelry, and sneakers. In William's restraint, Zac, Pete, and William end up partially naked increasing the intimacy of the touch. Not only do clothed bodies touch but naked bodies do as well.

Unlike in prisons, Tasers and other riot equipment are not used to dominate residents at Havenwood (Rhodes 2004). Rather, the logic of restraint is not to dominate. It is to physically intervene on dangerous behavior and show residents that staff *care* about them enough to not let them hurt themselves or others. Staff members do not touch a resident with anything but their own bodies, thereby maintaining an intimate interaction, despite the "distastefulness" of the act of restraining itself.

In addition to the intimacy of bodies touching, restraints are about "caring enough" about residents to do the distasteful work of physically holding them down. It might have been easier for Zac, Pete, Allen, and Steve to gang up on William and punch him out. In a fist fight, William, a big 16-year-old, would have been up against four large adult men. I'm not sure William would have been able to struggle so much, had Zac, Pete, Allen, and Steve not performed the restraint according to proper procedure. Had the four large men fought or punched William, they might have incurred less physical injury. However, Zac, Pete, Allen, and Steve did not fight William. Rather, they restrained William using therapeutic intervention strategies. It matters less that William attacked Allen; he was seen as a kid who was "struggling." This struggle outweighed how much his size or aggression hurt the staff members. The staff did not want to dominate him; they cared about him and they signed up to deal with the *crazy shit* he does.

As I mentioned earlier, Carter, Robert, Tina, Steve, Allen, Zac, and Pete could not claim to have a true understanding of what it meant to be restrained from the youth's perspective. However, they all engaged in the physical interaction. At some point, the reality of being restrained and having to restrain—the touching and being touched in this way—distinction gave way to the intimate intersubjectivity of being in a restraint. Everyone was in it, to some extent, together. The residents had to be restrained, but the staff members chose to work in a place where they might be attacked by residents and thus required to perform restraints.

When Sophie tells Zac that William wants him to restrain him and that he should "not get sucked in," she misses the intersubjectivity of the restraint. Zac has been hired to restrain, he has signed up to restrain, the youth sometimes need restrained, and, ultimately, restraints happen. Restraints mean that residents and staff members touch each other, often in violent, messy, and very intimate ways.

I have argued previously that often this touch is given meaning using Black Street Speech and African American ways of knowing (Hejtmanek 2010). In particular, I argued that restraints as a behavior modification strategy and other forms of touch, such as hugs or fist bumps, are made meaningful in comparison to the violence outside of Havenwood faced by the young men of Steele Cottage. Many of the staff members articulated that they would rather restrain a youth "in here" (meaning Havenwood) than have a youth "get shot out there" (meaning in society at large) (Hejtmanek 2010). Staff members informed me that if young men like William physically attacked people when they returned to their home neighborhoods, they would likely be the victims of gun violence. I argued that it was a Black Street identity, evinced in Black Street Speech and style-shifting linguistic practice in psychiatric custody, that allowed for a transformation of the meaning of restraints.

This Black Street identity I refer to in early work is the hip hop identity I focus on here. As we have seen in previous chapters, young men rap and talk about gun violence. Derrick states that he is learning to work without "havin' a gun" and SlowMo states, "niggas gettin' popped everyday." The perception of life outside of Havenwood for these young, urban, poor Black boys is a gun-violent life. Therefore, the reality for staff members and for young men like Derrick is to be able to make a life without dealing with guns or gun violence. Restraints are articulated as part of this learning process (Hejtmanek 2010). In particular, restraints are seen as the way to teach young men not to do *crazy shit*. Restraints are not just mental health treatment practice, but they are framed as an important intimate, yet violent, alternative to urban street or police violence that many of these Black boys might face (Hejtmanek 2010).[11]

Despite the desire to deal with *crazy shit* at Havenwood rather than have youth suffer consequences of such behavior in the community, no one I spoke to liked to restrain or be restrained. In fact, nonviolent or tender touch is often articulated as a healthy alternative to restraints. Steve tells William, "If you want a hug, ask for a hug. I'll give you a hug." Robert covers and gently leads Travis to the bathroom. Carter gives me a side-hug and he fist bumps Mike and Jason. Havenwood has taught staff members to view behavior like William's as a reactive attachment due to a traumatic past. The staff members know their job is to work with the residents during noncrisis times so that rather than be restrained, William will one day ask for a hug, an intimate, caring form of touch. Steve tells him—if you want one, I'll give it to you, just ask. In fact, Steve sees a hug as a healthy alternative to William's *crazy shit*. Steve does not want to physically punish William for causing the restraint. He wants to give him a hug; he hopes that one day William will be able to ask for one.

Conclusion

Crazy Shit is an integral part of daily life at Havenwood. It unmakes the world, as the cottages get shut down and residents act in ways that are extremely bizarre. However, *crazy shit* also makes the world at Havenwood. The fact that people do, witness, and participate in *crazy shit* reveals how it is included in the daily lives of those who live and work in this psychiatric center. What I found precipitated out of *crazy shit* was the cultivation of care, empathy, and loving touch. Staff members would perform restraints to deal with the *crazy shit*. In some cases, the restraint would be understood as an acceptable alternative to perceived gun violence that shapes many of the Havenwood youth's lives. But ultimately, a hug is desired as the acceptable alternative to a restraint. Love is preferred to a violent attack.

Chapter 5
A Keepin' It Real Group

[Inmates] can become objects of fellow feeling and even affection. There is always the danger that an inmate will appear human.

—*Erving Goffman*, Asylums

I stand next to Robert, who was introduced in the previous chapter, outside Bradley North waiting for the residents to arrive from school. I had just finished observing clinical and administrative meetings; Robert had just clocked in. It is 2:45 p.m. in the afternoon. We are facing the on-campus school, which is about one hundred yards north of Bradley North, past the female cottages, Shelby North and Shelby South, the two therapy cottages, the swamp area, and the building where I stay. Like clockwork, we see the single file lines of residents dispersing in all directions. The young men of Bradley North walk our way. Tina is leading the line and another staff member brings up the rear. School has just ended and the residents are making their way back to their cottages.

Robert unlocks the foyer door to Bradley—all of Havenwood's doors are locked. Once inside the foyer, we can turn right and enter Bradley South, or we can turn left and enter Bradley North. Robert unlocks the door to Bradley North and holds it open for me, "Take a seat, Katie, we'll see what they want to do." Recall from chapter 3 that the afternoon time, 3:30 p.m.–4:50 p.m. can sometimes be "free time" or "recreation time." Today, the residents of Bradley North's have a say in their afternoon activity. Robert props open the door with his foot as he watches the line draw near.

Tina, who was also introduced in chapter 4, opens the foyer door for the young men. Robert greets Garrett, the first one in line.

"What do you want to do today?" Robert asks Garrett.

I am sitting at the dining room table of Bradley North as Garrett walks through the door. His brow is furrowed and I think, "Something's wrong."

"I want to have group!" He states as he purses his lips together, further accentuating the furrowed brow.

Robert and I make eye contact; it looks like we are having group. It is noteworthy that Garrett, a teenage boy, would choose to have group therapy as his after school activity on a day when the scheduled activity is "constructive free time." He could have chosen any number of other activities including playing basketball, going to the field, going to the gym, playing cards, playing video games, listening to music, reading a book, watching television, sitting in his room, or drawing. However, after a few months in the field, I am also not surprised Garrett has chosen to have group. Garrett is visibly upset and he has learned, over the course of his time in psychiatric custody, that group therapy is a space to "make [democratic] decisions, air grievances, and seek collective solutions" (Waldram 2012:65). He knows that he lives in a "therapeutic community," or therapeutic milieu, designed to use therapeutic practice in all or most aspects of life.[1] Living in this environment, Garrett understands that group therapy is not only a viable option for an after school activity but, as he is clearly upset, it will probably help him deal with whatever is upsetting him.

"What kind of group?" Robert does not miss a beat. There are so many groups to choose from. Anger Management, Therapeutic Recreation, Healthy Choices, Needs and Issues, Goals, and Community are the official groups scheduled into the lives of Havenwood youth.

"A keepin' it *real* group!" He places particular emphasis on "real."

Yes, of course, I think, a keepin' it real group. Garrett wants to have a group "to tell the truth," doing so hip hop style.

"Hey ya'll, we're having group," Robert shouts, much like Allen hollers Quiet Time, so that all of the young men filing in from school hear him. Once the residents are seated on the living room couches for group, after Transition, Snack, and medication dispensing, Robert tells them, "Garrett wanted to have a group about keepin' it real, so we are going to talk about things that are bothering us."

I look around the room. Garrett, Mike, Russell, Terrell, Billy, and Travis are seated quietly ready to begin group. Both Billy and Travis are white. Garrett, Mike, Russell, and Terrell are African American. Travis, Terrell, and Garrett we met in chapter 4. Other residents are either off campus or in another kind of therapy—individual or family. Tina sits next to Billy.

Bradley North is home to mostly African American residents; however, a few white youth also live there. The staff members are equally African American and white. Bradley North even has a pretty equitable gender balance among line staff. While the racial identity was mixed between white and Black individuals, the influence of African American cultural practices is still very present. No one questioned the validity or possibility of a keepin' it real group. While Robert does tell the residents that they can "talk about what is bothering them," he does not rename the group to an officially recognized group name. No one challenges him on this either. Hip hop framing is being sampled into the psychiatric practices of Havenwood.

Robert looks at Garrett and asks him, "Do you want to start?"

"Yeah," Garrett is ready to keep it real. "I want to know why Travis keeps trying to provoke everyone." There it is, I think. We met Garrett and Travis in a moment of crisis—when Travis was suffering and vulnerable. In that instance, Garrett empathizes with Travis, in a quiet moment of compassion for his peer, his cottage-mate, and maybe, one day, his friend. Right now, in group therapy, Garrett is having it out. He turns directly to Travis, "You keep saying you have issues but we all have issues. We are all in treatment. You have to learn how to deal with your issues." In chapter 4, Garrett told me the same thing, that "We all have issues." Here he reminds Travis of it. He also pushes Travis to learn to deal with his issues, that this is in fact why they all are in treatment to begin with. Garrett tells Travis the truth; he keeps it real.

Travis whines, "Why does everyone target me? I just got here and I am trying to deal with my stuff but I feel like everyone is against me." Garrett rolls his eyes, sucks his teeth, and throws his hands up in the air in a gesture of exasperation.

Travis is new to treatment and is less familiar with the protocols of the institution and its paradigms and how to conform to them. He does not know that group is a collective event, where one is challenged to reflect on one's own "long-standing beliefs, values, and attitudes and to do so with the active assistance of others" (Waldram 2012:65). An anthropologist of therapeutic intervention, James Waldram argues that group therapy is the process of therapeutic self-reflection undertaken with the help of others. Travis has yet to learn the script of group therapy and the mechanisms through which to use the event (Carr 2011).

Group therapy is an intersubjective process, a practice by which one learns about one's issues by listening to others' views on them. This learning happens through sincere, honest, and occasionally confrontational interactions with others. Garrett does not pull Travis aside and tell him that he needs to deal with his issues. Nor does Garrett pull Robert, or another staff member aside and tell on

Travis, thereby hoping that a staff member will deal with the tension. Instead, Garrett asks for a group therapy session where the collective members of the cottage can come together to help Travis deal with his issues.

The rest of the group begins to mutter and Robert has to shush the youth. Russell, another veteran of Havenwood, raises his hand. He knows the Cottage Program's rules of group: raise your hand to speak.

"Russell," Robert calls on him.

"I think what you need to do is, when you are angry you need to talk about what is wrong. You just can't get aggressive. It is hard but you have to learn how to deal with your issues." Everyone but Travis claps at this statement.

Russell echoes Garrett's use of institutional speak: Travis is *provoking* everyone, he is *angry*, and he gets *aggressive*. Travis does not have to say that he is angry, what is assumed is that "provoking" or antagonistic behavior toward others is considered "aggression," the behavioral manifestation of anger. While in treatment, Russell has learned that he, and his peers, have anger issues. (I do not question the legitimacy of anger issues here, but I return to anger in chapter 7.) He also has learned that anger leads to aggression if it is not dealt with, as reflected in the Conflict Cycle and Life Space Crisis Intervention (LSCI) logic (see chapter 2) and restraints (see chapter 4). It is easy to deal with anger; just talk about what is wrong. Russell, like Garrett, can seamlessly articulate the institutional and therapeutic logic of Havenwood. However, this articulation of the institutional logic is also understood as "keepin' it real." Travis, as we have seen in chapter 4, reacts bizarrely when he is upset. Russell, Garrett, and the others know this. Therefore his peers remind him of the goal of psychiatric custody, the overarching aim of the institution: to deal with one's issues, not act them out. Everyone claps in agreement with Russell's statement.

"Now all you have to do is follow your own advice," Robert teases him. Russell smiles and hangs his head. The group laughs in response.

* * *

This chapter aims to describe the group therapeutic work that makes up so much of daily life at Havenwood. I situate the group therapy session within the organization of a total institution. However, my focus is less on how the residents of Havenwood reveal the structuring aspects of total institutional life, and rather on the messiness of their humanity, how they add to and challenge the structure in various ways.

I begin this chapter with Garrett, who knows how to walk in a single file line home from school and to ask for a group therapy session as an afterschool activity. However, Garrett does not want to have a formally named group. Rather he wants to have a "keepin' it real" group. The framing of "keepin' it real" does two things: first, it demands that the discussion remain "real" or sincere and truthful, and second, it demands this using hip hop framing. Therefore, my discussion of therapeutic work includes a discussion of sincerity and racial sincerity as lynchpins of the therapeutic process at Havenwood.

Here I explain how sincerity is a critical aspect of therapeutic treatment. This both exemplifies the work of therapeutic intervention—to get people to work together to deal with their issues—as well as illustrates the "give" in the total institution framework. I will also explain how racial sincerity is mobilized at Havenwood to challenge some of our existing notions of institutional life. I conclude that these aspects of sincerity allow for "mad love" to emerge as an emic framework of the practice of institutional psychiatric treatment. Through genuine or sincere subjective and intersubjective experiences in group therapy, residents sample hip hop into the structure and practice of psychiatry custody.

Group Work—Therapeutic Logic in Psychiatric Custody

As discussed previously, psychiatric custody falls within the genre of "total institutions" that completely organize the daily lives of those who live in them. These total institutions not only strip the messiness from those who live in them, but the goal is to fulfill the aim of the institution. One of the main goals of psychiatric custody is to take in "troubled youth" and make them "productive citizens." The therapeutic milieu, the home-like environments found in total institutions, is a way to achieve this end.

Psychologists Albert Trieschman and Larry Brendtro and social worker James Whittaker define a milieu as "a group living situation for children, specifically for children with emotional problems, children who must live away from home and whose lives are full of crisis" (Trieschman, Whittaker, and Brendtro 1969:2). They argued that the milieu could be the "other 23 hours of care" in addition to the hour of individual therapy, thus cultivating an environment of constant therapeutic intervention. At Havenwood, group therapy was ubiquitous within the milieu and was a significant part of the "other 23 hours of care."

Group therapy is a collective event found in various psychiatric treatment programs, therapeutic environments, and healing communities.[2] Group therapy sessions remind me of a ritual. "Ritual" is defined as formal social acts that have stylized, repetitive, and stereotyped performances. Rituals usually have set times and spaces and include highly regulated behavior. As anthropologist James Waldram (2012) maintains, group therapy sessions are ritual events where democratic decisions are made, grievances are aired, and collective solutions are sought when a group of people come together to share their beliefs, attitudes, and values. In the ritual events of group therapy, the method of speaking is also ritualized. Summerson Carr (2011) in her work on addiction and therapeutic talk in the United States, argues that therapeutic talk is highly ritualized, reflecting how political sharing of inner states can be within the context of therapeutic intervention. Therefore the group session and the manner of speaking are ritualized. At Havenwood group therapy is, in essence, a ritualized space where people come to share their problems, to seek group assistance, and to help others in their healing process.

Unlike individual therapy, group therapy requires collectively working together in the treatment process. Travis is new to psychiatric custody and wants to know why everyone is against him. However, the point of group therapy is that it is a joint therapeutic effort. The objectives of the keepin' it real group are: (1) the session is called to collectively deal with Travis's issues because he is disruptive to the group; and (2) everyone works together to encourage, challenge, and to get him to deal with these issues.

James Waldram finds that group therapy sessions are inherently performative acts, where an individual tells his story, his narrative, "in presentation to the group" (Waldram 2012:66; see also Carr 2011). Unlike this method of narrative construction and presentation, group work at Havenwood is often much more spontaneous. Travis did not know that the keepin' it real group Garrett wanted was going to focus on him and his issues. The group is less about a presentation or narrative storytelling and more about the collective work of talking about one's issues and confronting one another about provocative behavior.

At Havenwood, group therapy is codified in a few ways. For example, the Bradley North Cottage Program outlines "Group Therapy" by discussing the daily, weekly, and biweekly group sessions that occur. The topics to be discussed in these group sessions are also mentioned, including daily goal achievement, managing anger, and learning to manage one's finances or plan one's career (Figure 5.1). Appropriate behavior in group therapy is also codified in the Cottage Program, as evinced in Steele's Cottage Program (Figure 5.2). Residents are to avoid side conversations, to pay attention to and respect one another, to not touch others, and to raise one's hand for permission to talk. If youth cannot follow these rules, they will be subject to intervention, consequences, or be removed from the group. Residents know the kinds of groups available and how to behave in them. Russell, raises his hand to speak, which is proper conduct in group therapy.

In this chapter I use ethnographic data from three group therapy sessions (other group sessions are present in other chapters, see e.g., chapter 8). In each of these sessions, young men sit in a particular formation, and they follow the rules of raising one's hand to speak, one person speaking at a time, keeping hands to oneself, being respectful, and not indulging in side conversations. In essence, they follow the rules of Group Therapy outlined in the Cottage Programs (Figures 5.1 and 5.2). In addition, they know when to sit for group therapy (see the beginning of the chapter) due to the overall structure of institutional living; group is after the youth walk in a single file

<u>Group Therapy</u>

Each day, the residents meet at the beginning of the day to identify a daily goal. At the end of the day they meet in group to evaluate there progress about that goal. Cottage staff meet with the residents to assist them in completing this group.

Each week, residents attend a life skills group led by the Clinical Program Manager and the Transition Worker. Topics for this group include money management, career planning, food preparation, health and safety and community services.

Every other week residents attend an anger management group, which teaches the use of anger. This group regularly processes situations that residents identify as crisis.

Further, groups are regularly utilized to talk together about issues involving many or all of the residents.

Figure 5.1 Group Therapy in Bradley North Cottage Program

GROUP

- No outside objects.
- Raise hand to be called on.
- One person speaking at a time.
- Be respectful of others and to what they are saying.
- No side conversations.
- Keep hands and feet to yourself.
- Residents who are unable to follow group expectations or who are disruptive are subject to interventions, consequences, and/or removal from the group.

Figure 5.2 Group Behavior Steele Cottage Program

line home from school, medications are dispersed, and snacks are eaten (see Figures 3.1 and 3.2).

Youth even know how to use a therapeutic register, how to perform the ritualized speak (Carr 2011). Garrett and Russell can easily articulate their anger and aggression "issues." They know that they are all in treatment precisely to deal with their issues. Russell states that when he and his fellow Bradley North residents get angry they should talk about what is wrong, rather than to act it out by provoking others. Others clap when Russell makes this statement; clapping was common in group sessions. Clapping honors the veracity of Russell's statement and his ability to articulate it. His statement means that he is learning what he is supposed to do in treatment.

Despite the ritualized nature of the group therapy sessions, they were often not simply orchestrated events, filled with rehearsed narratives or social script performances. Rather, even group therapy sessions, highly structured and structuring aspects of total institutional life, are rife with spontaneity, playfulness, and, most importantly, sincerity.[3]

Sincerity

Anthropologist John Jackson (2005) asks us to think about the importance of sincerity, rather than authenticity, in the ethnographic endeavor.[4] Authenticity "presupposes a relation between subjects (who authenticate) and objects (dumb, mute, and inorganic)" (Jackson 2005:15). Using this framework we can imagine how someone is "authenticated" much like an object would be—through the social scripts or collective identities found in our cultural worlds. In addition, one adheres to social scripts, hoping to communicate one's authentic-ness to others. Jackson argues that we use scripts as "easy shorthand for serious causal analysis" (2005:13) and authenticity, the relation between subject and object, is the means by which we do this. Authenticity is about content.

Sincerity, on the other hand, Jackson states, "presumes a liaison *between subjects*…questions of sincerity imply social interlocutors who presume one another's humanity, interiority, and subjectivity" (Jackson 2005:15). Sincerity allows for the messiness or "liveness" of human interaction and it privileges intent (Jackson 2005:18). Sincerity, then, is about an intersubjectivity that allows for doubt and the ability to not always following social scripts. Sincerity is also about the way people shirk social scripts, or in the case with the keepin' it real group, might intentionally build a messy something else using available therapeutic and hip hop scripts. From the ethnographer's perspective, sincerity allows for a method of understanding those we work with. I cannot know that Garrett is truly speaking from his heart, but I understand that his asking for a particular kind of group gets at something more than just a performance of a hip hop identity or the social scripts he has been socialized to use. In addition, as we will see in ethnographic vignettes later, the men of Steele also trust one another in their group sessions. The trust in the sincere intention of the individual allows for an understanding of self-transformation and love to emerge from the confines of psychiatric custody.

Sincerity in Psychiatric Custody

Sincerity operates on two levels at Havenwood. The first is the group therapy sessions themselves as ritualized, standardized events that require sincere performances of discussing inner states (Carr 2011). The second is how engagements and interactions in group therapy at Havenwood are often spontaneously sincere, challenging the performative aspect of sincerity (Jackson 2005).

Therapeutic frameworks and practices in psychiatric custody require sincerely discussing inner states (Carr 2011). Social theorist Nikolas Rose argues that in group therapy people allow the "more intimate regions" of their lives to be seen, judged, evaluated, classified, and corrected by others (1999:240). Group therapy is about the revelation of internal worlds to others, and these intimate regions become the topic of group discussion, evaluation, and correction.

For example, Travis's issues become the topic of discussion: he is told that he has to deal with his provocative behavior (classified), and to do this, others give him feedback about proper behavior (corrected).

Group therapy and sincerity are part of the performative work of a "therapeutic community" defined earlier. Garrett is "airing a grievance" by seeking a group therapy session to confront Travis about his "provoking" behavior. Travis's behavior, his perceived inability to deal with his issues, disrupts the therapeutic process of his cottage mates. Garrett uses the group to seek a collective solution to Travis's issues. Russell supports the group process by telling Travis how he could better deal with his issues and be less aggravating to his peers. However, being new to treatment, Travis thinks that Garrett, and others, are singling him out unnecessarily and perhaps insincerely. When he voices this perspective, Garrett gets frustrated; group discussions and the airing of grievances are sincere exchanges, no one is "picked on" unfairly or insincerely. Group therapy asks that individuals sincerely examine their "more intimate regions" with others. Group therapy is a ritualized therapeutic event that requires sincerity's intersubjective interaction.

At the beginning of this chapter, I use a quotation from Goffman's *Asylums: Essays on the Social Situation of Mental Patients and Other Inmates,* which reveals anxieties about working with humans in total institutions—inmates might appear human, they may become objects of fellow feeling and affection. He describes how staff members might actually come to like, care about, or emotionally engage with inmates. He states, "Staff...may come to view inmates as reasonable, responsible creatures who are fitting objects for emotional involvement" (Goffman 1961:82). Rather than *maybe* appearing as human, I found that life at Havenwood required that we think about psychiatric custody, and group therapy in particular, through the lens of sincerity and thus the "liveness" and humanness of the residents who live at Havenwood. Many of the group sessions, like those mentioned below, are more "messy" than the defined, ideal, or social scripted group therapy sessions Havenwood imagined, as the residents and staff members cultivated a space of sincere interaction between subjects. Let me use two ethnographic examples from group therapy to illustrate my point.

"Role Model Behavior"

"Ok, needs and issues?" Steele Cottage staff and residents are concluding their weekly scheduled community group therapy session.

Allen, the staff member leading the session, wants to know if anyone has any needs or issues that require the group's attention.

William raises his hand, following group rules of speaking and turn taking.

"William," Allen calls on him.

"I have an issue with two peers," William states calmly. William is often seen as the last person to have issues with his peers, as he is often the one causing the issues (see chapter 4). However, William has been working on his issues and he is, what he calls, "improving." He uses this moment, as did Garrett earlier, to talk about the "issues" he is having with two of his peers.

"Okay…" Allen hesitantly replies.

William continues, "I have an issue with two peers who are on Gratis who should be showing role model behavior and they get into arguments and take advantage of the times when staff aren't around."

"What does that mean?" Allen asks.

"They were cussin' when staff wasn't around."

Like Robert mentioned earlier, Allen does not miss a beat. He looks around the room, makes eye contact with the rest of the young Steele Cottage men and states, "Ya'll got that?" While no one says anything, heads nod in acknowledgment. After a brief pause, Allen asks if anyone else has any other issues. William shakes his head. No one else comments. "Ok, constructive free time."

* * *

In this portion of a group session, William is using the group therapy to share an issue he is having. His issue, however, is not that residents are "provoking" him, like it was for Garrett. Rather, William wants the young men who have earned the Level of Gratis, the highest Level of the cottage, to role model good behavior for him, even and especially when staff members are not around.

Later I asked Allen about William's group "issue." I wondered what he thought William was doing in the session. He did not think William was "snitching," a common term used at Steele Cottage to mean tattling, nor did William want to confront anyone specifically about his behavior. Rather, Allen said William is working really hard and he wants his high status peers to role model good behavior for him, to encourage him by their example, even and especially when staff are absent. I interpreted the session similarly. William used group therapy—a time to collectively seek democratic solutions and to share one's "more intimate region"—to ask that his peers not curse, in order to help him in his treatment. I, and others, see William as sincere in his issue. He was not trying to get anyone in trouble and thereby seeking the punishment (per the Level System) of his peers for cursing. He could have named the guilty but he does not. William is not being "provoked" by his peers, nor is cursing seen as a behavioral manifestation of issues. Rather, cursing is just not role model behavior. The peers who are on Gratis are his role models and William needs them to act like it, for his sake.

While William brings up the "issue," the rest of the group understands the significance of the situation. Allen asks everyone, "You got that?" and the group nods. Allen is justified to ask who is cursing—he is after all a staff member enforcing the Cottage Program and the Level System in psychiatric custody. The rest of the boys respond with nods. Like the youth of Bradley North, the young men of Steele do not just acquiesce in group if they differ in their opinions. If they feel that they have been unfairly attacked or misunderstood, they confront one another, suck their teeth, or roll their eyes, much like Garrett did. However, in William's case, the group simply nods. I interpreted this to mean that they not only understood the collective decision that has just been made: do not curse when staff are not around. Affirmative nods also might indicate that role modeling good behavior, even and especially when staff are not around, might be an important part of the therapeutic process for them as well (I come back to this in chapter 7). In addition, affirmative nods indicated to me an acceptance by Allen and the other boys of Steele that "not cussing when staff aren't around" could be and is an issue for William. The men trust that William is not snitching but that he really needs others to behave well for him. They believe him and trust in his intentions. Therefore, group therapy is used to articulate needs and as a space to trust others' sincere engagement in their treatment.

Sometimes, entire group therapy sessions are modified to allow and cultivate the sincere subject-to-subject interactions we have seen from Garrett and William. In the next vignette, we see Steve take an entire formal group therapy session and use it to encourage sincere and trustworthy engagements among the young men of Steele.

"You're Gonna Help Me With Levels"

"The holidays are coming up and it is going to be difficult. I see it in your eyes, Manny. I see it in some of your eyes. It is going too good here. It is going to be difficult." Allen tells the group, comprised of

Andy, Dontay, Derrick, Lamar, Dwayne, Mark, Manny, Jonathon, William, Wesley, and Marlon. These young men sit on the couches in Steele's living room waiting for group therapy to start. The young men are silent. Allen sits at the dining room table, behind the couches.

Community group is a weekly group therapy session where the functioning of the cottage and the functioning of the community of residents who live in this institution are discussed. Topics include room assignments, group living dynamics, and interpersonal problems. Unlike the keepin' it real group earlier, where the point of the group is to talk about what is bothering people, community group is about maintaining the community and learning about weekly plans. In community group, residents learn about their weekly Levels as well. Community group includes staff members and residents, allowing everyone who lives and works in the cottage to bring up issues or share with the group. Today however, Allen bypasses all of the typical business of community group and goes straight to the heart of the matter: the upcoming holidays, Thanksgiving and Christmas, are going to be difficult and he does not need a piece of paper to tell him that; he can see it in their eyes.

Steve echoes Allen's sentiment, "I also want to say that the holidays are going to be hard. You want to go home but that isn't going to happen for all of you. But we are going to have a good time here, maybe go to Dave and Busters." Steve does not lighten the tone of group, instead he adds to the severity of it: who *gets* to go home for the holidays will be quite different than who *wants* to.

Manny sits still looking straight ahead, his eyes glazed over. Derrick, Lamar, Jonathon, Dwayne, and Andy have a similar gaze a slightly different head-cock. Mark, Dontay, and Wesley are looking down, also barely moving. Marlon is looking from Allen to Steve and Steve to Allen as he fidgets in his seat. William watches Steve with his hands folded on his lap. Pete, another staff member, is sitting next to Derrick on one of the couches. Zac is sitting near the cottage telephone at the staff desk, ten feet to the right of Allen. Jim and Sarah sit at the dining room table with Allen.

Steve lets the tension hang in the air for a moment, then he changes the subject, "Also I want to talk about jockeying for position. Who knows what I am talking about?"

Wesley raises his hand. Steve nods at him.

"When you do things so others will look at you?"

"That's part of it. Anyone else? Manny?"

Manny shakes his head. Pete, a staff member, raises his hand.

"Pete," Steve calls out.

"Who is going to take Chris's spot now that he is gone." Rather than defining "jockeying for position," Pete has it out: Chris left; he moved from Steele to a group home, and his position as a leader and role model in the cottage is vacant (I return to Chris and his process of leaving in chapter 8. Chris and Manny were the only residents I discuss in this book who left Havenwood—Manny ran away in the middle of the night.).

Steve nods. "I was with Chris for almost four years. He worked damn hard to get where he is. Damn hard. He was a leader around here and I know that some of you are looking at filling the spot. I don't discourage that. I think it can be a good thing. This is the stuff that is going to help you out there. You have to think about if you are going to be a leader or a follower. Like when you get out: are you going to be a follower and go back to what you were doing, or are you going to be a leader? I encourage leaders to step up. So I say: try to be leaders but know you aren't going to be perfect. You are 15, 16, 17 years old; you need to step it up. I think you have changed a lot. You aren't going to be perfect but your recovery is improving. For example, Mark," Steve turns to Mark and looks him in the eyes, "You and Derrick got into a fight and you were speaking the next day."

"That day," Allen corrects.

Steve nods and raises his eyebrows, acknowledging the accomplishment of recovering from a fight on the same day.

Mark nods in response.

Steve continues, "Dontay, you were upset yesterday and it took you 15 minutes to recover. That is a beautiful thing. You have to look at how you are changing and how you are recovering."

Marlon raises his hand, but does not wait for a nod, "But it isn't really changing, it is adapting."

Steve interrupts him, "No, I'm not going let that go on. You are changing. There are some things about yourself that are who you are, but you are changing. You aren't going to be perfect but you have to change. Like the other day when we were talking about 'can men cry?' That is a difficult thing, how to get in touch with your emotions besides anger. That is something we can talk about. But you are changing and that is a beautiful thing. You want to call it therapeutic or whatever, but you are changing." I underline the phrase "therapeutic or whatever" as I take down the conversation in my notes.

The quiet returns, however, the silence is less tense.

"You, Steve, are doing Levels today" Allen tells him as he takes the tally sheet over to him (see Figure 2.2).

Steve looks at the sheet, folds it, and puts it underneath his chair. Usually the staff member leading community group tells each resident what Level he earned over the course of the previous week. As I mentioned in chapter 2, Levels are tallied from various point sources—school, group therapy, therapeutic recreation, doing chores, everyday life—and these points are added up at the end of the week. Each Level corresponds to a certain number of points. Each resident's Level, and progress, has been discussed and agreed upon at Team Meeting earlier in the day. Today, however, Steve does something different. He disregards the piece of paper and looks up at the young men sitting in group, "You are going to help me do Levels."

Allen has returned to the dining table. He turns to me and whispers, "This is great, watch this. They say what Level they think they should be on and they hold each other accountable." Allen knows what will happen in this abrupt change of plans; he has obviously seen Steve do this before, even though he is quick to inform me that it "doesn't happen very often." Allen tells me that rather than the staff deciding the residents' Levels, the group will decide together. Spontaneously, peers will weigh in on one another's progress or not, and decide one another's weekly Level.

Steve looks to his left at William.

"I was on OOP but I think I should be on Level 2," William tells the group.

Derrick raises his hand. He apparently knows what to do in this situation as a group session, and also how to discuss William's Level. Steve nods to him. "I think he should be on Level 2 because he has been doing his thing and he hasn't been provoking as much." (Note the "doing his thing" and "provoking" framing in one sentence.)

Steve looks at William. William looks back at Steve waiting for his answer. Without consulting the Level sheet, Steve nods, acknowledging that William will be on Level 2. All of the young men clap.

Mark sees it is his turn, "I was on Level 2 but I think I deserve to be on Level 3 even though I still provoke my peers and got into a fight."

Derrick raises his hand. Steve nods to him knowing that Derrick was the one that Mark got into a fight with. "I think he should be on Level 3 because like you said we got into a fight but we recovered quickly and we were able to work together later."

William raises his hand.

Steve calls on him, "William."

"I think he should be on Level 3 because recovering quickly and working with Derrick later is role model behavior."

Steve looks at Mark, "I think you need to watch how you provoke your peers."

Mark nods. Steve nods. Everyone claps. Mark is on Level 3.

It is Manny's turn. "I'm on Transition and I want to stay on Transition."

After being given the go-ahead look by Steve, Lamar agrees with Manny, "He has been really helpful, giving advice to his peers and we think he should be on Transition."

Steve nods. Everyone claps.

"I want to be on Level 3," Wesley states.

Mark gives feedback to Wesley, "You came here and said you wanted to get to Level 3. You have done that, you said that from early on and you have done your thing." (Note that getting to Level 3 is understood as doing one's thing.)

Pete decides to participate, "I think you are doing well but I don't think you are working. I think you are just sliding by."

Wesley does not respond and the room becomes quiet again.

Steve addresses Wesley, "Do you have anything to say? You need to say it. If someone says something like that, you need to learn to stand up for yourself and say what you think. Wesley, what do you think about that? Use your words." Residents are rarely allowed to "talk back" or challenge staff members, especially about behavior issues, on their comments. Here, however, Steve encourages Wesley to stand up for himself and respond to Pete's critique. This is identified as "using one's words."

"I think I am kind of working but I am also sliding," Wesley states, providing an honest self-assessment.

Pete and Steve nod their heads. It is true that Wesley is working and sliding and they agree. Their nod also acknowledges Wesley's honesty.

It is Derrick's turn. "I am on Level 2 and I think I should be on Level 3 because after the fight, we did OK."

Marlon responds, "I think you are doing a good job but like the rest of us…." Marlon pauses, he seems unsure of whether to say what he is going to say.

"Just say it, man, come on," Derrick demands.

"OK. I think you could work harder," Marlon tells Derrick.

Derrick accepts this with a nod and "OK." Derrick can hear Marlon's critique and appreciate his honest assessment.

Allen breaks his silence, "Derrick, I think you are working but I am not sure about Level 3. I'd say 2 plus (2+)."

"To be honest, I don't think you should be on 3." Steve echoes Allen. "You have been doing a good job but we need to think about earning the Levels and you did some stuff that isn't Level 3. So I think you should be 2+, so 2+."

Derrick nods; he can accept and see how he is at Level 2+. It is better than Level 2. Everyone claps.

Turning to Andy, Steve asks, "Andy, what about you? You are already doing well but are you working? Are you changing? Here is your chance to tell me if you think you are."

Andy pauses, then nods, "Yeah. I think I am changing a little bit."

Marlon raises his hand.

Steve turns to Marlon, perhaps anticipating that Marlon is going to argue that they are just adapting and not changing, his latest argumentative stance in group sessions and in daily life, more generally. "No, you are not talking. That is something about you [that] you need to realize. Sometimes you just need to listen. You are always responding. Put your hand down. Close your mouth. Listen. That is an important skill. Sometimes I have to remind myself to shut up and I will say that out loud: Steve. Just. Shut. Up. Sometimes you have to just listen to what others are telling you." Steve wants Marlon to listen, using his own honest self-talk to illustrate his point.

Marlon puts his hand down and remains quiet.

"Ok, is that it?" He asks the group. If someone has anything to add to community group, this is the time when they know to raise a hand to do so. Most of the youth nod.

"Go have free time," Steve ends group.

In unison the 11 young men stand up and disperse from the living room area. I make eye contact with Derrick who is on his way to get his coat, which is hanging in the foyer, and then go outside for constructive free time. I wonder about his interpretation of the spontaneous group interaction.

"How'd that go?"

Derrick smiles and shakes his head, "Steve's got mad love for us."

* * *

I use this vignette to illustrate the structure and the flexibility of group sessions, the intimacy of the interaction, and the way that honesty, trustworthiness, and sincerity are cultivated as part of the group therapeutic process. Rather than simply follow a strict group therapy agenda, one that has been codified on a piece of paper and preserved in the daily cottage log, Steve places this sheet of paper underneath his chair. I liken this piece of paper to how group sessions are codified in the Cottage Program. Groups, like other aspects of total institutional life, are scripted. The tally sheet evinces how each resident earned his Level through the scripted process. When Steve folds the sheet and places it underneath his chair he limits the script's grasp on the therapeutic process. In that moment, it did not matter that Allen had tallied the weekly Levels or that the Team had discussed them at Team Meeting. Instead, Steve asks that the residents help him decide one another's Levels. He does this without pushback from any of the staff members; if, like me, they had not seen this kind of thing before, they trusted Steve enough to know what he was doing.

Steve uses the group structure to do something more complicated, more "alive," more sincere and honest than to simply "give out" the weekly Levels. He asks the residents to be honest about their work and progress in treatment, to allow their peers to comment on their claims, and to allow the group to work together to agree on these claims. I underlined Steve's comment "therapeutic or whatever." He knows how the group is *supposed* to go, which is per psychiatric custody's grand plan and treatment practices; it is supposed to be "therapeutic." However, Steve decides to be more flexible in the structure, which he states may or may not be interpreted as therapeutic. It might be "whatever." However, I believe his effort is to be more "real"—both sincere and honest—in the group therapy session and the distribution of Levels. Steve knows he is not following group rules per se, but he believes that allowing the young men the space to speak for themselves, to comment on one another, and to respond to their own critique are important skills of "being leaders" and standing up for oneself. Allen informs me this "doesn't happen very often," but as is obvious from how the group plays out, everyone knows what to do.

Within the spontaneous group interaction, the young men are encouraged to be honest and sincere in their interactions. Take Mark, for example, without knowing what "Level 2" means, it is clear that Mark is on Level 2 but thinks that he should be on Level 3. The reason he gives is because even though he got into a fight, he recovered quickly. Mark is honest about the circumstances of his situation; he does not try to deny that he got into a fight. Derrick, the young man with whom he fought, agrees with Mark. Derrick does not have to agree with Mark. But he does. He is sincere in his agreement that they recovered well and fast from the fight. Steve is also honest; he thinks Mark "provokes" his peers too much and that he needs to watch that behavior. However, in the end, Mark is on Level 3. Derrick, however, is not so lucky. He is challenged in his quest for Level 3 by his peer Marlon and other staff members, Allen and Steve. But Derrick accepts their critique of him: that he can work harder and that he is not quite up to Level 3 standards just yet. Finally, staff members challenge Wesley and Andy. How hard are they really working in treatment? Pete and Steve think these young men are "sliding by." When offered the space to deny this accusation, both Andy and Wesley admit that they are working but yes, they are sliding by too. Even Steve, when he intervenes on Marlon's discussion of changing versus adapting, is honest about how he sometimes has to tell himself, "Just. Shut. Up." Sometimes, "shutting up and listening" is a lesson even he needs to learn and reflect on.

While Havenwood has social scripts and Cottage Programs that dictate that group be about "daily goals" or "career goals," sometimes the staff members allow the residents' treatment progress to be discussed, negotiated, and decided through honest and sincere group conversations. The group session just mentioned even begins with Allen stating that the holidays will be difficult, and that he can see this in the youths' eyes. Allen begins with sincerity by indexing the emotional toll that being in psychiatric custody over the holidays can mean for teenage boys. In addition, Steve brings up conversations the men have had about crying. While Havenwood has anger management groups, these youth want to talk about crying rather than about anger. Steve is willing to have a group session on this. Both the conversation about crying and Steve's discussion of it in community group reveal how group sessions can become about meaningful topics, external to the official program of the session or the tally sheet. The interactions are spontaneous, allowing for the young and adult men to engage with one another honestly and sincerely, subject-to-subject. The Levels still need to be earned as Steve says—and they are still a critical way for the youth to understand their treatment process—but earning them can be accomplished not by only following the social script but by sincerely engaging the young men to participate in the honest and sincere assessment of their own change.

Racial Sincerity: Racializing The Clinical Encounter

Erving Goffman's *Asylums* was based on a year of ethnographic fieldwork at St. Elizabeth's Hospital in Washington DC He passed his days with patients, although he did not sleep there, nor did he conduct interviews with the inmates. His goal was to "learn about the social world of the hospital inmate, as this world is subjectively experienced by him" (Goffman 1961:ix). Goffman's ethnographic work in *Asylums* has provided the foundation for understanding the lived experience of total institutional life. My research at Havenwood supports much of what Goffman stated more than 50 years earlier.

However, Goffman is also quick to note that his particular social position might have influenced his analysis. He states, "I want to warn that my view is probably too much that of a middle-class male" (Goffman 1961:x). While he identifies that his middle class and male status might affect his analysis, he does not indicate how his white racial identity might do so as well. What he does not mention is how race shaped the practice and life of institutional living, especially in a deeply segregated United States society in the mid-1950s.

As mentioned in chapter 1, historian and psychiatrist Jonathon Metzl "tells the story of how race gets written into the definition of mental illness" (2009:ix). He argues that unspoken codes for normal or abnormal behavior reinforce mainstream racial hierarchies, with madness being overwhelmingly associated with Black men. As I mentioned previously, the majority of the young people—boys and girls—at Havenwood are African American. This simple observation, along with the national statistics, reveals that Black men, in particular, and people of color, more generally, populate American prisons and institutional treatment centers. However, I want to push our understanding of race in psychiatry further, past the statistics and incarceration rates. Goffman's analysis does not include how race might shape the institutional organization or therapeutic practice therein. My research, on the other hand, illustrates how race is an integral part of the *practice* of psychiatric treatment in the clinical encounter and the definitions of treatment success as I saw it at Havenwood. (I return to definitions of treatment success in chapter 8.)

John Jackson's work provides a way to think about racial identity and cultural practices in psychiatric custody through his work on what he calls "racial sincerity." Racial sincerity allows one to think about racial subjects and subjectivities in ways that push past authenticating measures of racial identity or identity politicking. Furthermore, because of its focus on subject-subject interaction, interiorities, and intent, racial sincerity asks scholars to think about "how (and why) race is lived so intimately and affectively" (Jackson 2005:13).

I use Jackson's framework of sincerity and racial sincerity to think through some of what happens at Havenwood, especially in group therapy sessions. I find that the framework of sincerity has broad applications. Sincerity not only allows me to think about the therapeutic practice of group therapy, but also about the ways race plays out in these clinical encounters. For example, I think Garrett is sincere in his treatment practice; he wants to have group therapy after school. He is also sincere in the ways he views his peers, he wants to engage others in intimate, affective, and subject-to-subject ways. Sincerity as a conceptual framework helps me understand how interactions like those between subjects privilege intent, the intentions and motivations of individuals (rather than content), are intimate and affective, and allow for the messiness of human "liveness" within the project of psychiatric custody.

Racial sincerity allows me to see the intention of mobilizing *race* in psychiatric custody through the sampling of hip hop into therapeutic practice. When Garrett asks for a keepin' it real group, he is indexing both hip hop and group therapy. Garrett, as an African American teenager, provides a window into how race might disrupt the psychiatric logic of the institution, carving out slippage in the otherwise hermetically sealed total institution. He walks in a single file line and wants to have group as an after school activity. But he wants a keepin' it real group. Keepin' it real is a hip hop phrase, which is often associated with African American cultural practice and black communities. In hip hop language, "to keep it real" means "to tell the truth" (Westbrook 2002:81).[5] While "keepin' it real" has become vastly popular in mainstream America, I argue that Garrett and other young Black men like him use it to index hip hop, sampling hip hop into group therapeutic practice. What is most interesting is that the language of hip hop became a way to frame therapeutic intervention, especially a group session. Garrett is not just keepin' it real, he is asking to have a *keepin' it real group*. Robert allows the keepin it real group. In instances like this, the vision of Goffman's total institution breaks down.

Throughout the larger group therapy vignette earlier we hear Derrick, William, Wesley, and Mark evaluate one another on "doing their thing" as much as "staying on level" or not "provoking" as much. The young men are evaluating one another not just on Level performance and dealing with their issues, but they do so using a hip hop framing. (I will come back to "doing you" and "doing your thing" in chapter 8 but this phrase indexes hip hop sensibilities.) They sample hip hop into the formal, ritual event of group therapy. Allen, Steve, and others allow for this framing to be sampled into the formal ritual of group therapy. As with Garrett, this is an integration of racialized knowledge (hip hop) with therapeutic practice resulting in a racial sincerity that cannot be authenticated using just hip hop scripts. Racial sincerity allows us to look at the ways race is lived "intimately and affectively," rather than just according to social script (Jackson 2005:13). Rather their racialize way of being in world is a sincere enactment of their Black identity as an integration of hip hop and therapeutic practice—a keepin' it real group and a doing his thing by not provoking as much.

Derrick interprets Steve's unscripted group therapy session via hip hop as well. Mad is used in hip hop linguistic practice as a modifier to indicate "a lot" or "great" in other nouns and verbs (Westbrook 2002:89). "I have mad respect for you" translates to "I have great respect for you." However, when mad is used in this way, more is being communicated that a simple synonym to "a lot." Using hip hop terminology indexes a whole set of cultural forms, political frameworks, and racial affiliations. Derrick states that Steve's ability to be flexible and sincere in group therapy is "mad love." He understands that it takes a particular kind of affective interaction, the subject-to-subject interaction of sincerity, to engage in group therapy the way Steve does. And Derrick demonstrates his understanding of this sincerity in therapeutic practices in psychiatric custody by interpreting Steve's behavior using hip hop: Steve has "mad love" for them.

The hip hopification of therapeutic practice complicates the straightforward psychiatric and therapeutic logic of the institution. It brings "liveness" and sincerity to the treatment process and psychiatric custody for the African American youth of Havenwood. In these moments of sincerity I think about the earlier Goffman *Asylum* quotation: "[Inmates] can become objects of fellow feeling and even affection. There is always the danger that an inmate will appear human" (1961:81). Rather than thinking that it is dangerous for the "inmate" or resident to appear human, the men of Bradley North and Steele Cottage cultivate the humanness of the residents and of themselves. They disrupt the structure of the institution by integrating hip hop into therapeutic practice revealing a "live" and sincere, messy and human, treatment process.

Steve's Got Mad Love For Us

Derrick's comment at the end of the group session above when I ask him, "How'd that go?" he states, "Steve's got mad love for us." Goffman is correct, "inmates can become objects of fellow feeling and even affection." In fact, Derrick interprets the sincerity Steve brings to the group session that day as love, "mad love" to be precise. In answer to my question about how the spontaneous group therapy session went (where Derrick asked for Level 3 but got Level 2+, where his peer Marlon told him he could work harder and Allen and Steve agreed) Derrick sees this as Steve being loving toward the residents of Steele. Derrick interprets Steve's action of folding the tally sheet and placing it underneath his chair and allowing for an honest and sincere subject-to-subject group session as Steve having a lot of love—mad love—for them. Derrick interprets Steve actions as loving, hip hop style.

While I know Derrick meant "mad love" in the hip hop style, I cannot help but appreciate the double entendre of "mad." Mad is a synonym for crazy; someone who needs psychiatric institutionalization is mad. Texts devoted to incarcerated populations use the term—Michel Foucault's *Madness and Civilization: A History of Insanity in the Age of Reason*, Lorna Rhodes' *Total Confinement: Madness and Reason in the Maximum Security Prison*. The young men at Bradley North or Steele would have been, perhaps in a different historical time, labeled mad. "Mad love" then indexes for me the love that emerges as hip hop is sampled into therapeutic practice within the confines psychiatric custody.

Love at Havenwood and Steele Cottage has various meanings and usages. Here Derrick sees Steve's ability to be spontaneous, to allow the young men to participate in Level assignments, to be honest about their work and progress in treatment, to allow others to comment on their claims, and for sincere subject-to-subject discussions of therapeutic progress as loving. Derrick modifies this love using hip hop framing. For Derrick, it takes "mad love" to allow the residents so much latitude in their treatment. Using group in this way, as Steve states, might be therapeutic or it might be "whatever." I suspect the "whatever" includes the "loving" orientation the men have toward one another. The residents and staff alike become "objects of fellow feeling," as Goffman would say.

The staff and residents appear human, rather than function simply as individuals who implement psychiatric discourse, when their interiorities are shared and recognized. William's asks others to trust that he not snitching but sincerely needs his peers to act like roles models. Steve and other staff members see the residents as young men who need to learn the skills of sticking up for oneself, of negotiating a difficult conversation, of being confronted and responding without physical aggression, of being honest and sincere in their conversations, and even in learning to support one another along their treatment trajectories. Derrick, Garrett, and other residents interpret this recognition as real and loving. I interpret it as sincerity. As these men negotiate the group therapeutic session, they sometimes shirk social scripts and authentic group therapy rules for sincere, honest, and even affectionate interactions with fellow humans living in psychiatric custody.

Chapter 6
Kickin' It

And the funny scene [in the movie about my life] would be . . . you know how we kick it . . . I might just get up and start break dancing, start singin' the old school [hip hop] songs.

—Derrick's Life History Interview

"Come on Katie, we're up!" Jonathon hollers at me from the dining room table. He has been watching the previous Spades games intently. I am sitting near the desk watching the evening unfold. I sit in between Steve who sits at his command center, and Allen who is cutting hair in the living room. Jonathon and I have paired up for the evening's Spades games and it is our turn to play. After months of watching the games and being taught how to play by Arthur, Jonathon decided I was a worthy partner. Tonight Jim and Arthur, who team up when they are both on shift, have won every game so far. It was our chance to beat them.

"Don't get comfortable, Lil' Bit," Arthur tells me as I sit down. Teasing and trash-talking is inevitable, and part of the fun of the game. Arthur had nicknamed me Lil' Bit, transitioning from the earlier nickname he gave me "Lily" for Lily White. Arthur's naming me "Lily" let anyone in earshot know that racial identity, politics, and inequality was up for discussion and that I was very different from everyone else in the room. Arthur's argument was that people were already uncomfortable with what I was doing and having me around because I was white. "Why not name it and talk about it?" He told me. Over the course of my research tenure, my name changed from Lily White to Lil' Bit. This shift meant that my relationship with Arthur was changing. Lil' Bit seemed to me a nickname based on our friendship, Arthur teasing me for my size, rather than a moniker that represents the legacy of racial inequality in the United States.

"You taught me all you know. If I suck, that's on you," I retort.

Arthur scoffs, "No baby, what you do with what I teach you is on you." Jim does one of those trash-talking snorts/scoffs/laughs.

Jim deals. I look down at my hand; I have no "books" or winning cards. Jonathon and I lose in short order. Jonathon is disappointed. "I told you, don't get comfortable," Arthur taunts us. Both Jonathon and I roll our eyes and suck our teeth.

Marlon and Robert sit down at the table. I hope that they fare better. "Don't get comfortable, yo" I hear Arthur tell the young men.

Steele Cottage's side door opens. This door leads to the 7- to 13-year-old males cottage, Roger Cottage, located on the other side of a 20-yard sidewalk. Reggie walks in, alone.

"They told me I could come over here, get lined up." Reggie, a ten-year-old African American boy informs both Arthur and Jim that he is there to have his hair cut, and the lines around his face and neck cleaned up. They are about to ask him where his staff is. It is rare to see one of the younger residents running around campus without a supervising adult. Reggie's staff members have let him walk by himself from his cottage; they probably watched him through the windows. He knows the structure well enough to anticipate Arthur and Jim's looks and forthcoming question.

"Reggieeee!!" Allen shouts out from the far side of the living room, "Come on!"

Reggie smiles and walks past the Spades table, behind the couches to the half brick wall in the living room. He fist-bumps Steve on his way past Steve's command center.

"My man," Steve smiles and chuckles.

Mark, Lamar, Andy, and Wesley greet him with fist bumps and head nods.

"Payment is in push-ups," Allen tells Reggie.

"How many I gotta do?!"

"100!" Allen tells him. Reggie's eyes widen and his mouth drops open. Allen drops his head and chuckles. "Na, man, I messin' with ya. Give me 10." He nods toward Mark, Lamar, Andy, and Wesley, "They'll count for ya."

Reggie walks the few feet over to where Mark, Lamar, Andy, and Wesley are. Wesley has been working on some dance moves associated with the very popular song "Goin' Down" by hip hop artist Yung Joc. Mark has been watching Wesley, giving feedback on his leg, hand, and arm positions. They play the hook over and over on the boom box: *Meet me in the trap, it's goin' down. Meet me in the mall, it's goin' down. Meet me in the club, it's goin' down. Anywhere ya meet me, guaranteed to go down.*

Lamar claps his hands and tells Reggie, "You got this, b."

Andy puts his hands on Reggie's shoulders, and faux massages, "Come on, I'll do 'em with you."

Reggie gets in a plank position on the floor. Andy faces him, also in a plank position. "You count," Andy tells Mark, Lamar, and Wesley.

"1, 2, 3, 4, 5, 6, 7…come on, Reggie, you got this!" Mark and Wesley are shouting and counting.

"Come on" Lamar encourages, clapping his hands as he counts. Reggie is working hard to complete the push-ups, struggling with the last few, "8, 9, 10!"

Reggie collapses on the floor. Andy jumps up from his plank position and pulls Reggie off of the floor. Andy and Wesley dust him off and slap him on the back. "Good job."

Reggie smiles meekly.

"Looked better than last time," Arthur shouts to Reggie from the Spades table.

"Ok, you're next, when I finish with Derrick," Allen tells him.

Mark and Wesley go back to working on their Yung Joc dance moves. Reggie joins them, practicing the simultaneous shoulder shrug and wrist flexion. Lamar and Andy discuss something about their biceps and chest muscles and they flex and touch various muscles.

During this time, Allen has been working on Derrick's hair. Almost weekly, Allen sets up shop in Steele and he uses his barber skills to trim and tailor the young men's hair. As Allen gently tilts Derrick's head by the chin I hear him ask, "What about your moms?"

Derrick's face says it all: he wrinkles his nose, scrunches his face, and sucks his teeth, "I don't know, man. Her number's disconnected." Derrick struggles with his relationship with his mom. Even though his legal guardian is the state, he wants desperately for her to visit or to pick up his phone calls. She visited once in the 18 months that I was there. However, she has a long history of substance abuse and she often disappoints him with promises of a visit and last-minute no-shows. Right now he cannot even reach her by telephone. He is just recently, after two years at Havenwood, thinking about alternative places to live once he gets out of treatment.

"You gotta focus on you, man," Allen tells him.

"I know." He sighs. After about 10 seconds Derrick states, "But she's my mom."

Allen nods, he understands that Derrick is going to worry about his mom and want her love, no matter how much he is told to focus on himself or he learns that her behavior is "unhealthy." Allen finishes Derrick's line, "Cool. All cleaned up." Allen turns to Reggie, "Next."

Derrick gets up out of the chair. Jonathon, who has been patiently waiting for him, joins him as they head toward me. "Katie, can we borrow your thing?" I look at Steve for permission. He sits at his command center watching the Spades games, the barbershop, the push-up contest, and the dance lessons. Steve nods, answering Derrick and Jonathon's question. I disappear into the staff office and grab my digital voice recorder out of my bag. I emerge to find Steve has moved to the back hallway. From the chair in front of the confinement room, Steve can supervise Jonathon and Derrick as they work on their music. Jonathon and Derrick meet me in front of Jonathon's room, the one at the very end of the hallway, with Jonathon's boom box.

"Listen, listen," Derrick tells me. "Katie from the Lou, is real coo', with her anthropology, she's here to study me."

"I'm cool?! Yes! Love it, D." I beam, as with the nickname "Lil' Bit." I find being "shouted out" in Derrick's lyrics a sign of friendship and fondness, especially when he raps about where I am from, how "cool" I am, and our relationship with "my anthropology" that I'm there to study him. When he shouts out other staff members, he usually references how they are from his neighborhood. He and I do not have that connection; we have my study and our lives at Havenwood. I respond to Derrick's shout out by calling him by his nickname: "D."

Jonathon and Derrick sit on the floor and begin collaborating on their latest rap, discussing the lyrics, hooks, beats, flow, and timing. I have watched them do this dozens of times. Derrick and Jonathon rap well together and their pairing has resulted in many CDs. I have made a deal with youth across campus interested in using my voice recorder. If they have permission, they can borrow my device. I will then burn them a CD of their music. Allen teases me that I am the local hip hop producer, the Def Jam Records of Havenwood. I pull up a chair next to Steve, as he sits in the back hallway watching Derrick and Jonathon. I spent time most evenings sitting next to whoever is sitting in the back hallway, asking questions about Havenwood. Today, our attention is pulled to the Spades table as Jim slams the ace of spades onto the table and dances about his win. Arthur joins in with a few taunts about being the best and rockin' the table tonight.

"Beatin' up on the kids! They're a mess," Steve tells me as he shakes his head and smiles. Not only is Steve the supervisor of Steele, but he is also the eldest and has worked there the longest. He has worked with Arthur for seven years, mentoring him as he has risen through the ranks of Havenwood employees. Jim is only three years in, having arrived from the rural South in the United States. Steve knows Jim's strengths and weakness in working with the city youth and he mentors him. These men are friends, they stand-up at each other's weddings, they pick each other's children up from basketball camps, and they help each other out during financial dry spells. Steve comments that "they're a mess" as a sign of endearment.

Allen walks past us just as Steve makes the comment about Arthur and Jim being "messes." "Get in where you fit in," Allen responds.

I watch Allen disappear around the corner toward the back staff office, as he leaves the pithy maxim in his wake. Allen is the youngest of all of the men who work at Steele, and he is the most recent one hired. Everyone mentors him, telling him he has so much potential and is excellent at working with "these kids." He laughs it off. In the years to come he would confide in me that he looks back on all that mentoring, cultivation, and encouragement that came from Steve, Arthur, and others. It is precisely his ability to sum up the situation with one true statement that means he has "potential" and is "good with these kids." He also hails from the same city as many of them, in some cases the same neighborhood. In this instance, in one short phrase Allen includes us all in the project of fitting in, finding our community, having friends, and figuring out our life paths. His logic puzzle is perfect: if they are a mess and you like hanging out with them and you get along with them, then you are also a mess. Much like Garrett's comments that "we all have issues," all of us at Steele are "a mess." I look behind me at Jonathon and Derrick, across the room at Arthur, Jim, Marlon, and Robert. I cannot see them, but I hear the hook again: *Meet me in the trap, it's goin' down. Meet me in the mall, it's goin' down. Meet me in the club, it's goin' down. Anywhere ya meet me, guaranteed to go down.* I think of Lamar, Mark, Andy, and little Reggie who will move to Steele in a few years, if he does not find an alternative less restrictive placement or returns home. I return my gaze to Steve, who is watching me look at everyone.

We smile and nod.

* * *

On most evenings, life at Steele Cottage resembled what I have just described. In addition to group sessions, like those found in chapter 5, or crisis events, in chapter 4, the majority of cottage life included Spades games, playing basketball, practicing dance moves, rapping, fist bumps, push-up contests, haircuts, going to the mall, movies, or skating rink, and, as Derrick states it in the quotation that begins the chapter, "kickin' it." I borrow from Thomas Csordas to identify this as a "cultural context of intimacy."

Thomas Csordas (1997) states that healing occurs in "cultural contexts of intimacy." A cultural context of intimacy includes a move toward community, the ways people are touched, the intimate relationships those being healed have with their healer, and the genre of ritual language known as "sharing" one's life experiences and inner worlds. Steele Cottage is a cultural context of intimacy. There is a move toward community, as the young men learn to live together, to find Spades and rap partners. People touch each other—they fist bump, they groom one another, they physically instruct each other about dance moves or give faux massage to psyche each other for push-up payments. This touch is a part of male bonding (Classen 2005b).[1] They share in the daily evening and weekend life at the cottage. While cottage life is a therapeutic milieu, we also see how life in this context allows for more everyday behaviors and practices. Finally, staff or peer relationships, those relationships predicated on psychiatric custody, are enhanced and mentor relationships and friendships emerge among the men at Steele.

In the "Introduction" I discussed the phrase, "It's all about the relationship." The "relationship" includes qualities of therapeutic intervention—of the staff member working with the residents as they focus on the youth's issues. However, the "relationship" also includes the work between young people in the therapeutic work of treatment and the less formalized relationships that emerge therein. In addition to the work of healing that occurred in healer/rehabilitant or staff/peer relationships, I found that the work of healing also occurred in other kinds of intimate relationships. Specifically, I believe that intimate healing relationships include the categories of "friends" and "mentors." Friendships and mentoring relationships emerged from this cultural context of intimacy and aided in the self-transformation that occurred at Steele Cottage.

Peers, Friends, and Love: Lamar's Perspective

"What is the worst part of leaving Havenwood?" I ask Lamar as we sit for our third and final life history interview. Lamar is a 15-year-old African American youth. I have asked this question in every formal interview and in casual conversations and the answers are often the same. As I wait for his answer, I assume Lamar will say something like Derrick does in the "Introduction": "staff and peers." Both terms index the institutional structure and therapeutic relationships among the people of Havenwood.

"Leaving friends and staff." He confirms my suspicions; however, he uses the term "friends" rather than "peers." The term peer indexes the histories the youth have in the various systems—foster care, criminal justice, and mental health. The youth are often referred to not as age-mates or cohorts but as peers. This is a common way to refer to the group categorization. However, Lamar references his "friends." Later in the same interview he uses the term "peer." In other contexts he uses hip hop terms for friendship including "homie," "boy," or as with Reggie, "b." In this instance, Lamar uses the word "friend."

"Yeah? Have you gotten pretty close to people?" I ask him.

"One person, one peer." He reverts to "peer" letting me know that his friend is someone his age. His use of "peer" to talk about the closest person to him at Havenwood leads me to believe that the switching from peer to friend to boy or homie is a rather fluid process. Lamar does not name him; he knows that I know he means Jonathon.

"Yeah. You're gonna miss him, huh?"

Lamar nods, "He's my boy. We think alike." Lamar switches to a hip hop term for friend, "boy," without missing a step or changing the kind of relationship he means.

"And staff?" I ask, following up on the "friends and staff" he mentioned.

"About 3 or 4. 5. I think it is 5." He names off the adults or staff members he will miss as he counts on his fingers, "Jim, you, Angie, Allen, and Steve. 5."

"Who helps you more?" I ask, following up on the two relationship categories and his understanding of their helping qualities that he mentioned earlier in the interview.

"My peers help me same as staff," Lamar tells me. "They give me good advice. And they're there, on my shoulder. They all do the same thing but I think staff do a little bit more." Lamar pauses, turns his head and thinks for a minute. "Na I think my peers do a little bit more. It's kinda awkward but, ah, I think my peers give me a little bit more advice than the staff."

I am not surprised by Lamar's difficultly in determining if the "staff" or "peers" are more helpful in his treatment process. From my anthropological perspective, I have come to think that both "staff" and "peers" are part of the cultural context of intimacy that cultivates healing at Steele. Not only that, I have seen Lamar interact with "staff" and "peers" and know that he is a very affable young man, quick to laugh and be playful with adults and other youth. He is smart and he knows it is kind of "awkward" to tell me that his "peers," the other young men at Steele, offer him just as much help in treatment as the "staff," or those who are paid to work with him. He knows this probably should not be the case, but it is, for him. But even if his peers help him more than the staff, he is clear that he will miss five adults when he leaves Havenwood.

I know Lamar has good relationships with the other young men of Steele. In fact, I have also seen him be particularly gentle and protective with a younger developmentally delayed boy at Steele Cottage, whom I call Tye. Lamar is quick to come to Tye's defense, seems to be endlessly patient with him, and makes sure that he is taken care of with knowledge of rules, programmatic routine, and even food. Lamar will explain the rules of the cottage in great detail and with patience as many times as Tye needs, trying to keep Tye out of trouble and thus earning higher Levels. While I am interviewing Lamar I know that Jonathon, Tye, and Derrick are waiting for Lamar to finish our interview so that they can all hang out together, at the court, or playing Spades. Lamar has positive relationships with his "peers."

"Why do you think that is the case? Why do you think your peers help you more than staff?" I ask him.

"My peers got much love for me."

Once again, love emerges as a reason for particularly significant and important work at Steele Cottage. Here Lamar uses it to explain why other young men help him so much. Love is the reason they give him good advice, and why they are there on his shoulder.

I end the interview with my final question: "If there was a movie about your life who would star in it and what would the plot be? Can you describe the movie for me?"

"It would be me, Jonathon, most of my friends. It would show people how to get along. It would be a positive movie so I can do something positive with my life, stop being negative. It would look real good if I did something positive."

"What would you be doing [in the movie]?"

"Helping kids, giving back to the community." I find it rather fitting that his movie includes working with his friends and doing the things that he says both staff and peers do, "helping kids."

I conclude the interview and let Lamar get back to his "peers." As we walk out of the office, down the cottage back hallway into the living room, Derrick, Jonathon, and Tye can be seen sitting on the couches waiting for him. Jonathon has the basketball in his lap and they all three have on their winter coats as it is early November. All three jump up when Lamar walks out. Derrick tosses him his coat. Lamar snags the coat and turns to face Allen, "Can we go to the courts now?"

"Yeup," is Allen's response. He is fully attentive to the young men, even as he organizes paperwork from a restraint that occurred earlier. He knows why Derrick, Tye, and Jonathon were sitting on the couch with their coats on during "constructive free time." They were waiting for Lamar and then they were all going to head over to the courts together. Part of Allen's job is to observe the relationships that the young men at Steele are making. Staff members, as part of their training (see chapter 3), are taught to observe youth for healthy and unhealthy attachments that emerge when these youth are thrown into this living environment together. As I mentioned in chapter 2, most of the young men of Steele and youth of Havenwood did not have any significant, long-term stable relationships. Part of the implicit and significant work of treatment at Steele is to teach the young men how to have friendships. Therefore, Allen took notice of a group of young men who seemed particularly fond of one another, discerning the kinds of the relationships formed among them.

I watch the group of four walk out of the door and across Steele field to the outdoor basketball court.

"They're a crew," Allen breaks into my own thoughts. After assessing the group, Allen defines the relationship among Derrick, Jonathon, Lamar, and Tye as a "crew." I know he is using a hip hop definition, interpreting the relationship among these young men as "tight-knit friends" (Westbrook 2002:31). I nod; they had waited for Lamar to finish with me before they went to the courts. They do seem rather close, supporting Lamar's description of love and friendship, even and especially among these "peers."

On Friendship

"The study of friendship is haunted by the problem of definition. 'Who (or What) are friends?' is a common refrain in much of the sociological and anthropological discussion of the subject" anthropologists of friendship Evan Killick and Amit Desai state (2013:1). Often in anthropology, friendship is eschewed in lieu of "adolescents," "peer groups," "cohorts," or "age-mates."[2] The focus is often on the group as a meaningful social organization, rather than on the quality or kind of relationship among these individuals. However, in some cases anthropologists investigate how *friendship* is defined and practiced in different cultural settings.[3]

Friendship, as a meaningful social relationship, is often juxtaposed with or compared to kinship.[4] Friendship is also compared with romantic or sexual love because of the emotional bond associated with both relationships.[5] Often friendship is linked with exchange, and it is understood in terms of reciprocity.[6] And yet, friendship—despite the ways people link it to kinship, romance, or exchange—is its own meaningful relationship. Friendship has its own norms and practices that are dependent on place, context, and history.

While friendship is predicated on the social and historical context, two important aspects of the relationship can be found cross-culturally. Anthropologist Daniel Hruschka (2010) offers an extensive and comprehensive review of ethnographic and quantitative literature on friendship, in order to understand how friendship is similar to and unique from other social relationships. Hruschka finds that a variety of practices are associated with friendship cross-culturally. These practices include gift-giving, mutual aid, ritual initiation, self-disclosure, informality, frequent socializing, and touching (Hruschka 2010:69). In addition to social practices, Hruschka also finds that "psychological constructs" are common to how people talk about friendship cross-culturally. Hruschka identifies the "psychological constructs" of friendship as feelings such as closeness and love (2010:18).[7]

In his analysis, Hruschka offers a workable definition of friendship across cultures. His definition of what he calls a "friendship-like relationship" is "a social relationship in which partners provide support according to their abilities in times of need, and in which this behavior is motivated in part by positive affect between partners" (Hruschka 2010:68). Friendships are characterized by support in times of need, and positive affection.[8]

I will use Hruschka's definition and framing of "friendship-like relationship" to ground and understand the relationships of help and affection that emerge at Havenwood and Steele Cottage. However, I will use the term "friendship" in my analysis rather than the phrase "friendship-like relationship" because of its succinctness.[9] I will also use the term "peer." Peer is almost synonymous to friend; however, it reveals the importance of living in an institution, removed from mainstream schools, social networks, and other cohort-based social experiences (e.g., sports teams, music groups). However, just as "peer" and "friend" are often used interchangeably, so are hip hop terms such as "homie," "boy," "b," and even "crew" to indicate a larger group of friends. Regardless of the term used, each indexed a particular kind of close, intimate relationship. Friendships were formed among the men of Steele.

In the vignette just mentioned, we see young men at Steele acting like what we might normally identify as friends. The young men are playing games together, they are encouraging one another in push-ups, they are rapping together, they are practicing their dance moves, and they are intimately touching. The older men of Steele are also acting more like friends than colleagues or coworkers. Arthur and Jim are teamed up against the youth. Steve affectionately calls these coworkers "a mess." Arthur uses a term of closeness, "baby," to refer to me. As I mentioned, the adult men of Steele are friends not only while at work, but they provide all kinds of support outside the work space as well. The youth who live at Steele Cottage know this; they can tell that Steve, Allen, Arthur, Jim, James, Zac, and Pete are friends. They know that these men have affection for Angie, the lone women of the group. Friendships are important relationships for the men of Steele.

The men of Steele "kick it," as Derrick states, a phrase meaning to "indulge in a relationship" (Westbrook 2002:81). "Kick it" is indulging in a friendship; it is what friends do. "Kickin' it" is a phrase rarely used to identify therapeutic intervention or life in psychiatric custody. However, this relaxed or indulgent way of life was meaningful for the young men of Steele, so much so that it is one of three scenes in Derrick's movie about his life found in the quotation that begins the chapter: *And the funny scene would be…you know how we kick it…I might just get up and start break dancing, start singin' the old school [hip hop] songs."* Friendships and kickin' it are significant aspects of the therapeutic life that unfolds at Havenwood and Steele Cottage.

Kickin' It with Friends and Mentors

"You comin' with, Li'l Bit?" Arthur asks me. It is a Saturday afternoon in May, and Arthur has requested a Havenwood van to take Derrick and Wesley to a local youth-league basketball tournament about a half-hour drive away. He is inviting me to come along.

"Yeah, thanks," I tell him as I grab my bag and jacket head for the van. I see two other young African American men sitting in the van already. I greet them, recognizing them as Arthur's son and James' son. I have seen them, along with Steve's son, around Steele. Derrick and Wesley have followed me out of Steele and jump into the back of the van. They give the high-five handshake common among young hip hop oriented men, although the usual hug is omitted in the greeting. I get into the front seat.

"You ready?" Arthur asks us. We all say something in the affirmative. He begins to back up the van when Steve comes jogging from the cottage. He hands Arthur some cash, just in case there is an entry fee to the tournament.

After we turn onto the main state highway that provides the southern boundary of Havenwood, we roll down our windows. It is too pretty a day not to let the wind blow through my hair. Arthur enjoys the breeze as well.

"Ahhh, this is my joint right here," Arthur exclaims as he blasts the radio. He starts nodding his head to the beat as "Hypnotize" by The Notorious B.I.G. comes on the radio. I look behind me as the wind rips through my hair and the four young men are leaning back, two basketballs are on the seats, and they too nod along to the beat. We make our way to the basketball tournament listening to Biggie rap about Brooklyn as his chorus lauds his flashy ways.

We arrive at the tournament venue, a public school in a neighboring suburb. "Don't do anything stupid," Arthur tells all four of the young men. We all pile out of the van and enter the building; Arthur pays with the money Steve gave him. We sit in the gym, halfway up the bleachers. We sit in twos, I sit next to Arthur, Derrick pairs with Arthur's son, and Wesley sits next to James' son. At halftime, the young men ask if they can grab something from the concession stand.

"You got money?" Arthur asks.

"Yeah," they all reply. Wesley and Derrick had used some of their allowance money, money generated from chores (see Figure 2.2), for the day. Steve had given it to them right before they left.

"Don't do anything stupid," Arthur reminds them. "D," Arthur states to Derrick as he reaches into his pocket and pulls out a couple of dollars. He hands the money to Derrick, "Get me some chips."

All four youth stand up. Derrick pockets the cash and then hikes up his jeans. Derrick has paired his jeans with a black T-shirt, a black hoodie, and black Nike Air Force Ones. James's son does the same thing, hikes up his jeans. All four of the young men are wearing similar outfits—jeans, T-shirts, hoodies, and tennis shoes, either Nike Air Jordans or Nike Air Force Ones; hip hop inspired outfits. The young men then file down the bleacher steps together, out of the gym doors and into the foyer area. I lose sight of them.

"I like to give them a little latitude, let them be regular kids without me standing over them so much," Arthur tells me, reading my mind. I was wondering if I should follow them, observe them like a good anthropologist. I also wonder if Arthur is afraid that Derrick or Wesley might run away while on this excursion, a common fear for Havenwood staff members because youth would run away often enough while off campus. He seems to trust them; he gives them "a little latitude." It does not hurt that his and James's sons are along. Arthur probably informs me about his desire to "let them be regular kids" as much as to ask me not to embarrass them by following them here. I also notice that Arthur treated all four of the young men similarly. In fact he even gives Derrick money, not his son, to get him some chips. No one is singled out for extra supervision or behavior regulation.

The four young men return at the beginning of the second half. Derrick hands Arthur his chips and his change. "It's yours," Arthur tells him, referring to the change.

We sit in our pairings and watch the end of the game. After the game we head back to Havenwood, stopping for lunch along the way. Arthur buys all of us lunch, as we eat at a local burger restaurant. On the ride home, Wesley, Derrick, Arthur's son, and James's son talk about basketball, describing the events of the game. When we arrive back at Steele, James is there to pick up his and Arthur's sons. Derrick and Wesley give the same high-five handshake as they head into the cottage. Arthur and I follow them in.

* * *

I went on similar off-campus trips with Steve during football season, with Allen to the skating rink, and with Angie to the mall and Laundromat. Most of the time only Havenwood youth would go but in some cases, as the one just mentioned, youth not in treatment but the sons of the men who worked at Steele would also come along (although this was not officially allowed). These off-campus excursions were part of the therapeutic process at Havenwood; youth had to earn the privilege of going off campus. However, once the youth were off, everyone seemed to relax a bit and behavior regulation became less noticeable. The "give" in the institutional life was much more obvious in these contexts, as the kids were allowed and encouraged to be "regular kids." This was not difficult to do because evening hours, as described earlier, allowed more of a *kickin' it* therapeutic practice than the strict behavior modification one encouraged by the Program and organization of the institution.

As I became more a part of Steele Cottage life and spent time within each cottage across Havenwood and on off-campus excursions, I realized the significance of *kickin' it*. *Kickin' it* was as much part of psychiatric custody as were the group sessions or restraints. *Kickin' it* allowed for the young men to act and live like typical teenagers who were not living in psychiatric custody. Times of *kickin' it* allowed for a respite, when the youth did not have to think about the fact that they lived in treatment, that they did not really have much of a family life, or that they had been sent away by the state. *Kickin' it* allowed for friendships to emerge within the confines of the treatment center. It also allowed for mentoring relationships among the youth and adults. *Kickin' it* allowed for Lamar to see his peers as friends and to think about the ways he would give back to the community alongside his friends. *Kickin' it* allowed him to see the staff as the people he named who he was going to miss when he finally left Havenwood. Friendships and mentoring relationships were a significant reason why "staff and peers" were so frequently mentioned as the most important aspect of treatment, from whom the youth learned to change in treatment, and whom the youth would miss when they left treatment.

When we went to the basketball tournament, we were *kickin it* together off-campus. The trusting relationships that Arthur had developed at Steele could transcend campus time and be relied upon, while at a basketball tournament. Derrick and Wesley could be friends and *kick it* together off campus, with two other young men not from Steele. Friendships and trusting relationships were not just part of the daily life at Steele and part of the therapeutic context, but they were relied upon during trips outside of the institution.

Mitchell Duneier (1999) discusses the importance of mentor-like relationships and friendships among African American book vendors in New York City. These African American book vendors occupy a similar social position to the youth of Havenwood; they are also socially marginalized and stigmatized people—unhoused and operating in the informal economy. Duneier finds that mentor relationships serve an integral role in the lives of these men. Duneier argues that "the friendships on the street were crucial in crystallizing the importance of a life devoted to some moral ideals" (1999:74). Friendships, mentoring relationships, and the strong support social support, particularly wisdom, in these relationships helped some of these men "to make positive changes" (Duneier 1999:74). Duneier argues that it was mentoring relationships and friendships cultivated in the context of book vending that encouraged these stigmatized men to respect themselves and to be responsible to others.

The friendships at Steele also encouraged young men like Lamar, Derrick, Wesley, and others to make positive changes (I will come back to what these positive changes are in chapter 7). *Kickin' it* allowed for the adult men to relate more closely with one another, to relate with the youth more intimately, and to build a sense of community grounded in positive male relationships. *Kickin' it* allowed for a cultural context of intimacy that facilitated self-transformation. It was through *kickin' it* that "staff and peers" became so meaningful and important male friendships emerged. The friendships of Steele are in direct contrast to other discussions of residential treatment, and relationships among young men of color.

Deviant Youth Cultures and Peer Groups: Pushing Past Initial Stereotypes

Based on the literature, I was not ready to find friendship or love at Steele. It is rare to find the theme of friendship or love in studies of young men, institutionalized, transitioning back to society, or living on the streets. Much of the literature on these subjects focus on the "deviance" of the youth institutionalized, the deviant youth culture that emerges in the residential treatment center cottage, and the "peer group" or gang that is influential in these young men's lives, often leaving them at odds with the criminal justice system and mainstream society.

In 1962, sociologist Howard Polsky published a short sociological account of cottage life in a residential treatment center.[10] He found that the culture and social structure of the cottage significantly impacts the boys who live there, despite the structure of the larger institution. His investigation was to uncover the workings of cottage culture as it related to the functioning of the therapeutic milieu. As I pointed out in chapter 1, research on therapeutic milieus was to investigate how the milieu itself shaped treatment. Polsky's (1962/1977) research was part of the mid-twentieth century analysis of residential treatment living, and the use of the cottage or therapeutic milieu in the process of treatment.

Polsky found that cottage life impinged on the way the youth related to one another. Polsky concluded that rather than milieu therapy working to change problematic persons, a "deviant subculture" emerged in the cottage (Polsky 1962/1977:18). He argued that this deviant subculture was a battlefield predicated on manipulation and power struggles among the institutionalized men.

As a sociologist, Polsky did not focus on individual deviancy but rather on patterned social relations. Polsky found that the young men of the cottage he studied, Cottage Six, represented deviant subculture patterns because they related through "aggression, deviant skills and activities, threat-gestures, ranking, and scapegoating" (Polsky 1962/1977:55). Cottage life was a deviant subculture cultivating deviant social patterns among the men who lived there. Friendships or tight-knit friends groups were not part of Cottage Six life.

In James Waldram's (2012) analysis of a prison therapeutic unit, the staff encouraged a therapeutic "cohort" among the men, which was difficult to form. Waldram states the men were "strangers to each other, the suspicious demeanor needed for survival in the penitentiary made any chance of bonding quickly rather remote. There was not 'crewing up' against the staff either, because the inmates had yet to trust each other…it was an 'every man for himself' attitude" (2012:87–88). In Waldram's study of institutionalized men, suspicion limits the bonding, and crews or friendships were nonexistent.

I had somewhat assumed that young men and cultural patterns in residential treatment would conform to these analyses. I had anticipated limited bonding and fear-based relationships, a cultural context predicated on fear and distrust. I did not anticipate that friendships would be important or that there would be meaningful relationships among the institutionalized cohort based on my reading of other literature.

Even Jamie Fader (2013) who found that male peer groups were important, and perhaps even positive, does not discuss friendships in her contemporary ethnography on institutionalized youth and their transitions to adulthood back in their communities. Fader follows the young men as they integrate into their home environments, their neighborhoods, and, presumably, their relationship circles. Fader finds that the male peer group is important, as are significant girlfriends.[11] One interlocutor in particular, "only felt like a man on the rare occasions when [his girlfriend] recognized him as one, and when he spent time with his male peer group" (Fader 2013:159). In her text, Fader does not discuss the "male peer group" or push this categorization further by investigating the significant male friendships. Instead, Fader focuses her analysis on the relationships these men have with their girlfriends.

As I mentioned earlier, friendship is often not part of anthropological inquiry. Even ethnographies that focus on relationships among men identify male peer groups as significant, but not friendships. In his classic ethnography, *In Search of Respect: Selling Crack in El Barrio,* Philippe Bourgois (2003) analyzes "peer groups," talks about the power of "youth gangs," and analyzes "street culture," a place familiar to the young men with whom I worked.[12] Bourgois's analysis focuses on the economic agenda, the hustling and drug-dealing of this "peer group." He even pushes a "functionalist interpretation," stating that the "crowd of friends" who hang out at the crack house are there to provide physical protection rather than because of any meaningful relationship (Bourgois 2003:107). This interpretation "insults" one of his interlocutors, Bourgois tells us (2003:107). But despite the fact that those he interviewed used the term "friend" to label these relationships (revealed in his transcripts), and even though Bourgois identifies the men as *his* friends, he does not discuss the friendships that were formed among his informants. Instead he focuses on the male "peer group" and the functions of these male relationships in economic terms.

It is not hard to imagine why friendship would be a difficult relationship to investigate in general, or how it might be challenging to see friendships emerging in such stigmatized and precarious situations. In fact, as mentioned earlier, Allen, a line staff member, was interested in the kinds of relationships that emerged among the young men of Steele. These young men had long histories of disrupted social relationships; they were removed from homes, schools, and neighborhoods. Case file narratives described problematic peer relationships. Before he was able to talk about his friendships or to identify that his peers had "much love" for him, Lamar articulated his fear of living in residential treatment, in a cottage comprised of young men. When he first arrived and we conducted our first life history interview, Lamar told me that he was scared to live at Steele because he had to live with "a buncha dudes." I asked him to elaborate and he told me what it was like to "live with a buncha dudes" he did not know. He states, "All of us in here is criminals. We all been locked up, we all did stuff to get us locked up. We all did stuff to get here. We broke the law some way, some how." I asked him, "That is what gets people here?" I wondered if he will focus on the criminal part rather than on his psychiatric illness, disrupted home life, or on parental failures. "That's most of the reason. That and not knowing how to participate at home. But I know if you ask 100% of these people in here, they all been to jail. They did a crime." I asked him, using his word "scared," "And you find that scary?" "Yeah," he tells me, "that's real scary!"

However, as he settles into Steele Cottage and Havenwood, Lamar makes friends. He tells us this in a later interview. He even states that his peers, those he previously identified as fellow criminals, have much love for him because they actually help him more than staff.

I use Lamar's words because initially he was fearful of his peers. He echoes some of what scholars like Polsky, Waldram, Fader, and Bourgios find—that men living in treatment, or who come from precarious social positions form basic relationships predicated on functional needs and therapeutic contexts. However, as Lamar continues to live at Steele he comes to see his peers as the most helpful in his treatment process. In fact, he comes to identify them as friends and he states that they have love for him. Much like Duneier's mentor relationships and friendships, the young men of Steele build relationships predicated on helping one another and on mutual affection. They build friendships; they make friends.

Lamar and others echo some of Greg Dimitriadis's (2003) conclusions in his research with young Black men in urban America, particularly those labeled "at-risk." "At-risk" youth are similar in definition to the troubled youth of Havenwood, young people who find themselves in socially precarious situations. Dimitriadis finds that the young Black men "had to struggle individually and together by drawing on the range of resources—local institutions, key older figures, and friends—in navigating their own largely improvised pathways out of adolescence" (Dimitriadis 2003:5). The resources young "at-risk" Black men use to navigate through adolescence include mentor relationships and friendships. Like the young men in Dimitriadis's study, Lamar and other young Black men at Steele, navigate their way into adulthood through important relationships with "staff" and "peers." Friends and mentors give Lamar advice and show him much love.

Limited research exists focusing on the emotional lives of men and boys (Way 2011), and even less on the emotional lives of Black men associated with criminality or aggressive physical activities such as football. One exception is the work of anthropologist Micah Gilmer (2008; 2009). Gilmer finds bonds of affection between African American male coaches and athletes and argues that Black men in his study understand the relationships among themselves as friendships based on intimate, emotional, and affectionate interpersonal interactions. He juxtaposes these friendships and feelings with the image of a big, Black, male football player, which is usually understood as dangerous, intimidating, and aggressive because Black men "are badly misunderstood" in the United States (Duneier 1992:25; see also Rios 2011).

Lamar echoes this sentiment—he and everyone at Steele are "criminals."[13] However, like Gilmer, Duneier, and Dimitriadis, Lamar also understands his relationship with his "peers" or fellow criminals as complex, friendly, and even loving. In fact, his life movie would be based on them and the "positive things" he wants to achieve. While he may have "committed a crime" he is also more than his crime, more than the label of "deviant" that he brings to the cottage and psychiatric custody. Despite Lamar's understanding of the criminality and fear of living life in a household with "a buncha dudes," friendships and love emerge in this cultural context of intimacy.

Befriending Me

Over the course of my research at Havenwood, I spent holidays, weekends, and birthdays with the men and woman of Steele Cottage. Not only did I learn about the life histories and current treatment life of the youth, I also learned about the adults of Steele. I learned about their children, their purchasing of houses, their new puppies, their engagements, and their divorces. We spent Saturday mornings debating controversial issues, including interracial dynamics in the United States, the role of hip hop and the Black church in romantic relationships, and whether or not the local sports teams were heading to the postseason. We cooked together. We celebrated together. We opened presents together. We learned how each other preferred our food and we were sure to pick up another's favorite drink at the store if we were off campus. Money was lent. Advice was given. Cars were borrowed. Occasionally, we even met up for dinner or a drink after shifts. We became friendly. Here I am reflecting on the friendships I built with the men and woman of Steele and I was a significant outsider, taking notes on meetings and in everyday life. And I was only there for 18 months. The friendships established over the years between Angie, the lone woman, and the men of Steele go beyond my own friendships. Most importantly, this method of relating, of supporting and actively caring about people, created a space in the cottage, a cultural context, not predicated on aggression and manipulation, as Polsky would have us believe, but on friendliness and love.

One of the most telling ethnographic examples of the friendship-like relationships and love at Steele includes what happened at my going away party. I was rarely the topic of formal discussion, and I never voiced my opinion in group sessions or Team Meetings. Therefore, my role in the cottage and the relationships I was building were rarely openly discussed at the cottage level (although I had long discussions with Steve, Arthur, and Allen, in particular, about whom I was and my role and relationships in the cottage). But my going away party was different.

I did not know a party was going to be thrown for me; the people of Steele had surprised me. But as was the case with Transitions or going away parties, we shared food and we shared advice or feelings. Someone had remembered one of my favorite foods and Angie made sure we had a feast. Steve used cottage funds to throw the party and everyone knew about it but me. Derrick, Lamar, and William were particularly proud to have kept it a secret from me. People knew what was coming and could prepare what they would share with me, the advice they would give me on my "transition."

Most of the young men shared wonderful comments, thanking me for being me and for helping them. I was told I was going to be missed and that life at the cottage would be vastly different without me there. I had become part of the intimate community at Steele. I had felt like I had befriended the men and woman of Steele and I was happy to hear, during my going away party, that we were friends, that we had built bonds of affection and we had helped one another. One particularly telling comment came from Jim, and it was not advice for me. Rather, Jim decided to thank me and to label the content of my role at Steele.

Jim and I had a tenuous relationship. Sometimes we were close, sharing long conversations or off-campus adventures. Sometimes our vastly different backgrounds caused ruptures in our rapport. When I saw that he was going to share something, I wondered what he might say. He kept it real, "You and I haven't always gotten along." I nodded; it was true. He also kept it friendly and kind: "But I want to thank you for what you did for these boys. You showed them a lot of love."

Gregarious and better-self-cultivating Steve laughed when Jim said this. Steve jumped up from his chair and ran over to Jim and gave him a huge bear hug, almost tipping over the chair where Jim sat. Steve had no problem hugging Jim full on and Jim had no problem being hugged by Steve. Loving touch among the men of Steele was common. Jim had decided to be kind to me in front of everyone, honoring our challenging relationship, while still respecting me and the relationships I had built with many of the youth of Steele. Steve, who was friends with Jim, his boss, and the leader of the cottage, gave him a big hug to honor Jim's respect. The genuine affection that Jim showed me and that Steve showed Jim were possible because of the cultural context of intimacy nurtured at Steele Cottage. The general atmosphere of the cottage was one of genuine affection for one another and for me.

The young men of Steele are aware of this too. Derrick, Lamar, William, and Jonathon (to name a few) befriended me rather quickly as they sized me up. They also knew I had a more difficult time befriending the staff of Steele. While many of the young men liked the idea of me studying their social situation, the adult men were much less accepting. But over time I became a Steele Cottage member evinced by my inclusion in Spades tournaments and rap lyrics, by my invitation to off-campus trips, by my name change from Lily to Li'l Bit, and by the affection shared at my going away party. Not only could real friendships emerge among the "criminals" of Steele Cottage, but they could also be cultivated between me, a white female anthropologist, and the African American institutionalized men and the adults who worked with them. In the end, like many anthropologists, I was more than just "the anthropologist," I was a member of the community; friendships are forged within and even despite radical difference. When Lamar spoke at my going away party he thanked me for "teaching him to read." After that he said, "no one had done that before, that was love" he choked up and covered his eyes with his hands as tears ran down his face. The young men of Steele did not have to look far to learn how friendship-like relationships work, how help is given, and how affection is cultivated. My inclusion in life at Steele is a testament to the openness and fairness by which friendships could be formed: across racial and gender lines and among "criminals."

I agree with Polsky that the cultural environment of the cottage profoundly shaped the relationships that the youth had with one another. However, I think that rather than a cottage culture predicated on deviance, aggression, and manipulation, Steve, Allen, Arthur, Jim, James, Zac, Pete, and Angie cultivated a friendly, loving environment. The environment of Steele was, as Derrick states it best, *kickin' it*. Being able to *kick it* at Steele allowed for friendliness, and real help and affection won out over deviance and criminality.

Conclusion

During a Team Meeting one Tuesday Angie invited Sarah to come to the cottage at night. "Come to the unit at night," Angie told Sarah, "See how we work with these kids." Sarah politely declined, stating she believed that they all did what she identified as "important work" on the units at night. What Angie meant, and Sarah failed to understand, was the cultural context of intimacy that emerged at Steele, the significance of *kickin it*, and the friendships that emerged during these evening hours.

The adults of Steele did not just use the therapeutic modalities found in psychiatric custody to encourage healing and treatment progress. They used their own relationships with one another, the Spades table, the barbershop, off-campus excursions, and their own knowledge of rap and hip hop songs as the work they did in the unit at night. In this work, friendships emerged. Friendships, teasing, supporting, encouraging, positive touching, laughing, being playful, having fun, and enjoying life were all part of daily life at Steele. This environment and the friendships that emerged, among the residents, between the adults, and between the adults and youth resulted in love and positive self-change. Residents understood that both their peers and their staff had love for them, a common and necessary part of friendship. The youth of Steele were enculturated in this environment, learning to make positive male relationships predicated on helping and loving one another. These relationships were nurtured even with people they never thought they would come to appreciate, care about, or even like. The young men of Steele Cottage were taught to be respectful and inclusive and that friendship was part of therapeutic life in a psychiatric custody.

Chapter 7
Becoming Good Men

In our society, [total institutions] are the forcing houses for changing persons; each is a natural experiment on what can be done to the self.

—*Erving Goffman* Asylums

Alls I gotta do is stay focused. You know what I'm sayin'? 'Cause I can leave here, master everything, the skills . . . but I don't use it? I don't stay focused? What I have? Nothin'. But if I use them to stay focused, I'm a good man.

—*Derrick's Life History Interview*

"Katie, what're you doing sitting back there? Move up to the big table. This is my Staffing and I want you at the big table." Derrick tells me as he saunters into the meeting room of the main administration building on Havenwood's campus. I am sitting at a smaller table tucked in a corner, trying to be the unobtrusive anthropologist in the room, taking verbatim notes from afar. I collect my stuff and move to the "big table," the large round table that fills the room. I spend every Monday morning from 9 a.m.–12 p.m. at this table, observing the Intake Meeting and taking notes about who is being admitted to Havenwood and why, what their initial treatment plan will be, including treatment objectives, goals, and interventions. Today, I am observing Derrick's "Staffing," a quarterly meeting where the initial treatment goals, objectives, and interventions are reviewed, discussed, and revised.[1] Unlike other assessment meetings, Staffings include the youth and external individuals such as parents, state workers, lawyers, and representatives of the funding sources paying for the child's treatment. Havenwood employees who attend Staffings include teachers, individual therapists, music or art therapists, the director of religious services, line staff, cottage directors, cottage case workers, and cottage supervisors. The point of the Staffing is to have a discussion among all of the players, including the youth, parents or guardians, and funding sources, about discharge plans: when the youth can leave treatment, and where he will go when that time comes.

Staffings are notoriously anxiety provoking. They are events where residents defend themselves and their progress against people who are reluctant to acknowledge that they are improving, to accept that their change is genuine or sincere, and who remind them of how much more work they need to do. The resident must listen to this feedback and respond without getting angry or frustrated. The feedback is often hard to hear because, I had been told, the "youth could always be doing better, that's why they are in treatment." Today, I hope for the best for Derrick.

Derrick seems to be in high spirits as he walks into the meeting room and makes sure to include me in the Staffing. I am a familiar face and he wants me to have a front row seat. I am the only person "from his cottage" at his Staffing today; it is 10 a.m. and too early for Allen, Steve, or anyone else who come to work at 3 p.m. Sarah, Steele Cottage's director, walks in right after Derrick and sits down next to him at the head of the table. Paige, Derrick's individual therapist, arrives next and sits to their left. Craig, Steele Cottage's internal case worker, and Ernest, Derrick's teacher, walk in together. Sarah is trying to call Derrick's state worker but is unsuccessful. Derrick is in the foster care system and his legal guardian is the State. The person representing the state, and making decisions that any legal guardian would, is going to attend the Staffing by phone. After a few more failed attempts, Sarah gives up and begins the Staffing without the state worker.

"OK, well no state worker. We will try again later. Craig, do you want to go over the Staffing report?" Sarah asks Craig. The Staffing Report is the cottage's official report on how Derrick is doing.

"Derrick is doing pretty well. He is doing his thing. He is working. He is on the highest Level. The most significant thing is he has a matching meeting on Friday with a prospective Big Pal. This could be a permanent arrangement for discharge. It would mean being with a family. We would like it to move quickly but this is the hand we are dealt. Derrick hasn't flown off the handle. He is taking it in stride. He is doing really well working during this time-table." With the Staffing Report in hand, Craig informs the group, a quick assessment of how Derrick is progressing in treatment. He is working, and this is articulated using the hip hop phrase "doing his thing," on the highest Level, and "hasn't flown off the handle" despite how slowly his discharge plan is progressing.

"Staff said yesterday in Team [Meeting] that he is doing his thing. He is a leader, responsible and that he has come a long way." Sarah added to Craig's report, also using hip hop phrasing.

"Good job, Derrick," Paige smiles.

Derrick nods in response.

"Any questions so far?" Sarah turns to Derrick.

"When am I going to leave? I want to leave." Derrick does not mince words. He knows he has a match meeting with a Big Pal, an adult in the area who volunteers to build a relationship with him. Sometimes Big Pals turn into permanent homes.

"We will start with the match meeting, see how the relationship goes. You have been opposed to moves. I am not writing off the family but let's say it takes six to nine months to set up a foster family. But in the meantime, do you see another avenue, seeing as it has taken so much time? I don't know why you should stay at Steele because you are doing so well. You need to be in on the plans."

"Can I have home visits then?" Derrick asks.

"Derrick, you know your mother is unable to supervise you. She is sick. And as far as we know she doesn't have adequate housing. You can't have home visits with her until she can supervise you. You know that."

"I want to live with a family. My sister." Eight months earlier, two Staffings ago, Derrick brings up home visits with his sister and having her serve as a possible discharge plan, the place he will go to when he finishes his treatment at Havenwood. He stated that he wanted to live with her then. He repeats this desire today.

"That may not be an option," Sarah states.

"You said you will move me where I want to go. This is my life and I want to live with my sister."

"Is that an option?" Sarah asks Craig.

"Yeah, I will talk to his state worker."

Paige interjects, trying to contextualize the discussion for Derrick, "I think the problem with that is that you run away. That's what you did before. If I were in your state worker's shoes....I'm just trying to prepare you for what the worker might say." Paige is referring to the time when Derrick went AWOL, when he first arrived at Havenwood almost three years ago. Paige is worried that this would be held against him.

"You have to look at that, your past behavior" Ernest tells Derrick, reminding him that behavior from three years ago, the one time he ran away from Havenwood when he was 12, might hurt his chances of returning to his family now.

"But I already talked to my worker and he said it was cool." Derrick informs the group.

"Ernest, can you give your report?" Sarah halts the impending debate about who knows what the state worker thinks.

"He will say it." Ernest states, nodding towards Derrick.

Sarah turns to Derrick, "OK, Derrick, how have you been doing?"

"I don't know. You all tell me how I've been doing." Derrick seems to be confused about what is going on. Ernest, and other teachers, usually report on a youth's school performance, much like Craig reported on his cottage performance. However, here Ernest has asked Derrick to provide his own report. Ernest is known for being fairly antagonistic toward the youth; this kind of behavior is called "provoking" at Havenwood. Derrick does not easily acquiesce to Ernest's decision to have him report on his schoolwork.

"This is the real you: rude, trying to control the situation," Ernest states.

"Yeah," Derrick scoffs, "I haven't made any progress."

"Ernest, how is he doing?" Sarah, who is leading the meeting, decides who will report.

Ernest shrugs almost dismissively, "It's a mixed bag. He gets upset over little things but can process. He says he is tired and sleepy. Academically he is OK."

"I've said I was sleepy one time, yesterday." Derrick responds. I sense a pending heated debate between Ernest and Derrick.

"He wants you to believe it because he says so. He needs to be controlled, authority figures need to be listened to," Ernest tells Sarah.

"How is school, Derrick? Academics? Pretty good?"

"I hate academics. I hate school. I hate pretty good," Derrick tells Sarah. He then turns to Ernest, "I am tired of you lying on me. I haven't gotten any Majors [consequences for bad behavior]. I've been good. I should be getting As not Bs."

"You are trying to manipulate now. You are arguing. You aren't a stellar student," Ernest tells him. Ernest then looks at Sarah, "He still needs a lot of help."

"OK, what are some good things?" Derrick does not miss a beat. He hears Ernest's critical feedback but now wants him to tell him some of the good things he does.

"I've already said them."

"No you followed them up with the bad things," Derrick reminds him. I look up from my note writing and pause. I think to myself, Derrick is trying to teach Ernest how to help him improve, how to give positive and negative feedback, and how to keep calm and open-minded during a rather tense discussion or confrontation.

"Why don't you tell me the good things," Sarah asks Derrick, as it seems that Ernest will not do so.

"I do my work. I don't care if I need help but I do my work. You tell me to do things, I do them. I'm not in the hallway every five minutes. And I am working, at the greenhouse." For Derrick it doesn't matter than he needs help, he does his work. He has a job at Havenwood's greenhouse, and he does as he is told. He has recently moved from a more remedial classroom to Ernest's classroom and this shift means that he is doing much better academically. I have spoken with Derrick about his progress and he is proud of himself for doing as well as he is. He has not spent much time in formal schooling, resulting in significant deficiencies in reading, math, and other academic skills. He does not say all of this, he just states, "He does his work" and he does what he is told.

"This is your version of how you have been doing? This is what I asked you to do from the beginning. So thank you. You do good things, you needed to say what I asked you to," Ernest states.

"So he is pretty accurate?" Sarah asks Ernest.

"Yeah. But there are things to work on…"

Sarah interrupts Ernest and asks Derrick, "So what do you need to work on?"

"I need to see my family. I haven't seen them in three years."

"Say it differently, say…" Ernest begins to tell Derrick how to rephrase his statements.

Sarah once again interrupts Ernest and reminds Derrick, "But you said you didn't want to go to the city."

"Can I talk please? Let me talk." Derrick takes a deep breath and no one breaks the silence. "I am doing really well. You don't see me. My mom had a heart attack. A heart attack. That is it. I need to see my mom. My mom doesn't live in [name of a particular housing project]. My sister lives in a good neighborhood. I need to go see my mom. I don't care if six staff have to be there. I need to see my mom. Ernest told me I was doing good. My file says that. My old file says I go AWOL, smoked. I don't do that. I've changed." Derrick makes his case about why he wants to go on a home visit (to see his very sick mom), and how that can happen (his sister lives in a good neighborhood and he can be supervised by as many staff as they want to send). He refers to his file, which he knows that Sarah, Craig, and others read and add to using events such as the Staffing. He uses this index to evince his change, how his files used to say one thing (that he went AWOL) but now it says something else (that he is "doing good"). Derrick realizes that others might believe his "file" over his own presentation.[2]

"OK so you need us to know you've changed and that you want to see your family," Sarah reiterates what Derrick says.

"Yeah." Derrick responds. There is a pause in the conversation then Derrick asks, "So when can I have home visits?"

"Let me talk to your state worker." Craig tells him.

"Thank you," Derrick tells Craig. After a brief pause, Derrick asks Sarah, "Why didn't we do this two years ago?"

"You weren't ready two years ago."

"Yeah," Derrick says and he nods.

The Staffing ends with Craig's plan to speak to Derrick's State worker about home visits and to prepare for the pending Big Pal meeting. Everyone files out of the room and I finish writing up my notes. When I leave, I stop by Sarah's office, "How do you think that went?"

"Pretty good. Derrick pulled himself together. But what was Ernest's problem? He provokes so much."

I see Derrick walking to lunch about an hour later. "How'd that go?" I ask him.

"I got mad. But then I recovered. That's what Steve be sayin', 'It's all about the recovery.' I didn't snap on [Ernest]. I used my words. That's what Steve be sayin', 'Use your words.' I thought I did good."

* * *

Goffman, quoted earlier, states, "In our society, [total institutions] are the forcing houses for changing persons; each is a natural experiment on what can be done to the self" (1961:12). I also quote Derrick, who links mastering the skills he learns at Havenwood and staying focused with being a good man. Therefore, this chapter links what is done to the self in treatment at Havenwood with producing and cultivating particular kinds of racialized, gendered selves. In particular, I focus on the process of change, the *becoming* that happens while living at Havenwood, participating and performing in Staffings, and working toward a goal of leaving psychiatric custody.

In this vignette, we see how Derrick enacts and reflects on his behavior, especially in relation to how he is changing: he got mad, but then recovered; he wanted to snap, but he didn't, he used his words. In real time, we see Derrick *living out* his recovery, illustrating that he is really changing. He is enacting the change, becoming a good man, that he is learning from "staff and peers" such as Steve. Other young men at Steele also see and experiencing themselves as changing and *becoming* good men. In this chapter, I juxtapose these racialized gendered selves-in-process with other selves that bear down on African American boys, especially those linked to criminality and villainy.

Hateful Unminding Bastard

"Can you tell me who you were before you came to Havenwood?" I ask Lamar in our interview session. I am trying to get a sense of how the young people of Havenwood talk about who they were before they arrived at Havenwood.

"A bad kid who didn't do too much but was very defiant. And I had no remorse for anything. And it was just basically if Lamar didn't get what he want, he do what he want. I had a lot of stress on me and a lot of anger built inside of me so I just let it all out in one place, in one area and it just flew everywhere."

I have heard the residents talk about being "angry" and "aggressive" as the reasons for why they were at Havenwood. In fact Garrett, Russell, and Travis discuss this in their group therapy session in chapter 5. I wondered what Lamar was angry about; how he would articulate the source of his anger. I ask him.

"Not being at home. Not knowing my parents. You know? Not being able to have a father or, you know what I'm sayin', a mom. Just bein' on my own, just my auntie and that's about it. I lived in foster homes. I lived in group homes. [My auntie] couldn't pay the rent and stuff. So she had to put us somewhere, so we could be safe and grow up a good person."

It is not difficult to understand Lamar's anger, especially as he shares that he does not have a family, a dad, a mom, and that he had to enter the State foster system. He sees this placement as a way to be sure he is "safe" and can "grow up a good person." According to his case file, Lamar's aunt had been arrested for drugs and for harboring her fugitive boyfriend during a police raid at her home. It was at this time that Lamar and his cousins were removed from her guardianship and placed in the foster care system. Lamar was around 10 years old at the time. He is currently 15, and has been "in the system" for five years, a full one-third of his life.

"When you think about your past, what sticks out to you?" I continue asking him about his past, and who he was back then.

"Me runnin' away. Runnin' away from people, places, just bein' me. That's what I do, that's what I'm used to. I'm used to runnin' away." Lamar continues the interview, telling me about the shelters he has lived in, the residential treatment centers he has run away from, and the foster homes he has ditched as he "does what he is used to." Currently at Havenwood, he is on "high alert" for AWOL as his file concurs that he is apt to run away.

I push him to tell me more about how he remembers who he was before Havenwood. "Tell me about who you were before you came to Havenwood."

"I told you already. I told you I was a hateful unminding bastard. All that. I didn't do nuthin' nobody say. You ask me to do something, I wouldn't be doin' this [interview]. I would be very ungrateful, play hard to...play hard to mess around with."

* * *

Like many residents of Havenwood, Lamar frames his early childhood (he is still barely 15) in terms of being "bad." He defines his younger self as "a hateful unminding bastard" with a lot of stress and "anger built up inside." Lamar can also articulate why he was so stressed and angry. He does not have a family. In chapter 6 Lamar talks about himself and the other residents of Steele Cottage as "criminals," and that he was scared to live with a "buncha dudes." In these narratives and discussions, we hear how bad, hateful, criminal, and even "hard to mess around with" Lamar, and in his estimation, the other young men of Steele Cottage are. We get a sense from his narrative that he has come to see himself in very stereotypical ways. He frames himself, not as a victim of adult violence or poverty and trauma. Rather, he presents himself as an angry, dangerous Black male, recapitulating the most legible way to read the Black male body (Neal 2013).

American media representations of Black boys and men in the United States shape how they are perceived. African American Studies scholar Mark Anthony Neal (2013) argues that the general framing of Black men in the media is negative—a Black male in need of policing, surveillance, or incarceration. Neal calls this the legibility of the Black male body. He argues that, "black men are seemingly bound to and bound by their legibility" (Neal 2013:6). The media is not alone in constructing this legibility, Van Deburg (2004) argues. The US's criminal justice apparatus reflects "the larger society's tendency to conflate blackness with villainy" (Van Deburg 2004:186).[3]

Research on urban youth, particular Black and Latino boys, argues that various historical and cultural trajectories lead Americans to view these youth as criminal, dangerous, and bad based strongly on skin color alone (Anderson 2008:3; see also Van Deburg 2004). "Even as a child, the black male is subject to the remnants of suspicion that go along with that racial and gender position. His identity is shaped by the repeated expression of these attitudes, and he inevitably becomes alienated," Elijah Anderson, a leading sociologist of race and discrimination against African American men, argues. (2008:15). Sometimes, in a proposed act of empowerment, young Black men might use the outsider status thrust upon them to express themselves in their own terms, taking up the mantle of being "oppositional" to mainstream society (Anderson 2008; Van Deburg 2004). Anderson argues that "the young black male becomes invested in his outsider status and buys into it as an end in itself" (2008:25).

African American Studies and hip hop scholar Imani Perry argues that this outsider status and investment in the outsider status is a particular kind of masculinity, one that is present and embraced by hip hop. As mentioned earlier, hip hop is situated within an urban context and it speaks to many young men who have felt disenfranchised and misled by progressive social movements, urban deindustrialization, the crack-cocaine epidemic, and police brutality. Hip hop has been a terrain for asserting a particular kind of Black masculinity, one linked to urban America and to the exploitation of Black male identity (Perry 2004). This Black masculinity has embraced and celebrated the struggles of life in the urban terrain, while rejecting the continued oppression by white society. Hip hop masculinity is linked to a real or authentic Black urban male experience, and a confrontational social rejection of mainstream American values.[4]

Young men of color who embrace a hip hop masculinity come to be read and regulated because of what this masculinity represents. Sociologist Victor Rios (2011) argues that these urban, hip hop identified and identifying young men come to be hypercriminalized by the criminal justice and education systems. As with Anderson, Rios (2011) argues that this hypercriminalization has significant consequences on these young people's life trajectories. With the mainstreaming of gangsta rap music and the rise of films depicting a particular kind of inner-city life (for example, *Menace II Society*), African American men associated with hip hop have been narrowly confined to particular kinds of hip hop masculinities. The contemporary hip hop masculinities are represented by the essentialized tropes of "playa," "pimp," "hustler," and "thug" (Neal 2013:35). These hip hop masculinities are social problems, read to be violently and criminally inclined (Neal 2013; Van Deburg 2004). Anderson, Rios, and Van Deburg argue that young men of color in general, and those who embody hip hop masculinities in particular, are in almost constant negotiation of identity in relation to criminalizing stigmas and systems of oppression.

The African American boys I worked with could also be categorized as "urban, young, male, and poor" as Anderson classifies them in his text. They can be identified as having hip hop masculinities, as they embrace hip hop cultural knowledge, representation, and location. Take Dwayne, for example, the young man I discussed in the Intake Meeting in chapter 2. Dwayne is identified as "tough," "noncompliant and aggressive," and is diagnosed with Conduct Disorder. Dwayne is not unique. In fact, he is "like the other kids of Steele Cottage." Dwayne, and others at Havenwood, embody Anderson's depiction of the young, urban, Black male as they are ensnared by the criminal justice system (perhaps more so than young men who live outside of psychiatric custody). Young men like Lamar and Dwayne (and others) do not just act oppositionally. They are institutionalized by the State and are diagnosed with a mental illness called "Oppositional Defiant Disorder." These young men must spend their days proving that they are no longer oppositional and defiant, bad, criminal, or threats to society.

If one arrived at Havenwood and researched how young Black men are diagnosed, medicated, and how they themselves initially talk about who they are, one might leave thinking that the youth there are in fact "criminal," "bad," "tough, aggressive, and noncompliant" or "unminding bastards." Narratives like Lamar's and Dwayne's recapitulate the most common or legible ways in which young Black men are identified in the United States, as criminals in need of policing or containment (Neal 2013). It might even seem as if these young men are invested, as Anderson identifies, in their outsider status, being "hard to mess around with," like Lamar states or "argumentative," as Tricia defines Dwayne. Without further investigation, these stereotypical stories might be the only stories that the research would tell because they are the stories most easily imagined (Neal 2013:180).

However, as I have tried to show, this is just part of the story. I quoted Tricia speaking about Dwayne: "He tried to be tough but a piece of him felt bad about being tough. He tried to be oppositional but he had a nice piece to him." Young men like Lamar and Derrick challenge Black male hip hop stereotypes and indeed invest in a status that renders them "good persons" who are not oppositional, defiant, or "unminding."

Derrick is a hip hop aficionado. He raps constantly—in individual therapy, in informal conversations, into my recorder. When he raps, he talks about urban living and working a hustle to "make it" (see chapter 1 for this rap). Derrick dresses in hip hop clothing, the visual representations of hip hop masculinities (Perry 2004:122). Derrick's masculinity is a hip hop masculinity. However, Derrick's hip hop masculinity includes a desire to not need a gun, or to know how to work without owing people money, as he explained in his life history interview (see the "Introduction"). Also, Derrick discusses feelings about how he engages with the world despite his world crashing down on him. During one rap session, Derrick asked me to "interview" him as part of a rap, using my ethnographer position and my interviewer status creatively in his rap. He used this moment to discuss the pain of having his world destroyed, and yet, his desire to be happy and to make others happy despite these circumstances. He wrote out my questions ahead of time, and made me practice my lines. This interview led straight to the beat:

Katie: So Derrick, where you from?
Derrick: I'm from [name of housing project], [number of building]. You know? I useta always go there. I used to live in [number of original building]. Now I live in [different number building] since [number of original building] went down. It's been painful.
Katie: What's been painful?
Derrick: You know, livin' without [the name of the housing projects], man. That's all in my heart, you know. That's what's up.
Katie: Derrick, what makes you happy?
Derrick: To see people smile.
[*At this moment he pushes play on the boom box.*]
Derrick: [rapping] It's D here, man. It ain't all about killin' and you know doin' all that other stuff man. Long as I see you smile I'm happy if the world blow up....

Derrick's shares his feelings about the demolition of his housing project and yet his desire to make people smile, even if the world (or his housing project) blows up. Derrick used his rapping in a meaningful way to discuss feelings, and his goals for how to be in the world with others. While rap and hip hop are often linked to villainous Black masculinities, Derrick and his rap illustrate that they need not be. Derrick's version of hip and hip and rap here includes wanting to make people smile and be happy, despite the pain experienced by the rapper himself.

Challenging Urban, Black, Male, Poor Stereotypes: Complicating Manhood

Mark Anthony Neal (2013) provides an analysis of illegible black male bodies as represented by African American cultural icons, including musicians Jay-Z, R. Kelly, and Luther Vandross, and actors Avery Brooks, Michael K. Williams, Wood Harris, and Idris Elba (and others from *The Wire*). Neal illustrates how these African American male entertainers challenge mainstream notions of Black masculinity (i.e., the essential tropes in hip hop masculinities). His argument, and that of other Black masculinities scholars (see, e.g., Alexander 2006; Allen 2011; Anderson 1990; 2008; Cohen 2004; Davis 1997; Duncan 2002; Duneier 1992; Gordon 1997; Hall 1997; Harper 1996; hooks 2000, 2004; Van Deburg 2004) is that despite larger American culture's inability to imagine Black men beyond narrow definitions, African American masculinities are complex and numerous.

The African American masculinities offered by Mitchell Duneier (1999) in his ethnography *Sidewalk* illustrates how complex and numerous masculinity is for many poor, urban, adult African American men in New York City. His ethnography explores the worlds and lives of these men, as they sell written matter (books and magazines) on the streets. Many of these Black men are "unhoused" (the term Duneier, uses rather than "homeless"), have histories that include drug and alcohol abuse, are disconnected from family and friends, and have interactions with the criminal justice system, including spending time in prison. Many of the Black men in *Sidewalk* embody an older version of "the Black male" that Elijah Anderson describes.

Duneier examines how many of the men come to be unhoused, disconnected, substance dependent, and even involved in criminal activity. For many, social withdrawal and an "I don't care" frame of mind allow them to disengage from their families and mainstream social life. However, by investigating the vibrant social dynamics of the book vendors and others involved in this economy, Duneier illustrates how men do not just give up and retreat or remain oppositional. Rather, these poor and urban African American men come to see themselves as living a self-respecting, society respecting, and entrepreneurial way of life. Duneier complicates the idea of the urban, poor, African American male stereotype through his rigorous and extended ethnographic research. Much like his first book *Slim's Table: Race, Respectability, and Masculinity*, Duneier illustrates the complex ways in which African American men can be men, despite their social disenfranchisement and marginalization. As anthropologist Edmund Gordon, Duneier provides a window into the "rich and diverse Black-male cultural repertoire" (Gordon 1997:36).

In his text, the African American men discuss the integral role of the mentor, and of close, personal, trusting relationships among themselves as critical (Duneier 1999). Friendships, mentoring relationships, and strong social support and influence, in the form of wisdom, among the African American men helped some of these men "to make positive changes." Duneier traces how one informant's "panhandling led to scavenging and vending, which have given him a trade of sorts and a mentor, who in turn encouraged him to take care of his [elderly] Aunt Naomi" (1999:79). Duneier argues that these mentoring relationships, through the avenue of book vending, encouraged these men, usually external to mainstream social opportunities, to respect themselves and to be responsible to others.[5] Unlike other ethnographies and studies of urban Black males, Duneier's research asks us to question some of the logic that extreme social precariousness (including being unhoused, or as a child understanding life as a constant hustle) inevitably leads to violence among men, to criminal lives, and to a giving up mentality.

Following his Staffing, Derrick tells us that he takes Steve's mentoring, advice, and teachings. Derrick allows Steve to mentor him and Derrick has come to believe Steve so much that Derrick changes according to Steve's advice. It can be argued that Derrick *must* incorporate Steve's advice into his life in order to prove that he is changing or to get out of treatment. However, I do not believe that this is the primary motive for Derrick to change. I begin the chapter with a quotation where Derrick tells us: "Alls I gotta do is stay focused. You know what I'm sayin'? 'Cause I can leave here, master everything, the skills…but I don't use it? I don't stay focused? What I have? Nothin'. But if I use them to stay focused, I'm a good man." Derrick *wants* to be a good man, to use the skills he has been taught, to "use his words," and to rap about his pain, and his desire to make others smile. Derrick is making positive changes. Derrick is in the process of "buying in," and Derrick is not alone.

Good Manhood as Improving and Becoming Trustworthy

I sat down with William for a life history interview. William, as I have mentioned in previous chapters, is a particularly difficult resident. He gets violent and attacks staff members or he attacks himself, which inevitably results in his being restrained. William is seen as "struggling" in treatment. In addition to being a difficult resident, William is also extremely bright. He reads self-help books, trying to understand more about his problems. He even challenged me to think about the nature of anthropological research. He called me "nosey," and when I responded that I was "curious," he scoffed and quipped, "curious is just a fancy word for nosey." Sitting down with William is very informative as he is a very thoughtful, discerning young man.

William and I are sitting in the back staff office at Steele Cottage for one of his life history interviews. We are talking about him getting angry and hitting people, and why it has taken him a long time to learn to talk to people instead of lashing out.

"I wouldn't wanna be listenin' to anybody. It was either my way or the highway. I wasn't listenin' to nobody else way. 'Cause I thought they was just doin' that cause they not in the situation."

"What made you change your mind and want to listen?" I ask him.

"Because if I talk with somebody about my anger and then if I forget what they say, it will be on me for ignorin' what they say. And that went on my record of ignorin' people, not bein' trustworthy. I thought about that. Around here if you do a lot a positive things, people start trustin' you. Staff be tellin' me I'm doin' good. Then I talk to staff about it and they say he movin' on up, he talkin'. They see that I'm not lying. Then they believe what I say."

"So telling the truth is a positive thing. What are other positive things?" I ask, following up on his "a lot of positive things" comment.

"Talkin' to staff or talk to someone about [something that is bothering you]. Or leave it alone and if it gets to a point where you can't leave it alone, talk to staff."

I think about William asking for what he needs. Not only have I seen him pull Steve or Arthur aside and talk to them about what he needs, we also saw him ask for what he needs in group. He asked for his high Level peers to role model good behavior for him even when staff aren't around to punish them (see chapter 5). William did not tell on anyone, but he asked that his successful peers act right, even and especially when staff members are not around.

Over the course of my time at Havenwood and Steele, I have seen William changing. When I first arrived he was so often in trouble, always in the confinement room or serving out some sort of punishment for a Level infraction (his punishment per the treatment protocols mostly included sitting at the table or not being able to go off campus). William would "self-harm" or he would attack the staff, as we saw in chapter 4. He was even frustrating his peers, much like Travis frustrated Garrett in chapter 5. However, over the course of my 18 months at Havenwood, I watched William earn higher Levels, more privileges, and go off campus on Friday nights. In our interview he is telling me that he is trying to do "a lot of positive things," including telling the truth and talking about his problems. I wondered how he came to this realization. "How do these things change?" I ask him.

William is quick to tell me that he does not like to use the word "change." It carries too much weight. "We don't talk about change though 'cause change is like turnin' your whole life around. So we use improve. I brought it up in group 'cause I didn't like people usin' change. Because change is like when you hit somebody every day and then you change and don't hit 'em. That is change. But if you hit them some days then that is improving."

So I ask him, "How do things improve?"

"I'm getting' tired of being here. I realize the things I do and I can stop 'em. But big things, like my anger, it is in my head and it comes out when I am angry. So that is the one thing I try to change. So they trust me. If they trust me, I can go on home visits."

William is not looking to manipulate the staff members into letting him go on home visits. Rather, he wants the staff to trust him. He knows that trust is very important in his treatment progress. I ask him to clarify why this is the case: "Seems like trust is a big deal to you. Why is that?"

"Because if you in a placement or anywhere and you not trusted you can't do that many things, privilege wise. Like you can do the basic Program but you can't do nuthin' like get passes or get out of people's eyesight. But if you bein' positive and you got trust, they can trust you anywhere you go. And when staff aren't around, they can trust you to do the right thing instead of sneakin' around. That is why trust is big to me." It is important to William to earn privileges, such as to get passes or "get out of people's eyesight," which means that he can go around or off campus without a staff member. He understands how using the Cottage Program is important. However, what is most important to William, he has learned, is beyond the Cottage Program. It takes more than just following the Program to be able to do things outside of the institutional rules. Improving in psychiatric custody is about *trust*, it is about being trustworthy and earning the trust of the staff members.

Trust is, inherently, an intersubjective experience, a "medium of interaction" (Giddens 1991:3). Much like touch is a social sense, trust is something established *between* people. Anthony Giddens (1991) provides a very detailed analysis of the way trust is linked to both initial caregivers (basic trust) and to an abstract social system, a result of modernity.[6] Here I do not mean the trust that an individual has in others, where the individual is the subject of the trust sentence: *I* trust you. Rather, William and others want to earn the trust of the staff members, they want to be worthy of someone else's trust, to be on the receiving end of the trust: They trust *me*.

To be worthy of trust is to be understood as a reliable person. More importantly, one has to be reliable to be good, to follow the rules, to do the right thing. William wants the staff members to believe in the reliability of his goodness. In order to achieve this, he tries to do more positive things like telling the truth and talking about things, rather than getting mad. For William, as it was for Derrick, being good means being able to talk about one's feelings or difficulties and to tell the truth. Trust is more than just about earning privileges, it is about being relied upon to do the right thing, even and especially when staff are not around to structurally regulate you. For William, what is changing the most is his ability to earn the trust of the staff members. This trustworthiness is not only tightly bound within the relationships with others, but it also cannot be disarticulated from being good. William is improving because he is becoming a good person; someone who can be trusted by others.

I conclude my interview with William by asking him about how he sees success at Havenwood and beyond. I want to know if and how he links his improvement with success. How will he know when he has improved so that he can leave the institution?

"To me being successful means like taking the information that they gave me and usin' it in the real world or society. Like if staff tell me to stop a behavior and I take that [knowledge] out to the streets or to society or community and be like 'I'm not even gonna fight you, man that's a waste of my time.' Or something like that. I don't want to do this right now or I don't want to do this at all and then I am being successful 'cause I am using what I've learned. Here [at Havenwood] using it, and in the real world."

"What about when you leave Havenwood, what does 'successful' mean when you leave Havenwood?" I ask. I am wondering if the youth in general, and William in this case, will see what they have learned in psychiatric custody as applicable in what he and other youth like to call the "real world." Can they see "using their words" and "talking about what is bothering them" as transferable skills from psychiatric custody to mainstream social life?

"Being successful here is leaving and doing what they told me to do, and following their directions. Usin' stuff that I learned here. And then when I leave, it will be the same because I learned the stuff here. Then I am using it when I get out. Successful to me right now is being able to accept change and stuff. Acceptance. But long term successful is to become a police officer. That's one of my goals."

William is integrating the skills, such as talking things out and being truthful, that he is learning at Havenwood in his everyday life there. As he does this, he sees himself improving. Not only does he think that he is improving, but William practices this improvement by attacking people less, achieving increasingly higher Levels, and behaving well when he is able to go off campus. His less aggressive behavior, his higher Levels, and his earned privileges support his claims of improvement. Everyone is impressed and happy about William's marked transformation. William chalks it up to learning acceptance—learning to accept that he has to change, and accepting that the staff members might be able to help him. He hopes to one day put his skills to good use in society by becoming a police officer.

Learning to Read as Manhood

Despite his bad-boy reputation and the rough exterior Lamar brought with him to Havenwood, I found it very easy to be around him. I did not interpret him to be a "hateful unminding bastard" over the course of my time at Havenwood. In fact, Lamar and I became close.

One day, after school, I was sitting at the picnic bench outside of Steele Cottage. I was watching Shelby North and Bradley South play a therapeutic game of kickball. Mark and Jonathon were dribbling basketballs on the concrete just outside of Steele. The campus was fairly busy; youth from every cottage were out and about enjoying the beautiful late August day.

Lamar joins me at the picnic table. "Can you teach me to read? I got a kid now and I don't read too good. I seen you helpin' Jonathon. Can you help me?"

I have been tutoring Jonathon in preparation for the ACT college entrance exam. My role in the cottage has expanded to include helping young men with schoolwork, reading, or college preparation. I am not surprised that Lamar has asked me to help him learn to read. He has articulated to me in previous conversations that his problems—which he identified as not having a family, not being able to read, being in an institution, and having a kid at 15—are much more important to him and worse than his issues—which he identified as his anger and aggression. He sees much of his work at Havenwood as dealing with the problems rather than the issues. I have met the mother of Lamar's baby, whom he called his "girl," and his baby boy. Lamar and the baby's mother were at the same residential treatment center (not Havenwood) when she got pregnant. The baby's mother and the child now live in a group home for teenage mothers already in the foster care system; mom, dad, and baby are wards of the State. Lamar is trying to learn how to use the public transportation system so he can take the bus and train to visit his family. However, he cannot read the signs or schedules. I know this because I have gone with him and Pete to visit his baby and his "girl."

"Sure," I tell him. Lamar's teacher allows me to come in three days a week for about an hour to teach him to read and work on his reading and English schoolwork. For almost five months Lamar and I work together toward his literacy. Some days he would be so frustrated with his inabilities that he would want to quit. Other days he would be resolved to improve his reading; "I'm a father now," he would tell me.

Lamar's own life history includes "not being able to have a father," and the anger and stress that welled within him. Against so many odds—life in psychiatric custody, not being able to read, not having parents or guardians himself—being a good father is a challenge. He does what he can, he enlists help to learn to read, and he regularly asks for visits with his son, even though at 15 years old, he is still legally a child.

The Lamar I tutor and observe hanging out and having fun with his "friends" is far from the "hateful unminding bastard" he describes in his first life history interview. Rather, I see him more akin to the idealized version of himself that he provides. The ideal version of himself would work with his friends to help kids and give back to the community. In his "movie," Lamar projected himself into an ideal future, where he worked with his friends to show people how to get along, help kids, and give back to the community. Currently, he is helping Tye, a developmentally delayed youth at Steele, to learn the Program, calm himself rather than get upset, and integrate into the community. His ideal future and his current present are very different from his identification as a "hateful unminding bastard." Being a good Black man is what Lamar wants to be, and this version of manhood includes learning to read, visiting his son, and helping kids and giving back to the community. He not only wants to be this, but he goes about the process, by mentoring others and spending hours and days learning to read, during his tenure at Havenwood.

That's What Steve Be Sayin': Making Good Men

"An important element that limits and destroys the lives of young black men growing up in concentrated areas of poverty, especially the violence and social disconnection ghetto youths experience, is that adult men are basically absent" (Anderson 2008:22). A great deal of literature and public discourse on the struggles of young African American men lays the blame on the shoulders of missing Black fathers. Popular American culture and criminal justice scholars also argue that gang life fills the void of kinship structures and serves a social (read: negative social) support for youth in the inner city.[7] Sometimes the more neutral "peer group" is used in lieu of "gang," but the point is similar: inner-city young men fill the gap of family, particularly male role models with a negative peer group.[8] What I argued in chapter 6 is that rather than just finding peers or peer groups, perhaps it is the real friendships that might be important for the youth at Havenwood and Steele Cottage. In addition, I believe that the positive relationships that the youth have with the adult African American men are crucial in cultivating positive change and allowing the youth to become the good men they envision themselves as and desire to be.

As we have seen earlier, the adult men of Havenwood and Steele Cottage provide various examples of how to be men. Steve is the supervisor of Steele with a gregarious personality and almost heroic dedication to the youth of Steele. We have seen him tell the youth to "use their words," to "stick up for themselves." We have seen him tell youth in chapter 5 that sometimes you have to tell yourself "Just. Shut. Up." when you should be listening. Also in chapters 4 and 5, he discusses that it is important to get in touch with emotions besides anger, to learn to cry, and to even "ask for hug," if you know you need one. Steve shows up for work every day, except Sunday, dedicating much of his life to Steele and Havenwood youth.

Steve, while a dominant figure in their lives, is not alone in his dedication to the young men. Jim also engages jovially and talks some trash at the Spades table. Allen teases the youth from a neighboring cottage about push-ups, as he grooms and talks to the young men who visit his barbershop. James cultivates the athletic gifts and talents of the Steele youth. While he is not as easy to play with as other staff members, the young men of Steele seek advice from James. Arthur, who self-identifies as a "40 year-old-thug" and adjunct professor at the local community college, is known for being a strict rule follower. Despite this orientation toward rule following, we see Arthur give the youth "a little latitude" when we are off campus at a basketball tournament. Angie, the matriarch of the cottage, has a positive relationship with the men of Steele and they are tender toward her. Angie has been known to two-step with the young men, when they *kick it* during evening hours, especially if one of her favorite songs comes on. The staff members of Steele, most of them men, are complex people from all kinds of backgrounds. These men and woman are not only implementing the institutional Program and facilitating therapeutic practices but they are raising and changing the young Black men of Steele.

Staff members influence youth across the Havenwood campus. Many are known for particular traits. Steve is known across as campus as the father figure, his nickname is "Papa Bear." Brenda, a girl who stays at Evelyn's, told me that Allen is her favorite staff member because he "keeps it real" and she trusts him. Arthur is admired by many of the youth for being fair. For different reasons, these men are identified as significant in the lives of many youth across campus.

In addition to individual personality traits, it is also significant that many of the leaders at Havenwood are African American. The vice president of Havenwood's residential program and the principal of the school, both African American men, are identified as individuals you can go talk to if you need extra guidance. One of the important directors of the residential program is an African American woman. Seven of the cottage supervisors are African American men, one is an African American woman, and one is a white male. In other words, Havenwood youth see African Americans in important positions of power, with a range of personalities, and having experienced various kinds of life trajectories (from the rural South to New York City). Many of these individuals share their own histories of growing up poor, in the city, and within the various oppressive social systems like the young Black male residents. Therefore, a youth like Lamar, can envision himself one day "giving back to the community" by "helping kids" much like the staff members currently do, whom he will miss when he leaves.

Once again, I return to Duneier's discussion of mentoring relationships. Mentoring relationships do not negate the reality that the men in his study were unhoused and had suffered from an oppressive social system. However, these relationships are a significant part of the lived realities and daily lives of the men. The realities of American racial inequality, poverty, childhood histories of abuse and neglect, and mass incarceration rates influence and affect the African American youth at Havenwood. However, their lives are not just the culmination of abstract or oppressive systems. On a daily basis and even in projected futures, the youth of Havenwood define and go about becoming good men; they do not invest in their outsider status, as Anderson argues. The youth are not becoming good Black men because they no longer have issues or never get upset. Rather, they are becoming good men because they learn the skills important to them—not snapping on people, talking about feelings, recovering when they get mad, using one's words, and learning to read. And they learn these skills through important mentoring relationships and the love that was said to be shared.

As I have illustrated before, actions in restraints, discussion after restraints and crisis intervention, group therapy sessions, and the cultivation of friendships and just hanging out together in the cottage allow for the young men of Steele and youth across Havenwood to build relationships with others, to improve who they are, and to learn to be good men. Leading scholars of masculinity, and in particular, African American or Black masculinity, argue that masculinities are constructed and defined based on cultural or social contexts.[9] The masculinities cultivated at Steele are complex. Often they incorporate hip hop identities, therapeutic identities, and a positive or good personhood, where one gives back to the community.

Conclusion

Demographically these young men resemble the young Black men Anderson and Rios discuss in their books on poor, urban, young, Black men. Both Anderson (1990; 2008) and Rios (2011) maintain that criminal behavior is a viable way for these young men to communicate, demonstrate, and develop their manhood.[10] In many ways these scholars recapitulate the most common ways in which African American men are identified, as criminals, as men needing to be contained or policed, often with essentialized hip hop masculinities (Neal 2013). While in many ways my research supports these claims, revealing the racial bias in the institutionalizing of young Black men into psychiatric custody, the perpetuation of criminal identities for these youth, and the power of hip hop in defining manhood, I also found these versions of manhood did not cover the ways in which youth at Havenwood and Steele defined themselves as men. Derrick, Lamar, and William propose other ways of demonstrating their manhood, ways not predicated on violence or criminality. Rather, these boys are becoming particular kinds of men by living in psychiatric custody.

In his Staffing, Derrick gets upset, but he quickly recovers and uses his words. He sees himself as changing along this path—from a person who used to smoke weed or fight to disengage from the world, to one who can talk about his feelings, not snap on people, and use the skills that he learned. If he continues to do this, he is a good man. William learns that honesty and talking about what is bothering him means that he is improving. Improving helps him to be trusted by staff, trusted to do what is right even when they are not around. Lamar wants to be positive in his life, to give back, and to work with his friends to help the community and kids. He begins this idealized future in small ways by being present as a father, one who can read well enough to take the public transportation to visit his child. He does this, despite not having his own father and living in psychiatric custody. Derrick, William, Lamar, and other youth not mentioned here, embed their emergent, rapping, reading, trustworthy masculine selves in mentoring relationships and in positive peer relationships or friendships, and enact it by learning to care about and trust other Black men.

Part III
Subjects and Power

Chapter 8

A Hip Hop-Therapeutic Subjectivity

The concept behind Do You is fairly straightforward: Always try and be yourself . . . The first step is knowing yourself—who you are and what you stand for. And the only way to do that is to be in touch with that higher voice inside of you.

—*Russell Simmons*

Do You!
Do you: Do your thing. Don't worry what other people think.

—*Alonzo Westbrook* Hip Hoptionary

"I want to say some things about Chris before we have cake and ice cream," Steve states. Chris and Derrick stop their dance-off and Allen turns down the music. Chris is leaving Steele and moving to a group home, and Steele Cottage staff members are throwing him a going away party. Everyone at Steele has been invited, as well as a few other friends from across campus. Like most events at Havenwood, the going away party is shaped by therapeutic and hip hop logic and practice. Steve asks that the dancing, laughing, and talking stop so people can share their thoughts and feeling with Chris, as he makes this very important life transition.

We know from an earlier group session in chapter 4 that Chris has worked with Steve for four years. He was 11 when he came to Havenwood and began working with Steve and others. He is now 15, and so successful at Steele that Havenwood has decided that it is time for him to move on. It has been difficult for many of the staff members to let Chris go, just when he is doing well and because he is only 15. Nonetheless, he is moving on and tonight's party is to share with him our good wishes and advice.

Steve looks at William and nods.

"We have been here together and you got your stuff together. Go out there and continue doing what you do," William tells Chris.

Chris nods.

Derrick sees that it is his turn, "Thanks for everything, go do what you do."

There is a short pause. Because it is a going away party and not a group session, everyone is not required to share.

Allen breaks the silence, "You have come a long way man and you got to go out there and do your own thing, keep your head together and do what you need to do." Chris looks at Allen for a few beats and nods in response.

"You got this, go out, do what you do," Manny tells him.

"Thanks, man," Chris responds.

Because Chris was so young when he arrived at Havenwood, he was first placed at the youngest boys' cottage. His supervisor from that cottage is at the party and shares with him some insight, "Remember Steele when you are out there. You learned a lot here and you need to remember what you were taught here when you are out there. Use those instincts you learned here and you can do it."

Arthur chimes in, "Keep your nose clean."

"Baby, you know we're gonna miss you around here. But go out there and do your thing," Angie tells him.

"Thanks, Angie," Chris smiles.

Steve looks at me. "I have only known you a few months but you have impressed me, I think you are a very talented and though it won't be easy, you can do it," I state.

"Anyone else?" Steve asks. No one offers to share anything else. Steve continues, "I am not going to tell you everything right now, I will wait and do my thing tomorrow...but you aren't going to be perfect, the thing is to think. You are getting older and things matter and you need to keep your nose clean. Do your thing." There is a pause to let the words sink in a bit. "Okay, let's get some cake and ice cream."

The latest Chris Brown song is turned on again, the young men bust out more dance moves, and we continue our celebration of Chris's success.

* * *

I began this chapter with Chris's going away party. Chris has been in psychiatric custody for at least four years, and it has been decided by clinicians that he no longer needs to be institutionalized. He "maximized the program," and thus has proven he can live in a "less restrictive environment." Chris is given a going away party where his friends, peers, and staff members remind him of the most important lessons they have learned together at Steele.

Allen and the young boys' cottage supervisor remind Chris that he has learned a lot at Steele. Allen, Arthur, and Steve remind Chris to keep his nose clean or his head together. And many of the other comments remind Chris to *do you*. In this chapter, I focus on the subjects cultivated at Havenwood and Steele. As we have seen, therapeutic logic and practice are mixed with hip hop sensibilities, frameworks, and practices in the treatment process. I argue that these logics and practices result in hip hop-therapeutic subjectivities.

Making Better Choices and Keeping Your Nose Clean

It is a common feature of cognitive behavior therapy and psychiatric treatment to get patients to make good choices in an effort to determine life trajectories (Brodwin 2013). The idea that there is a self that is in control, choosing either to behave badly or to follow the rules is endemic to American psychiatric ideology (Gaines 1992). Waldram (2012), in his work on sexual offenders in prison, illustrates how choice and agency are central elements to what he calls the inmates' "habilitation." Inmates are given considerable agency to either choose to offend or choose not to offend. In her work on maximum-security prisoners, Rhodes (2004) also illustrates how the *will* of the inmates is the focus of coercion. The will is the seat of agency, of control, of choice and, therefore, the will is what must be transformed. The overarching framework at Havenwood is also about getting the youth to make better choices. I began the book with clinicians struggling to understand how they can get young people to realize they need treatment and then to get them to make better choices, which illustrate that they are "really changing." This problematic—how do you get a resident to buy into his own treatment, a treatment that is predicated on "really changing" versus merely following the rules—is the cornerstone of psychiatric treatment at Havenwood, and it reflects cognitive behavioral therapy and psychiatric treatment paradigms.

I have illustrated throughout the book how young people come to integrate therapeutic frameworks into their lives. Garrett wants to have a group therapy session to discuss and work through problems in chapter 5. Derrick "uses his words" in his Staffing in chapter 7, when he "recovers" from getting mad at Ernest, but before he "snaps on" him. In chapter 7, we also hear how William learns to be trustworthy and how Lamar learns to read as markers of them making better choices and becoming good men. Derrick, William, and Wesley discuss in their life history interviews how they have changed while in treatment, honing in on the therapeutic logic they have learned:

Katie: What things about you have changed?
Derrick: A lot. For instance, the way I approach things. If I think you have on my shirt, I'm won't say "Dude, up my shirt!!" I'll say, "Man I got a shirt like that, you sure that's yours?" You know what I'm sayin'? Or when I'm mad, I rap insteada tryin' to fight or smoke weed to get away. Instead of smoking weed to clear my problems, actually talk about it, tell my momma how I feel. You know, let my family know from my point of view.

* * *

Katie: Why are you leaving Havenwood?
Wesley: [I'd leave because I] maintain my treatment. I show them that I am ready to leave, that I learned from staying here.
Katie: What kinds of things have you learned, can you list them?
Wesley: Social skills, peer interaction. Um
Katie: Can you give me a specific example of social skills?
Wesley: Talkin' with my staff, talkin' my problems out with my staff or my peers. If you got problems, solve them without getting in trouble.
Katie: What would it be like, what kinds of problems?
Wesley: Like if I was to get into it with one of my peers or like if we playing something together as a team and I started hollerin' at him I'd find ways to talk to him without bringing him down, encourage him to do better.

* * *

Katie: Why are you leaving Havenwood?
William: Because my behaviors have decreased, my aggression, restraints, my defiant behavior, my opposition, my thinking before I do something.
Katie: Can you explain those behaviors explicitly?
William: Like aggression, when I hit somebody or I feel I am being antagonized I try to defend myself with aggressive behaviors. Defiant I automatically...like when somebody tells me to do something I do the opposite anyway. Without thinking before I do something is like I like doing the wrong thing, I just don't think about it. Well I think about it but I don't think about the consequence.

Katie: How did those things change?

William: Well, the reason I think these things changed is because now I try to think about the consequences too. I'm not gonna say I don't do it, I still do it sometimes but I don't do it as much.

Katie: What things about you have changed? Or improved?

William: Like when I first got here, I couldn't take no redirection without giving lip back. I either yell or I'll curse or I'll give attitude. But now staff tell me to do something most of the time I do what they say. I still give lip back sometimes but I do what they say. If I have a question, I ask after I do it appropriately.

Katie: What's the difference between giving lip back and doing it appropriately?

William: I either yell or I'll curse or I'll give attitude. But when I do it appropriately I don't do those things plus I be calm. I talk to staff and I get a reply back. When I do it negatively, when I yell they don't listen. When I bring it to them calmly I get a reason and they talk to me. I speak up for myself but I do it appropriately.

Derrick learns to approach things differently. He will talk about his feelings, rather than get high to get away from them. He will also approach others who he thinks might have wronged him with respect, rather than be aggressive. Wesley will talk about his problems and try to solve them without getting into trouble. He will also encourage his peers to do better, rather than "bring them down." William's provoking behaviors have "decreased" by thinking about the consequences of his actions and rather than "give lip" or attitude, he talks to staff about his concerns and his need to understand why he is doing something. He still speaks up for himself but rather than yelling or cursing he does it "appropriately."

These young men talk about how they have internalized or "bought in" to their need to really change. I could argue that they are just following the rules. However, hopefully it has become clear that in most cases these actions can be interpreted as sincere, rather than manipulative. Having watched these young men engage in their treatment process, I err on the side of "really changing," or at least a desire to really change and to share feelings, talk about things appropriately so that others treat you with respect, and to encourage rather than bring others down.

However, these better choices are flavored with something besides pure therapeutic logic. Derrick's use of words is the most clear: I rap instead of trying to fight. As we have seen throughout the book, psychiatric frameworks are not operating alone at Havenwood. In fact, hip hop ideologies and practice shape daily life, as much if not more than therapeutic ones. Therefore, in his going away party it should not be that surprising that most of his friends and peers tell Chris to *do you* as a treatment achievement. They are sampling hip hop ideology into measurements of treatment success. And they are helping define the self or subject that has proven that he no longer needs treatment. This hip hopification of treatment success can best be understood through *do you*.

Do You—Hip Hop Culture and Ideology

I began this chapter with two quotations that define hip hop's *do you*. Hip hop culture producer Russell Simmons (2007) locates himself within a "hip hop nation." Simmons became a hip hop cultural producer and founded Def Jam Records to promote hip hop artists and musicians. From there, Simmons created a hip hop clothing line called Phat Farm, hip hop television programs including Def Comedy Jam and Def Poetry Jam, and even a hip hop social change initiative called Hip hop Summit Action Network. The thread tying all of Simmons's creative and entrepreneurial endeavors together is hip hop. When he decides to write a book about his success he titles this book *Do You!* in recognition of the hip hop phrase that he defines as knowing "who you are and what you stand for" and to "be in touch with that higher voice inside of you" (Simmons 2007:45).

The other quotation at the beginning of this chapter is from Alonzo Westbrook's Hip Hoptionary. Westbrook defines *do you* with "do your thing" revealing, as is evident in Chris's going away party, that these phrases are synonymous. He provides more clarity by stating that to *do you* means to not do what other people think. Both Westbrook and Simmons clearly understand the phrase *do you* to be grounded in hip hop culture and ideology.

Both Simmons and Westbrook hone in on hip hop's relationship with authenticity—a higher voice inside of you, do not do what other people think. "Staying true to yourself" is one of the most important aspects of hip hop ideology and identity (Harrison 2009; Perry 2004; Rose 2008). Remaining true to oneself is "something I've learned growing up in the hip hop nation, which has always put a priority on integrity and respecting what's real" (Simmons 2007:43). Hip hop scholars argue that hip hop has always cultivated a very dynamic interplay between structure and agency (Harrison 2009; Neal 1999; Perry 2004). The structure that shapes hip hop is an urban context formulated by a racially divided US society, very much a Black male experience (Perry 2008). The agency is the cultivation of an authentic self that prioritizes integrity and what's real.

At Havenwood, the structure that shapes hip hop in the institution is the practice of psychiatric custody that, like urban America and other forms of social abjection and confinement, reveals racial disparities in those who get sent there. The young men at Steele are identified as bad, wrong, and in need of becoming someone else and have been placed at Havenwood to change who they are. The agency cultivated by hip hop ideology, which as we have seen was remarkably not only allowed but also cultivated at Havenwood, helped the young men shape their structure in meaningful ways. This structure and agency relationship not only shaped the practice of treatment but it shaped the changed selves, the transformed subjectivities cultivated in psychiatric custody. *Do you* is an important intersection where the structural scripts that shape hip hop and hip hop's agentic subjectivity converge. On his departure from treatment, the men of Steele remind Chris to *do you*. When he reenters society, Chris should stay true to himself, a self that not only is shaped by hip hop, but by the life he lived and lessons he learned at Steele and Havenwood.

Do You—A Framing of Psychiatric Healing

In the following vignette, I discuss Jonathon and his process of learning *do you* as emblematic of the way do you was integrated in psychiatric practice. *Do you* emerged in other chapters, in other group therapy sessions, in Derrick's Staffing, and in milieu treatment. The phrase and frame is ubiquitous to the treatment process. Here I hone in on one young man's engagement with the framework through intensive work in group therapy and therapeutic conversations with staff members. Jonathon "reveals" his "buying in" to this framework in a discussion overheard, with his friend Lamar. Jonathon's learning process and subsequent revelation illustrate that he learns to integrate *do you* with making better choices, and thereby cultivates a hip hop-therapeutic subjectivity.

Jonathon—Learning *Do You* as Psychiatric Treatment

"Does anyone have anything to add?" Allen is concluding the group session he is leading. William, Lamar, Wesley, Derrick, Jonathon, Kyle, Mark, Marlon, and Dontay are seated on the couches in a horseshoe arrangement, as they often are during group sessions. Steve gets up from his small round table serving as command center and walks into the center of the group. He grabs a dining room chair on his way. The room falls silent; it is rare for Steve to commandeer a group session when another staff member is in charge. Steve flips the chair around and sits, straddling the back. He pulls up the sleeves of his Akademics sweatshirt, places his forearms on the back of the chair, and interlocks his fingers. Steve embodies a particular masculine demeanor; he comes off as tough. He looks around the room. If a pin were to drop, we would hear it.

"Okay, I've been hearing some talk around the unit about some of you bein' on some bullshit." He pauses and looks around at the young men staring back at him. Steve rarely curses. He continues, "You all are gonna get caught up if you continue to do stupid things. I mean I know you wanna smoke your squares, try to be all bad. But let me break it down for you." He pauses again, and tilts his head. Steve has code-switched into a hip hop register that includes phrases like "smoking squares," "breaking it down," and "getting caught up" by police. I've seen Steve use this hip hop register regularly, especially when he wants to relate cottage choices with real-world consequences, where the youth will easily get "caught up" by police if they do stupid things. He continues, "You need to stay on your squares, do your thing, step up and be a man. You can't be worried about what others are doin'. If they out doin' stupid shit, they gonna get caught up. Don't let another nigga try to use you, don't be a send off man." Steve pauses again and looks around to see if the young men are understanding what he is trying to say, especially in the therapeutic context of a group session. "What do I mean by send off man?"

Wesley raises his hand.

"Wesley."

"Doin' something for somebody else." Being a "send off man" is the exact opposite of doing you or "doing your thing," which Steve mentions in his lecture.

Steve leans back in his chair, opens up his hands, emphatically nods his head, and tells him, "My man." Steve sits up straight again and continues his lecture, "You need to do you, don't be anyone's little...." Steve pauses and looks at me, "Excuse me, Katie." I nod, excusing whatever is about to come out of his mouth. "Bitch." He pauses for effect. "You understand?"

The residents nod that they understand.

"Jonathon, you understand?" Steve singles out Jonathon who has been particularly quiet this group session. Jonathon's demeanor tells us that something is wrong: he has a long face, his shoulders are hunched, and he sits slumped over.

Today Jonathon had a Staffing, the quarterly progress meeting described in chapter 7. Jonathon's father came to the campus for the meeting. Jonathon had been excited to see his dad and he longs for his approval. Jonathon's mom is no longer in the picture, and although he has uncles who visited once, his father is his main family member. However, similar to other campus visits, Jonathon's dad had driven the two hours from the city for the Staffing and a family therapy session but spent no other time with his son. Allen told me later that because the Staffing and the family therapy session were scheduled a few hours apart, right over the lunch hour, Steele staff had decided to let Jonathon go to lunch off campus with his father without supervision. He was doing well enough in treatment that they trusted he would not run away. Even though his father seldom answered the phone when Jonathon called, Allen and others still hoped the two would spend quality time over lunch. However, Jonathon's father did not invite Jonathon along when he went to lunch. I attended the Staffing. Jonathon's father had been particularly hard on Jonathon, questioning his treatment successes, including what his dad called Jonathon's "so-called tutoring sessions." Jonathon had asked me to tutor him for a college entrance exam, and we met twice a week. Someone informed Jonathon's father that I was the tutor (sitting right there in the Staffing) and I was asked to report on Jonathon's work during our sessions. Jonathon's father responded somewhat sheepishly with an "Oh," after he learned that the so-called sessions were not only real but demanded a lot of work on Jonathon's behalf. In the Staffing, Jonathon's father was dismissive about Jonathon's treatment successes and did not believe that he was really progressing. After the Staffing, Jonathon seemed upset, extra quiet, distracted, and close to tears for much of the rest of the day. Jonathon is notorious for running away when he was upset; he went AWOL after most of the visits from his father.

Jonathon keeps his head down and nods almost imperceptively.

"Look at me, son," Steve softens and lowers his voice. Steve uses the term of endearment, a kin-term to make headway with Jonathon during their interaction.

Jonathon does not look up. He blinks hard.

"Do you want to go to the hallway? Look at me." Steve reminds Jonathon that not listening will result in a consequence; he will be excluded from group therapy and have to sit in the hallway to process with a staff member.

Jonathon slowly raises his head, his face has fallen and he looks on the verge of tears. He looks Steve in the eyes.

Steve meets his gaze, "You can't be worried about what others are doing. You gotta focus on yourself, do you. Do what you need to do to get up outta here. You understand?" Steve continues with the *do you* framework, reminding Jonathon that in order to successfully get out of treatment he has to focus on himself or *do you*.

Jonathon nods.

"Do you understand? Use your words, son," Steve's soft and low voice has returned and he uses therapeutic advice. Using one's words cultivates self-confidence and is identified as a "better choice" than fighting or getting angry. Steve also wants Jonathon to use his voice to articulate that he has understood what Steve is telling him.

"Yeah," Jonathon manages.

Steve takes the focus off of Jonathon, "You all understand?"

"Yes," and nods abound from the boys in group.

"Okay, constructive." Steve releases them to have "constructive free time" before dinnertime.

I watch Jonathon get up and slowly make his way outside. Derrick is trying to cheer him up by asking him if he wants to play some hoops. They are both on Levels that will allow them to walk over to the outdoor basketball court by themselves. Jonathon declines the offer; instead he sits on the picnic bench outside of Steele Cottage.

A few hours later, during the evening hours, after dinner, Quiet Time, and Chores, I once again notice that Jonathon is sitting by himself in the living room. His brow is furrowed and he looks deep in thought. Arthur is on shift tonight and Jonathon usually asks him to play Spades. However, Jonathon is not doing anything that usually makes him happy. He seems very pensive and quite uncomfortable.

Later in the evening, Jonathon walks up to where Arthur and I are sitting, near the staff desk and office in the main living room area. He looks at Arthur with a look of desperation. "What is the difference between being selfish and focusing on yourself?" Without waiting for an answer, he continues, "Because y'all say I'm supposed to be focusing on myself but my dad is selfish and I don't want to be like that. I don't want to focus on myself if I am going to be selfish." Jonathon needs help in defining the therapeutic concept such as "focusing on himself" especially in relation to his "selfish" father.

Arthur looks at me, he has teased me for being particular about my word choices but he thinks that I can be of some help at the moment. I take out a small pocket Merriam-Webster dictionary and hand it to Arthur. He reads the definition of selfish, "exclusively concerned about one's own well-being." We both look at Jonathon who is in psychiatric custody where his primary focus, his exclusive concern, is about his own well-being. Therefore, according to this definition, Jonathon should be "selfish."

"Maybe self-centered?" I say, thinking this might be a more discerning and helpful definition for Jonathon.

"Concerned only with one's own self," Arthur reads. Again, this is Jonathon's goal in treatment but he is neither selfish nor self-centered in the negative connotation of the words. Jonathon is being told to focus on himself and *do you* so that he can do the work of really changing in treatment and thereby one day "get up outta" there. However, this understanding seems rather close to being selfish, which Jonathon does not want to be. Jonathon understands his father's selfishness as the reason for their poor and disconnected relationship. Jonathon wants to know how to focus on himself without being selfish.

We both look at Jonathon, who seems more confused by the dictionary definitions, as his brow furrows deeper and his eyes move from Arthur to me and back again, pleading for some clarity

Arthur slams the dictionary close and looks directly into Jonathon's eyes and switches into a hip hop register, "I feel you, Jonathon. I do. But you gotta do you man. You gotta worry about finishin' school and gettin up outta here. You can't worry about what your pop's doin'. Do you. Focus on yourself means doin' you and not worrying about if your dad is gonna be there. You can't worry 'bout that." Arthur defines the therapeutic concept of "focus on yourself" with the hip hop definition *do you*. Arthur's move to a hip hop register illustrates hip hop cultural practice and his own hip hop subjectivity. As Arthur makes these shifts in speech style and terminology, he also changes the *way* he speaks. His hand gestures change and he takes on a stronger, more passionate demeanor. Arthur's subjectivity changes from therapeutic staff member to a hip hop-therapeutic staff member.

Arthur's closing of the dictionary and his move to hip hop language allows him to keep it real. He is sincere in his defining of the terms "selfish" and "focus on oneself". He empathizes with Jonathon's struggle and he speaks to him from his heart. The integration of hip hop into Havenwood's therapeutic practice here reveals the cultural embeddedness of hip hop within the treatment paradigm of doing what needs to be done to get out of Havenwood. Jonathon needs to *do you* to get out of treatment, and this includes not worrying about whether his dad is going to be there when he does.

I stand next to Arthur and watch him use a hip hop *do you* framing to better communicate therapeutic logic in real-time therapeutic practice. Silence fills the space after Arthur finishes speaking. Jonathon looks from Arthur to me. He lets out a heavy sigh, nods his head, and walks back to where he was sitting in the living room. Arthur cannot give Jonathon the answers that he desires, precisely because *do you* is an individual lived practice of integrating therapeutic ideals within a hip hop frame. What *do you* means cannot be defined by one person for another. Rather Jonathon has to define and live his own version of *do you*.

Allen, who has been sitting nearby hearing our conversation, breaks the silence, "How do you tell a kid his dad doesn't want him the way he wants him to want him?"

I turn to him and my mouth falls open as the gravity of the question sinks in. How do you tell a boy that his dad does not want to be in his life, even though he wants desperately for him to be there? When he realizes the desperation in Jonathon's gaze and question, Arthur chooses to step back from the therapeutic language of "self" and communicate in the way he is most comfortable with and in a way that he thinks Jonathon will understand. Arthur "feels" Jonathon, he empathizes with him and sincerely engages with him, heart-to-heart. Arthur tells Jonathon he's "gotta do" him in order to "get up outta" treatment. He does not necessarily tell him that his dad does not want him. Arthur and Steve use a hip hop *do you* to reiterate to Jonathon the therapeutic work he needs to do in treatment, he needs to "focus on yourself" and get out of there.

As we have seen throughout the text, hip hop registers are routinely integrated into the therapeutic practice of psychiatric custody at Havenwood. Often hip hop phrases are used to support therapeutic logic, to bring home particular therapeutic points, such as using one's words and not doing stuff for other people that will get you "caught up" by police. It is telling that Arthur slams close the dictionary, an artifact of the most dominant English in American society, when he cannot accurately define therapeutic concepts for Jonathon. The failure to define the concept is not because Arthur is not capable. However, he chooses to make his point clear, to communicate with Jonathon using hip hop language. "I feel you, Jonathon" but "you gotta do you" Arthur tells him. Steve also uses hip hop language to articulate what the young men of Steele want to do, and what will happen to them if they do not "do themselves." Both Arthur's and Steve's words flow smoothly, when they talk to the young men in hip hop language. In order to clear up the difference between "selfish" and "focusing on oneself," hip hop phrases are used. Hip hop is sampled into therapeutic interventions.

Months after this group session and conversation with Jonathon, I find myself talking to Allen outside, as he supervises an afterschool game of therapeutic kickball. In between arguments about who gets to pitch each inning, I ask Allen whether or not he thinks that the older kids "get it," that they need to make important changes, or whether they simply abide the structure of psychiatric custody. I wonder what Allen thinks: Do residents learn to make changes; do they listen to the lessons in group, in the evening hours when they ask for clarification? To echo the psychiatrist from the "Introduction" and the formal treatment paradigms: Are some older youth merely adapting to the structure, or are they really changing?

"Yeah, they get it." He pauses and then hits my shoulder with the back of his hand, a telltale gesture that he is going to relate a story to clarify his point. Allen is a good storyteller and likes to communicate his points with them. "You know when Marlon left and Lamar moved into Jonathon's room?" I nod. I recall when Jonathon and Lamar became roommates. They have been attached at the hip of late, and they had asked specifically to be roommates. "I heard them talking, you know, like the kids do when they become roommates. I heard Jonathon say, 'Fuck my daddy. He is so selfish. I got to do what I got to do. For me. 'Cause he is selfish and he doesn't really care.' I told him that one time [when he was] in crisis, 'Fuck your daddy, fuck your daddy.' He then told his daddy that I said that." Allen looks at me with a can-you-believe-he-told-his-dad-I-said-that look. I chuckle and he continues, "But it is true I mean the mug [Jonathon's dad] only comes up once in a while for a Staffing and then he just hates on you?" Allen shakes his head at Jonathon's father's actions. "But they get it, Kate, some of them do."

Jonathon is hearing *do you* and focus on yourself in various therapeutic modalities. Steve tells him so in group therapy, Arthur tells him so in a therapeutic conversation during milieu treatment, and Allen reminds him of it during a restraint or crisis. According to Allen, after months of treatment and the hearing of *do you* and focus on yourself, Jonathon is "caught" telling his friend and roommate Lamar that he is going to do what he needs to do for himself, that he is focusing on himself rather than on his distant father. Allen thinks that this illustrates how "some of the kids get it," as they are able to integrate the knowledge they are learning in various therapeutic contexts and demonstrate this knowledge and "buy in" during in an intimate conversation with a friend, outside of the earshot and thus the behavior modification system of staff members. In his sharing with Lamar, I argue that Jonathon is revealing a hip hop-therapeutic subjectivity that he is cultivating at Havenwood. Jonathon is learning from Steve, Arthur, and Allen and he is embodying positive self-change and *do you*, he is "buying in" hip hop-therapeutic style.

When *Do You* is Not a "Better Choice": The Fragility and Drama of Healing

I want to return now to Chris. Earlier I illustrated how *do you* is integrated into his going away party and that, at the culmination of four years of psychiatric custodial living, Chris is encouraged to keep his nose clean, follow his Steele-created instincts, and do his thing. However, staff members were very hesitant to let him leave. And when he does leave, he ends up making a therapeutically defined "bad" choice. However, I argue this does not mean he didn't "buy in" or really change. Rather Chris's story reveals the fragility and complexity of healing in this psychiatric context.

Weeks before his going away party the Steele Team discusses his pending departure during a weekly meeting:

"I am seeing Chris and I want to see if he is telling you guys similar things he is telling me. He does not want to go to the group home. He says everyone who goes there fails." Paige, Chris's individual therapist, wants to talk about her client Chris at the Steele Cottage Team Meeting. She looks around the room and continues, "Do any of you get any of that? Is he telling you the same thing?"

"Yeah, he will ask me, 'Angie, why do you want to set me up for failure?' And he wants to stay here with Steve," Angie shares.

This Steele Cottage Team Meeting takes place about a month before Chris's going away party. Steve, Allen, James, and Angie are meeting with Paige, Sarah, the cottage director, and Craig, the case worker helping Chris transition out, to discuss how well Chris has been doing in treatment. According to the clinicians he has mastered the Steele therapeutic program and needs to move on. Chris knows that he will be sent somewhere else to continue the "stepping down" process of therapeutic intervention for children in psychiatric custody. He tries to divert his transitioning-out process by sharing with his therapist and Angie his own trepidation about leaving Steele and being placed in a group home. While this is the logic of therapeutic intervention—Chris has earned the right to live in a group home, a less restrictive environment than a residential treatment—there are mixed feelings about him leaving.

Paige responds to this comment about failure, "Yeah, he will tell me he doesn't have any internal control or impulse control and I will say, 'Yeah, you do.'" He will give me examples of where he doesn't and I will give him examples of where he does. I am not sure if he is just saying this because he thinks this is what I want to hear. He says he won't have any freedoms there, like he does here, and he says he has more freedoms in jail than at the group home."

Sarah disregards the debate Chris has with his therapist about his internal and impulse control and asks about the difference in freedoms between jail and the group home Chris might be sent to, "Does he know that?"

Allen answers, "Well he has been out there [at the group home] and he has been in jail so...." Allen shrugs as if to say "Why not believe him?"

Paige continues, "He said his destiny is to go to jail if he goes to this group home."

Angie piggybacks on Paige's concern, "He will list the kids that have failed out there and he will say, 'I am going to be just like that, Angie'." Chris knows the kids who have been sent to this group home because many of them have come through Havenwood and Steele Cottage. Having spent four years at Steele, Chris knows the young men who he says have failed.

Craig sarcastically states, "Yeah that's right, he has no choice but to fail."

Sarah is intrigued by the "destiny" comment and the disregard for the ideology of choice which is important in the clinical program of Havenwood, "Do the kids think and talk this way, that they have a destiny? We want them to see that they have choices, and they have to make those choices for themselves. He has to make the most of the Program out there. He is done here."

Sarah has mobilized the therapeutic framework of choice and that it is up to Chris to make choices about his future because he has maximized the program at Steele. As a counter framework, Angie mentions the quasi-kinship ties between Chris and the staff members and peers built at Steele. "But this is the only family he knows. He has learned the Program but this is his *home*, he has nowhere else," Angie states.

Angie's argument of the familial ties between Chris and the staff, and is concerned about what Sarah is asking of Chris. "If a kid were in a foster family, he wouldn't do well and then the family would say, 'OK, now that you are doing well, time to move to another family.' I know this is treatment, but this is his family too. He is young; he is 15, not 17 or 18. He wants to know why you want to move him when he is finally doing well." James does not think that it is a good idea to move Chris right when he is being successful, especially being a young teenager. He believes that making Chris leave is not right, even if it is the psychiatrically defined next step.

Sarah, the constant professional, replies rather stoically, "It is unfortunate other kids haven't done well at the group home but we have to send kids there, it is part of Havenwood."

Angie tries to say something but Sarah cuts her off, "He has to leave, he has maximized this Program, he has done all he can do here at Steele. He has to move on. Our response to his fears about failure is to say, 'It is up to you, you can control what happens, it is on you to fail or make good choices'."

Angie does not want to accept this from Sarah, "But the Program at the group home...."

Steve interrupts Angie and speaks for the first time about Chris's plan. He knows, in the end, he and his staff have no say over the decision to move Chris, regardless of their family-like bonds or Chris's placement at Steele. "This isn't a debate. Chris is leaving and we have to prepare him. The agency has decided. We can't talk about their Program out there, we do what we do, and we prepare him for the move." This "better choice," to move Chris when he has performed so well in treatment is made palpable by reminding the staff members that they will "do what we do" to help him not fail.

Paige wonders, "When does he move?"

"Sometime between November and January, right Sarah?" James asks. It is October 10th, and this will give everyone some time to deal with Chris's pending move.

Craig, who is the liaison between the State and Havenwood, tells everyone, "His state meeting is next Wednesday and he could leave anytime after that."

There are murmurs around the table about the suddenness of this time frame. Chris, who has lived at Steele and worked with the staff there for years, and has built family-like relationships with the staff could leave in a week. Once he leaves, there is nothing that requires him to remain in contact with Steele, the people he cares about or who care about him. Rather, he will have a new treatment program to learn and new people to get along with.

"What about school? If he could play some sports out there that would be good," James states. He has known Chris the four years he has been at Havenwood and knows that he is particularly interested in basketball and football. He would like to see Chris be able to play some sports and this had been a significant way in which James had helped Chris while at Steele.

"I don't want to do that. I don't want to just throw him out into the school out there. He needs to make that transition slow. He will go to school here. And then maybe have one class at the high school. Once you start just throwing him out there, then he will fail. He needs to make a slow transition," Steve responds.

Angie, knowing who ultimately has the final say about Chris's plan, looks to Sarah, "I agree. Can we make it a slow transition, Sarah?"

Sarah continues with the treatment logic that Chris's choice will ultimately determine his fate and that the staff's feelings of loss should not limit Chris's future. "Part of preparing Chris to leave is to put aside your feelings that he will fail. It is not predetermined that he will fail. Put it on him. You have to believe in him a little bit and help him believe that his failure isn't predetermined."

"It isn't about that," Steve interjects. "Kids are changing and we need to remember where they come from and it can be scary for them. It is real for them. He is going. We will make it a gradual thing by getting him over there and then not throwing him out into the high school." Steve reminds everyone about the reality of Chris's situation without going into detail. Psychiatric custodial ideologies maintain that it is "on" Chris to fail or be successful. Steve knows that this is not necessarily true. Sure, Chris has been changing, but it is scary for him to return to mainstream social life. Not only has Chris been living in psychiatric custody for four years, but Steve refers to where Chris "came from." He grew up in foster care because he was removed from his biological family's custody due to abuse and neglect. In addition, he grew up in the poorer parts of the neighboring city and has been to jail. Therefore, on top of having lived in treatment 4 of his 15 years and his lack of family ties, Steve also knows that it is scary for young Black men in America to return to urban life without a strong family. Chris's fears of going to jail reflect not only his lived experience but the realities for young African American male teenagers. Even though Chris has proven that he has really changed, the social situation is precarious and scary for young Black men like Chris.

Angie sighs but states, "OK."

Chris's going away party is thrown a month after this meeting. As we saw, Chris is reminded to keep his nose clean and do his thing at the group home when he gets out. He is also called "baby" by Angie, and reminded that he will be missed at the cottage.

* * *

At first glance, it appears that *do you* and Sarah's phrases "It is up to you, you can control what happens, it is on you to fail or make good choices" are similar frameworks of choice, control, and agency. However, upon further scrutiny the differences between these two frameworks emerge. Because Havenwood is a psychiatric center and a total institution designed to reshape the individuals who live there, it comes as no surprise that in the Team Meeting about Chris, Sarah, the voice of psychiatry treatment paradigms, would instruct the staff members to focus on Chris's choices. They are to remind Chris that it is "up to him" to "fail or make better choices."

Do you is different than the psychiatric framework of choosing to fail or to make better choices. *Do you* is about "staying true to yourself." rather than following any particular orders, trends, or rules. Psychiatric logic maintains that there is a hierarchy of choices, some are better than others (Waldram 2012). These "better choices" are often in line with mainstream social parameters of good behavior. One makes "better choices" when one chooses to behave appropriately, according to hegemonic social norms, rules, and laws. Sometimes "staying true to yourself," doing you, or being authentic requires that an individual resists mainstream social protocol. In fact, Simmons (2007) and Westbrook (2002) argue that that is precisely what *do you* is—a staying true to oneself, no matter what other people think or what the current trends are. Black street culture, the home of hip hop, is predicated on an "oppositional" lifestyle or counterhegemonic ideology. *Do you* is a choice framework that not only allows for residents to not be perfect and to make bad choices. It also allows for oppositional behavior, especially because it is rooted in hip hop ideology. Sometimes, *doing you* means not making psychiatrically defined better choices.

Chris is an illustrative case, in the end he "does himself." Chris shirks psychiatrically defined better choices and runs away from the group home. However, he does not end up in jail.

On a Tuesday in January 2007 during a Team Meeting at Steele the phone rings. James jogs over to answer it. He talks for a minute, hangs up, and returns to the meeting.

> He looks at Steve, "Chris. Said he'll call back."
> "Chris calls you?!" Paige, Chris's individual therapist, almost shouts.
> "Yeah," Steve confirms, "He calls twice a week."
> "Where is he?" Paige asks.
> "At his Grandma's house. He's doin' his thing."
> Shortly after he moved into the group home, Chris ran away; he went AWOL.

Havenwood holds Chris's spot for 30 days, in case he is picked up by police and returned to the institution or he returns on his own (often at the behest of family members). It is illegal for Havenwood youth to go AWOL, and warrants are issued for their arrest until they turn 18 years old. Nonetheless, it was more common for Steele youth to run away from Havenwood than to "step down" along the psychiatric continuum of care—from custody to group home to independent living. Derrick, Lamar, Jonathon, Chris, Kyle, and Manny went AWOL and thus ended their treatment themselves.

According to the better choice model, the "better choice" for Chris, and others, is to work the Program at the new placement. However, by running away Chris is "doing his thing." Doing himself, included running away from the group home and "keeping his nose clean" so he can stay at his grandmother's house. Few staff members at Steele were surprised by the reality that most of the young men left Havenwood by running away. I was informed that the decision to run away meant a young man "got tired of being a treatment kid and was making his own way." In other words, doing you sometimes means making psychiatrically defined bad choices.

However, Chris calls Steve and Steele twice a week. When Steve says Chris is "doing his thing" this includes keeping his nose clean at his grandma's house and also his biweekly phone calls. Chris calls and checks in with Steve. Chris tells Steele staff members, usually Allen or Steve, him how he is doing, how he is not getting into trouble. He is also maintaining the close relationships he has built with staff members. I once answered the phone when Chris called. We talked for a few minutes about how people were doing at Steele, his peers and staff members. He even inquired about the status of my research project and book. He maintained, as closely as he could, the relationships that emerged from his stay at Steele. Despite the lack of proximity, he maintained emotional bonds with people and he ensured we all were aware of his life outside and successes outside of Steele. Many of the youth who went AWOL called regularly to check in. I argue, using Chris's choice to run away from the group home but remain in contact with Steve and Steele, that this is an example to reflect the hip hop-therapeutic subjectivity cultivated at Havenwood and Steele Cottage. Chris "does himself," which includes biweekly check in phone calls with staff members, as well as a decision to run away from psychiatric custody. *Do you* is a mixture of better choices and authentic, autonomous counterhegemonic practices, a hip hop-therapeutic subjectivity.

In their work with families in Los Angeles who have children with significant illnesses and disabilities, Cheryl Mattingly and Mary Lawlor argue that "beneath the highly visible machinery of the modern clinic, with its elaborate technology, mind-numbing routinization, and cool dispassion, all sorts of strange and even miraculous healing dramas may spring up, and in the most unlikely of ways" (2001:52; see also Mattingly 2010). In these healing dramas are significant moments of creation that "reveal possible worlds and possible selves" (2001:54). At Steele these healing dramas include a sampling of hip hop into the context and practice of the routinized and dispassionate psychiatric custody. The possible selves that emerge include selves that learn to talk about feelings with a parent rather than to fight, that encourage peers and friends rather than bring them down, and that respond to staff members without giving lip all of the time. These selves include those that can focus on oneself without being selfish. These selves can also not always make good choices, not be perfect, as Steve tells Chris in his going away party, but still do themselves and keep their noses clean. William states it best—healing is not an all or nothing kind of a thing. It is an improvement rather than a change, a giving of lip sometimes but sometimes doing it appropriately, a running away but calling to check in. It is both buying in to and opposing hegemonic psychiatric constraints. We see Jonathon learn, or as Allen would say "get it," this dynamic slowly, through the work of various interventions through the work of cultivating possible selves. While I have not focused on the outcome of treatment in this book, the practice of treatment has illustrated that healing dramas occur at Havenwood and Steele, as young men work with their staff members and peers to emerge from treatment with a better choice making, *doing you* self, a hip hop-therapeutic subjectivity.

Chapter 9

Mad Love: Theorizing and Politicizing Transformation

If black males were loved they could hope for more than a life locked down, caged, confined; they could imagine themselves beyond containment.

—*bell hooks* We Real Cool

"Lamar's not going to make the interview," Steve tells me as I walk into Steele Cottage. Earlier in the week I had arranged with Steve and Lamar to interview Lamar that fall afternoon. I had to arrange all of my interviews with the cottage supervisors.

"Why not?" I ask, as I pull up a chair next to him. I was expecting to hear that Lamar was in therapy, individual or recreational, at the moment or that he had chosen to do something more fun.

"He's locked up."

"What?!" I exclaim. "What happened?"

"He and Jonathon were out on a pass and they got picked up."

"For what?" I ask, still shocked.

At that moment Jonathon walks in the door with Allen. Jonathon looks sullen, dejected.

"You OK?" Steve asks Jonathon. He does not answer. "Go get washed up, we'll talk after that." Jonathon nods and heads to the back of the cottage to get cleaned up.

"They're transferring Lamar," Allen tells Steve. Steve purses his lips and shakes his head. He gets up and follows Jonathon to the back. Steve will probably "process" with Jonathon back there.

Allen looks at me and shakes his head. I have been sitting there, confused and fearful about what is going on. I wait; maybe Allen will tell me what is going on without my prying.

"They were out on a pass, walking to McDonald's. They get stopped by police. Apparently, Lamar has a warrant out for his arrest. He failed to show up for court last month. So they take both of them in." He pauses and shakes his head, "They weren't gone long enough to get into trouble."

I let the information sink in. It happens all of the time; police will stop Havenwood youth when they are walking off campus. Around campus they call it "walking while Black." Because Havenwood is located in a very white rural area of a midwestern state, African American youth stick out. They are also regularly profiled, assumed to be running away from campus or up to no good. Allen would not put it past them to do something to get themselves into trouble; they are teenagers after all. But today, he thinks they have not been gone long enough to do so. It does not sit right.

Jonathon and Lamar were doing so well in treatment that they had earned "off-campus passes." These passes allowed the lavish privilege of being off campus for an hour or two, once a week. Most of the time youth on passes walk to the McDonald's or Walgreens, a mile away. Jonathon and Lamar are close friends and they used their passes together. They saved their passes for the same day. It was rare to see the youth exploit the passes by misbehaving. They did not want to lose the privilege of not walking in a single file line or being off campus without supervising staff. It was in these rare instances that the youth were able to be regular teenagers for a few hours, hanging out at McDonald's on their own. In their few moments of freedom from supervising staff, just off Havenwood's grounds, Lamar and Jonathon get stopped by local police. Their two-hour well-earned pass to freedom cut short.

"What's the warrant about? What do you mean, court? Lamar has been here for four months, if he didn't show up for court isn't that the case worker's...." I let the accusation remain unsaid as I realize what has happened. Lamar's formal relationship with the outside world—his court appearance, his treatment meetings with state funders, and his ability to visit family members—is taken care of by Havenwood's case workers. Lamar has recently moved to Havenwood from another residential treatment center, which had been shut down. The case worker, who missed the court appearance, would link the missed court date with improperly filed paperwork or a misstep in the transfer process. Lamar is now in jail because police stopped him while he was out on a pass, "walking while Black," and his case worker had missed a court appearance.

Allen watches me as I make all of these connections in my head and my facial expression turns from confusion to anger. He curls his lips in and raises his eyebrows in a silent gesture of "Yep, that's right."

"And, of course, the police wouldn't just let him come back here with you and Jonathon. They know all of that. They know Lamar is not responsible for his court appearance as a Havenwood kid. He's fifteen!" I let out a heavy sigh, and then quietly curse. The injustice makes my stomach turn. Lamar has been doing so well in treatment. He has even taken Tye, a younger developmentally delayed resident, under his wing. He is easy to get along with, and laughs readily. The "hateful unminding bastard" with all of the "anger built up inside" is starting to be talk and work through his issues. And he and I are working three times a week, for an hour, to improve his reading skills, which he asked me for help with. He is becoming a good man, constructing a hip hop therapeutic subjectivity. None of that matters right now, as he is being transferred to a different detention facility and, because it is the weekend, will likely remain there for a few days.

Jonathon and Steve emerge from the back of the cottage. Jonathon remains sullen the rest of the evening. He is not in trouble but is clearly upset. I imagine that he is worried about his friend. Jonathon is patted on the back by a few of the other residents. Steve is also quiet.

Steve, Allen, and the other line staff of Steele Cottage and Havenwood are familiar with this situation. As African American men they are all too familiar with the injustices of the criminal justice system, racial profiling, and that the youth are bound to be stopped or picked up for "walking while Black." They have, throughout their lifetimes, experienced many of these same State aggressions and injustices. The line staff have a different set of knowledge than just the clinical knowledge of "making better choices"; they hold a different position on what it means to be a psychiatrically institutionalized Black boy in the racially oppressive United States.

Later in the evening Steve asks me if I want to "try and call up there," see if the detention center will let me, a white female voice, speak to Lamar. This was the only time I was asked to use my white privilege, and it was the only time I was asked to engage with the outside world on behalf of any of the residents.[1] As I dialed I felt like this was all we could do to connect with Lamar, to let him know that he is not alone or forgotten. I call and after they put me on hold for a few moments I am told that he "isn't taking phone calls." Lamar is on his own.

Lamar returns a couple of days later in the company of Steele's case worker, Craig. When Craig drops Lamar off Craig takes a form over to Steve who is sitting at his usual command-center table. No one says anything, but Steve stares Craig down. Craig groans, shrugs, and then sighs as he walks out the door. He does not make excuses, nor does he apologize for his part in Lamar's detainment. Steve does not make a sound.

Lamar's demeanor has changed. The once gregarious young man who usually displayed bravado and silliness at the same time is more on edge, quiet, and distant. He moves gingerly the first few days back; he seems physically sore. He is a small 15 year old, no bigger than 5'4" and 140 pounds and my mind imagines all of the horrible things that happened to him while he was locked up. He does not want to talk about it, and he remains distant for a few days. He does not share in group therapy sessions, he rarely really interacts with anyone, and he does not laugh. He is not pressured to speak in group sessions or to engage in his usual ways; his staff give him the space to negotiate his return in many ways.

After a while, however, Lamar returns to his "old self," the one who laughs, gives advice, and is a leader in the cottage. He and Jonathon are as close as before. Lamar and I restart our tutoring sessions and he is just as committed to his literacy. We reschedule our interview; he is as informative and forthright as ever. Soon he joined the other youth who could go off campus to the skating rink, the mall, and to the movies as a group, with staff supervising. It takes a few weeks for Lamar to go off campus on a pass, despite earning them repeatedly in treatment. But eventually he does. At some point he has to venture out again on his own.

Discipline: Psychiatry and Hip Hop

Foucault (1965/1988; 1977/1995) tells us that institutions like prisons and asylums change people through particular disciplinary procedures. These disciplinary procedures include infrastructural containment, discourses of proper subject formation, and the implementation of these discourses into organized practices for those contained. Through the power of these disciplinary procedures individuals come to see themselves through the discursive lens. Rather than simply changing behaviors and actions to fit with social rules, Foucault states that individuals come to believe in their own subjugation; their souls are transformed.

In psychiatric custody these disciplinary procedures include containment in the institution, the Cottage Program, the routine or schedule, and the use of physical restraints. The discourse of proper subject formation is psychiatry. The everyday practices—individual therapy, psychotropic medication use, group therapy, and milieu treatment—that shape quotidian life at Havenwood are psychiatric practices. Through these practices, the youth learn to deal with their issues; healing is framed using psychiatry.

Over the course of their tenure at Havenwood, youth come to participate in group therapy, and to help others do so as well. They learn to "use their words" and to "improve" by sharing their feelings. They try to and become role models, and they ask that others do so as well. Steele youth want to use the skills they learn at Havenwood to go out and be good men in the world. They do not want to snap on people, but rather, to treat them with respect. The youth of Havenwood are enveloped by psychiatry and this power shapes their experiences, practices, and understandings of themselves as subjects.

Those who work at Havenwood are supposed to implement these practices and use these discourses. They too are technologies of power, teaching the young men and women to understand themselves as psychiatrically ill, having issues, and needing to deal with their anger and aggression.

Although the adults are hired as technologies of government, to implement psychiatric practices and to discipline the youth according to psychiatric knowledge and discourse, many of these adults are African American and they exhibit considerable agency and conscious interpretation of psychiatric discourse. While they want the youth to heal and improve, many of the adults of Havenwood see a strong link between hegemonic discourses of psychiatry and white supremacy. In addition, many are familiar with counterhegemonic discourses, including and especially that of hip hop. Therefore, life and treatment at Havenwood and Steele are not just about proper behavior defined by psychiatry but include the hip hopified version of psychiatry, which includes hip hop uniforms, keepin' it real groups, and *do you* definitions of treatment success.

At Havenwood, the discourse of psychiatry shares power with hip hop framings; recovery is linked with *do you* and "not being perfect." As adults teach *do you* rather than to always make better choices, the African American adults are less technologies of government and more translators of discourses, they provide a buffer for the constraining treatment process. The staff members code-switch between these discourses, teaching the youth to learn how to discern and integrate the power of each one.

The integration of these discourses is fluid, live, and sincere. Ultimately, the goal is to have proper behavior (e.g., use one's words) and to be good men, but the discipline to achieve this is less fierce, less enveloping, and less demanding as it is diluted with other discourses and practices that encourage individual sincerity, allow for imperfection, and cultivate *do you*. When someone does not follow the contours of psychiatry at Havenwood the youth are not identified as "bad" or morally wanting. The integration of psychiatry and hip hop leaves room for all kinds of scenarios or healing dramas to play out—for white supremacy to shape the placement practices and policies, for people in society to make you angry, for the youth to mess up, for running away and calling to check in, for friendships among criminals, for keepin' it real groups, and for compassion despite and because of *crazy shit*.

The power that allows for such integration, for the live, spontaneous subject-to-subject translation of various discourses, for structural oppression to be integrated with human frailty and imperfection is love.

Love as Transformative Power

Foucault (1977/1995) argues that over time the prisoner comes to internalize the gaze; the prisoner comes to discipline himself according to systems of knowledge and discourses. In the panopticon prison, individuals come to internalize the gaze of the inspection house, disciplining their souls to the discourses of proper behavior. Power in this instance is the gaze, the perceived or assumed surveillance. Regardless of whether the gaze is actually present or not, the prisoner believes that he is being watched and he disciplines himself accordingly.

Much like the way the internalization of the gaze and the subsequent disciplining of oneself to its power works, the youth of Havenwood come to relate to themselves and others according to the disciplinary power of love. What is different is that love is inherently intersubjective. The "gaze" is replaced by intimate, interpersonal interaction. As we have seen in this book, close, personal interactions are the driving or disciplinary force of transformation, change, and healing.

Adults like Steve, Allen, Angie, and James struggle to let young men like Chris leave the institution because they are the "only family he knows." They work "damn hard" with the boys and love them all along the way. Youth like Lamar come to view the other men who live in his cottage not as criminals, but as peers, even friends. Lamar comes to see his friends as having much love for him. Garrett responds empathically and compassionately to Travis in crisis; he even asks for a group session to help Travis deal with his issues. Jonathon and

Chris learn to *do you*. Jonathon learns it as a response to his father "hating on him" and his lack of parental support. Chris learns it as he has to make his way back into society as an independent individual despite the fact that, as a 15-year-old African American without much of a family or social support, he is scared to do so. From the mad love of Steve, Derrick learns to tell his mom how he feels, rather than get high or angry. William is improving because he becomes trustworthy, and one day maybe, he will be able to ask for a hug from Steve, who will gladly give him one. Love allows Lamar to see himself not as a "hateful unminding bastard" but as someone who could do something positive with his life and be playful at times. The young men develop new subjectivities that relate to others and themselves in new ways. These subjects relate through kindness, compassion, understanding, affection, respect, and forgiveness. Taken together, I argue that the power at work at Havenwood is love.

In the vignette just mentioned, no one mentions love. However, what we have seen at Steele Cottage is how the context is set up to provide a safe place, a place where staff members are family and peers/homies/friends have much love for one another. This loving space at Steele not only cultivates change in the individual residents, but it is maintained as a safe space for abused and neglected children, who have and will face, throughout their lives, State violence and racial oppression.

All of the Black men of Steele understand what happened to Lamar when he ventured out into mainstream society. Lamar experiences institutional racism, in the form of policemen picking him up for "walking while Black." The officers do not let him go, once they have the information, reminding Lamar that he is powerless against the system, if they so choose. Jonathon is profiled and hassled by policemen; there was no warrant for Jonathon's arrest, nor had he done anything to cause him to be stopped. Steve and Allen know all too well the ways in which Black men are stereotyped, judged, and persecuted in the United States; they have decades of living there and history teaches of such violence. Allen has shared more of his personal stories of racism with me; Steve nods in agreement. Steve, Jonathon, and Lamar embody the powerlessness they feel by closing up, quieting down, and shrinking into themselves. As with restraints and crises, the cottage had a shift in energy with this event. Everyone seemed a bit ill at ease, laughter was heard less, voices were lowered, and play was rare. As a form of violence, racism unmakes your world (Scarry 1985). If you let it, racism can take the successes out of your treatment progress.

But the cottage eventually returns to normal and the Spades games return, the dance-offs are on, and laughter is heard. Eventually, Lamar goes out again on pass. Something more powerful than racism induced powerlessness, or the subjugation to the practices and enactments of white supremacy, operates at Steele. Jonathon finds a safe place to land, when he returns to Steele after being arrested and detained. Everyone lets him be for a while, allowing him to recover in his own time. The same treatment is true for Lamar. Friends try to get him to play, but they allow him space to say no, to *do his thing*, to recover in his own time. Much like the way disgust operates, as discussed in chapter 4, there is something that does not allow racism to discipline the young men to morally judge or subjugate one another or themselves. They do not come to see themselves or one another as bad, morally wanting, and deserving the harassment or punishment by police. In fact, most change their perceptions while at Havenwood. Something at Steele operates as a balm to the racism found in society. The balm is love—in the forms of kindness, compassion, understanding, affection, respect, and forgiveness. Love at Steele is not an antidote; racism shapes the youths' lives, as race shapes all of our lives. However, while the youth are still living at Steele, the intimate environment and loving relationships there provide a balm to the wounds that racism inflicts. Love in this case is the power at work as African American men go about healing and befriending one another, despite the broader, racially unequal US society. It is the power that encourages them to *do you,* because making better choices doesn't always matter. Steele's loving environment and the work that is done there is not just psychiatric treatment, but an African American counterhegemonic response to American racism, prejudice, and injustice.

In 2011, anthropologist Michael Hardt inquires into a political concept of love. "What if" he asks, "we were able to identify or invent another love, a love that is properly political?" (Hardt 2011:678). I would like to offer an ethnographic example of this kind of love: the *mad love* that emerges at Steele Cottage.

A political concept of love would have three qualities, Hardt (2011) continues. It would have to destroy conventional divisions between the pubic and private, it would have to operate through the encounter of difference, and it must transform us, somehow make us better (Hardt 2011:678). The *mad love* that operates at Steele Cottage does these things. As a concept, practice, and experience within a *living unit* in *psychiatric custody,* it is both private and public. It shatters conventional divisions between the spheres. Second, it operates through encounters of difference: the young men are strangers; they are a "buncha dudes" who come to live together, to befriend one another, and to help and forgive one another in treatment. The adult men of Steele are constantly engaging with new young men as the waves of intake, discharge, or AWOL are constant. It is what allows the Black men to befriend me, a white woman. *Mad love* shatters the boundaries between psychiatry and hip hop. Finally, the *mad love* transforms the men of Steele, making them better—they use their words, they share their feelings, and they allow for recovery rather than demand perfection. They do this despite all of the reasons not to cultivate this open, loving, and better self. Elijah Anderson (2008) and Victor Rios (2011) inform us of all the reasons why the young Black men should not be open and loving in a world that is biased and violent against them. But young men of Steele are just that—open and loving, even and especially when racism briefly takes the successes out of their treatment.

Love is the power that changes people in at Havenwood and Steele Cottage. This love is a politicized power, as it operates as a balm to racism and prejudice against Black men in America. bell hooks is correct: "If black males were loved they could hope for more than a life locked down, caged, confined; they could imagine themselves beyond containment" (2004:xii). I believe the men and women of Steele do—imagine a life beyond containment because of love.

Notes

Introduction

1. All the names are pseudonyms. In some cases, due to concerns about specific psychiatric issues, histories of abuse, or criminal behavior I conflate some individuals. I use quotation marks throughout to indicate conversation, even though the only actual recordings were during life history interviews. During formal sessions—groups, meetings—I took detailed, verbatim, real-time notes. I took jot-notes in other more informal settings and then typed them up immediately. The nature of my research demands the context of conversation and dialogue. Therefore, even while not recorded, I took great pains to capture the accuracy of the discussions. However, for narrative flow, I have deleted redundancies, cleaned up some of the dangling phrases, and sometimes deleted entire sections of a meeting or a life history interview. I also have occasionally added words or phrases to clarify meaning and intention. In some rare cases, I combined some conversations and events even though they took place at different times.
2. In addition to the therapist's comments, the title of a document prepared for the Colorado Department of Health Services, Division of Child Welfare Services is "Inside the Black Box: A Study of the Residential treatment Center Program in Colorado."
3. The framework comes from Wilhem Cauer's circuit theory. However, to refer to something as a "black box" is common in other fields as well. Jay Friedenberg and Gordon Silverman also use the term "black box" to identify how behaviorists viewed the mind—something too complex to understand the internal workings of—in their text *Cognitive Science: An Introduction to the Study of Mind* (Thousand Oaks, CA: Sage Publications, 2006) 85.
4. Havenwood identifies the youth that live there as "troubled" and the goal of the institution is in making them "productive citizens." The concept of "troubled youth" is pervasive in the field of residential treatment as is the framework of "at risk" youth. See, for example, Larry Brendtro and Mary Shahbazian *Troubled Children & Youth: Turning Problems into Opportunities* (Champaign, IL: Research Press, 2004), Larry K. Brendtro, Martin Brokenleg, and Steve Van Bocken's *Reclaiming Youth at Risk: Our Hope for the Future*, revised edition (Bloomington, ID: National Education Service, 2002), and Nicholas J. Long, Mary M.

Wood, Frank A. Fecser's (2001) *Life Space Crisis Intervention: Talking with Students in Conflict,* second edition (Austin, TX: Pro-Ed, 2001), Kenneth Cmiel's *A Home of Another Kind: One Chicago Orphanage and the Tangle of Child Welfare* (Chicago, IL: University of Chicago Press, 1995), Bethany Lee, Bright, Svobda, Fakunmoju, and Barth "Outcomes of Group Care for Youth: A Review of Comparative Studies," *Research on Social Work Practice* 21 no.2 (2011):177–189, and Bethany Lee and Curtis McMillan's "Measuring Quality in Residential Treatment for Children and Youth," *Residential Treatment for Children and Youth* 24 no.1/2 (2007): 1–17, Richard Barth's *Institutions vs. Foster Homes: The Empirical Base for the Second Century of Debate* (Chapel Hill: University of North Carolina, School of Social Work, Jordan Institute for Families, 2002), and Magellan Health Services Children's Services Task force 2010 report on residential versus community based treatment.

5. I use the pronoun "he" regularly throughout the text, rather than "he or she" or even "she." I do this because most of the individuals we meet in the text are men.
6. I use the framework of abjection based on Julia Kristeva's *Powers of Horror: An Essay on Abjection*, translated by Leon S. Roudiez (New York: Columbia University Press, 1982).
7. This is the case for centers and for youth whose treatment is demanded or paid for by the State. There are private institutions where parents pay for residential treatment and placement is external to State authority.
8. See Lorna Rhodes' (2004) discussion of this distinction and the lack thereof for adult populations in the United States.
9. One female resident climbed the tower during a crisis and fell (or jumped, depending on who is telling the story) off. She had to be life-flighted to a hospital.
10. I do not include any images of the grounds or people of Havenwood to protect anonymity.
11. *SmackDown* is a *World Wrestling Entertainment, Inc* (*WWE*) weekly program.
12. *Roc the Mic Right* is the title of H. Samy Alim's (2006) book on what he identifies as the language of hip hop culture. I will come back to how Derrick and others use Hip Hop Nation Language but I index it here now as Derrick does indeed grab the microphone and flow into my recorder.
13. I follow Black Language scholars and the linguistic structures and practices they document (Baugh 1983; Dillard 1972; Hecht, Jackson, and Ribeau 2003; Labov 1972; Labov, Cohen, Robins, and Lewis 1968; Mitchell-Kernan 1972; Mufwene and Condon 1993; Mufwene, Rickford, Bailey, and Baugh 1998; Smitherman 2006; Wolfram 1969). In particular, I follow John Baugh's (1983) description of Black Street Speech for my transcripts and dialogue as they illustrate style shifting. Style shifting is much like code-switching but it includes particular grammar and linguistic style in addition to vocabulary. Some of the syntax

and grammar of Black Linguistics can also be found in what H. Samy Alim (2006) identifies as Hip Hop Nation Language, which is also used throughout this book.

14. I based this assumption on Geertz's definition of experience-near ethnography, which is when the ethnographer tries to put oneself in the other's skin (1984:125). Other anthropologists have conducted similar kinds of research with psychiatric patients, specifically Sue Estroff in *Making it Crazy: An Ethnography of Psychiatric Clients in an American Community* (Berkeley: University of California Press, 1981).
15. In some research papers, some youth are interviewed about life in treatment (e.g., Epstein 2005, and Freundlich and Avery 2005). However, in the Colorado Department of Health Services, Division of Child Welfare Services document "Inside the Black Box: A Study of the Residential treatment Center Program in Colorado" not one resident was interviewed. Instead the data comes from social workers, psychiatrists, psychologists, state workers, and even parents.
16. This is in contrast to E. Summerson Carr's (2011) research on therapeutic talk and therapeutic contexts in the United States. While a therapeutic register was part of life at Havenwood, the integration of hip hop language and nontherapeutic framings diluted the power of therapeutic talk. I believe this has to do with the linguistic practices of adults and workers who used nontherapeutic talk when emphasizing "therapeutic" moments. I come back to this in chapter 8. Due to the way fieldwork unfolded, I found that narrative or scripts in the more standard sense were not the most salient aspect of the treatment. Rather, I found Cheryl Mattingly's (2010) understanding of dramas, which include gesture and lived experience as part of the "narrative," captured life at Havenwood more comprehensively.
17. Catherine Lutz's *Unnatural Emotion: Everyday Sentiments on a Micronesian Atoll and their Challenge to Western Theory* (Chicago: University of Chicago Press, 1998) provides the grounds for emotion as something that anthropology can investigate, as human emotions are not universal or natural, but rather contextual and differ cross-culturally. See also Robert Levy's "Introduction: Self and Emotion" *Ethos* 11 no. 3 (1983): 128–134, and "Emotion, Knowing, and Culture" in *Culture Theory: Essays on Mind, Self, and Emotion,* Richard A. Shweder and Robert LeVine, editors (Cambridge: Cambridge University Press, 1984) 214–237 and Michelle Rosaldo's (1984) Toward an Anthropology of Self and Feeling in *Culture Theory: Essays on Mind, Self, and Emotion,* Richard A. Shweder and Robert LeVine, editors (Cambridge: Cambridge University Press, 1984) 137–157.
18. See for example, Anthony Gidden's *The Transformation of Intimacy: Sexuality, Love, and Eroticism in Modern Societies* (Oxford: Polity Press, 1992), Jennifer Hirsch and Holly Wardlow's *Modern Loves: The Anthropology of Romantic Courtship and Companionate Marriage* (Ann Arbor: University of Michigan Press, 2006), William Jankowiak's

edited volume *Intimacies: Love and Sex across Cultures* (New York: Columbia University Press, 2008), and *Romantic Passion: A Universal Experience?* (New York: Columbia University Press, 1995), Perveez Mody's *The Intimate State: Love-Marriage and the Law in Delhi* (Delhi: Routledge, 2008), Elizabeth Povinelli's *The Empire of Love: Toward a Theory of Intimacy, Genealogy and Carnality* (Durham, NC: Duke University Press, 2006), and Linda Rebhun's *The Heart is Unknown Country: Love in the Changing Economy of Northeast Brazil* (Stanford: Stanford University Press, 1999).

19. See Christine Dureau's (2012) work on emotional communities and love between mother and child. Unni Wikan's (1993) work illustrate how love is a resonance between people.
20. See for example, Zoë Wool and Seth Messinger's "Labors of Love: The Transformation of Care in the Non-Medical Attendant Program at Walter Reed Army Medical Center," *Medical Anthropology Quarterly* 26 no. 1 (2012): 26–48 and Catherine E. Bolten's *I Did It to Save My Life: Love and Survival in Sierra Leone* (Berkeley: University of California Press, 2012).
21. I am indebted to scholars of and work on subjectivity and subject formation in anthropology. In particular, see João Biehl, Byron Good, and Arthur Kleinman's *Subjectivity* (Berkeley: University of California Press, 2007), Tanya Luhrmann's "Subjectivity," *Anthropological Theory* 6 no. 3 (2006): 345–361, Nick Mansfield's *Subjectivity: Theories of the Self From Freud to Haraway* (New York: New York University Press, 2000), and Sherry Ortner's (2005) "Subjectivity and Cultural Critique," *Anthropological Theory* 5 no. 1 (2005): 31–52. For a special focus on race and subjectivity I am indebted to Stuart Hall's (1997) "Subjects in History: Making Diasporic Identities," in *The House that Race Built: Black Americans, U.S. Terrain,* Wahneema Lubiano, editor (New York: Pantheon Books, 1997) 289–300, "Gramsci's Relevance for the Study of Race and Ethnicity," *Journal of Communication Inquiry* 10 no. 2 (1986): 5–27, and "Race, Articulation, and Societies Structure in Dominance," in *Sociological Theories: Race and Colonialism* (Paris: UNESCO, 1980) and John L. Jackson Jr.'s *Real Black: Adventures in Racial Sincerity* (Chicago, IL: University of Chicago Press, 2005).
22. I use both terms African American and Black to talk about the men and women in the book. I use African American to index a respect for the historical and contemporary significance that race has in the United States, especially for African American individuals. However, I also use the term Black. I use this term because only one person, Steve, ever used the term "African American" during my research tenure, and he only used it a handful of times. Therefore, I use both terms almost interchangeably.

    I am aware of ways that race shapes research and knowledge (Twine and Warren 2000) and interracial communication practices (Ray 2009; Spears 2007). I am familiar with the emergence of African American as a term during the shift in American social life to ethnicize rather than racialize difference (Hacker 1992; Omi and Winant 1994). I often thought about these ways and practices because Steve only used the term African American when he was speaking to me. When he did so he was teased by some of the youth for "talking white." As we became closer, Steve stopped using "African American" altogether. When most people at Havenwood talked about race they talked about white and Black. I understood the use of these terms as an important way that the men understood, experienced, and were communicating to me things about race. I want to respect these experiences, understandings, and ways of communicating here by using the terms most common in my field site.

As a critical race scholar adamant about pushing past color-blind ideology, I have come to use African American, white, Black, and European American. I do this in an effort to be more inclusive of the various ways to talk about race and to facilitate more open and honest discussions about race (Duncan 2002; Jackson 2008; France Widdance Twine, "Racial Ideologies and Racial Methodologies." In *Racing Research, Researching Race: Methodological Dilemmas in Critical Race Studies*, ed. France Winddance Twine and Jonathan Warren, 1–34. New York: New York University Press, 2000; Twine, France Winddance, and Jonathan W. Warren, eds. *Racing research, researching race*. New York: NYU Press, 2000).

23. See also Murray Forman's "General Introduction" in *That's The Joint!: The Hip Hop Studies Reader,* second edition (Middleton, CT: Wesleyan University Press, 2002).
24. For a detailed discussion of why she locates hip hop in a distinctly Black American tradition in contrast to Caribbean and Latin traditions see the chapter "Hip Hop's Mama" in Perry's *Prophets of the Hood: Politics and Poetics in Hip Hop* (Durham NC: Duke University Press, 2004).
25. Perry argues that the focus on the origins of hip hop shifts the focus from cultural form to questions of cultural purity. She maintains that hip hop can have multiracial origins and still be Black, much like something identified as French can still have Germanic cultural influence (Perry 2004:10–11). In fact, she states, "music is never compositionally pure, even as it exists within a culture and is identifiable with a community" (Perry 2004:11).
26. "*Do you*" as a concept of living authentically does not originate in hip hop. I appreciate my reviewer's comments on this point. "*Do you*" can be found in Isaac Hayes song titles in the early 1970s, "Do Your Thing" and the framework emerges in literature from the 1930 and 1940s as illustrated in Claude Brown's *Manchild in the Promised Land* (New York: Simon & Schuster, 1965/2012). Even today, neosoul artist India. Arie's titled a song off her 2013 album *Songversation* "Just Do You." In other words, "*do you*" did not originate, nor is it solely located, in hip hop. It, like hip hop, is a product of a long African American cultural and political history. Nonetheless, for the young men of Havenwood "*do you*" has salience as a hip hop phrase.

27. There are therapeutic programs however, which do explicitly and formally integrate rap into therapy, see for example, Susan Hadley and George Yancy's (2012) edited volume *Therapeutic Uses of Rap and Hip-Hop* (New York: Routledge).
28. This Certificate protects my research subjects in any court of law or legislative proceedings and is required if information might be collected about mental illness or illegal activity.
29. I only formally interviewed state wards who were 15 years or older. I interviewed both boys and girls. I focused on state wards because the majority of the youth at Havenwood are state wards and in the foster care system.
30. I did this in order to conduct experience-near ethnography (Geertz 1984).
31. See for example, John Jackson's *Racial Paranoia* and Amy C. Steinbugler's *Beyond Loving: Intimate Racework in Lesbian, Gay, and Straight Interracial Relationships* (Oxford: Oxford University Press, 2012).

1 Histories and Social Contexts

1. Historical texts of Havenwood were written by the founder and subsequent directors. These texts were published in 1926 and 1986 but did not detail life at Havenwood after the mid 1960s. I use these texts, which include local narratives and photographs, to evince how Havenwood has changed over time. I do not cite them here because they use the real name of the institution.
2. Most of the institutions in the United States were based on Christian doctrine. However, a few institutions housed Jewish children and were structured according to Jewish ideologies and practices (Robinson, Gardner, Greenwood, Hagan, and Richmond 1956:xiii).
3. Adherence to these standards is not policed or officially regulated. "These standards, and those provided by the Council on Accreditation, do not necessarily bear any relation to what actually goes on in the typical residential care setting, given that the vast majority of state and local governments do not require that providers be accredited or belong to the CWLA or other provider associations" (Courtney and Hughes-Heuring 2009:183; see also Hejtmanek 2014).
4. For extensive histories of psychiatry see Edward Shorter's *A History of Psychiatry: From the Era of the Asylum to the Age of Prozac* (New York: John Wiley & Sons, Inc., 1997), Richard Hunter and Ida Macalpine's *Three Hundred Years of Psychiatry 1535–1860* (London: Oxford University Press, 1963), Mary Ann Jimenez's *Changing Faces of Madness: Early American Attitudes and Treatment of the Insane* (Hanover, NH: University Press of New England, 1987), and Gerald N. Grob's *The Mad Among Us: A History of the Care of America's Mentally Ill* (New York: The Free Press, 1994).

5. See for example, Bruno Bettelheim's *Truants from Life* (New York: The Free Press, 1955), B. Bettelheim and E. Sylvester's "A Therapeutic Milieu," *American Journal of Orthopsychiatry* 18 (1948): 191–206, William Caudill's *The Psychiatric Hospital as a Small Society* (Published for the Commonwealth Fund by Harvard University Press, Cambridge, MA, 1958), R. E. Cohen and L. Grinspoon's "Limit Setting as a Corrective Ego Experience," *Archives of General Psychiatry* 8 (1963): 74–79, and Joseph Noshpitz's "Notes on the Theory of Residential Treatment," *Journal of the American Academy of Child Psychiatry* 1 (1962): 284–296.
6. Young women are not the subject of this text but it is clear that Havenwood not only excluded African American young men but also girls. Today, Havenwood houses girls. The shift to coeducational institutions is also limited in the historical accounts.
7. See also Robert V. Guthrie's *Even the Rat Was White: A Historical View of Psychology* second edition (New York: Pearson, 2003) for historical details regarding leading African American psychologists.
8. See also historian David Oshinsky (1997), who argues that even with the abolition of slavery the time of Jim Crow laws allowed for new ways to subjugate and exploit the Black population were created.
9. There are countless examples of this situation: Trayvon Martin's shooting and George Zimmerman's acquittal in Florida to the Michael Brown shooting in Ferguson, Missouri and the protest slogan, "Hands Up, Don't Shoot," which provide compelling evidence that the fear of the Black criminal contributes to Black death rather than simply a reality of the "Black criminal."
10. For more analysis on the ways color-blind ideology shapes American social life and institutional structures see Eduardo Bonilla-Silva's *Racism Without Racists: Color-blind Racism and the Persistence of Racial Inequality in the United States* (New York: Rowman & Littlefield, 2003), Brown et al.'s *Whitewashing Race: The Myth of a Color-Blind Society* (Berkeley: University of California Press, 2003), Joe Feagin's *Systemic Racism: A Theory of Oppression* (New York: Routledge, 2006), Wahneema Lubiano's (1997) "Introduction," in *The House that Race Built: Black Americans, U.S. Terrain,* Wahneema Lubiano, editor (New York: Pantheon Books, 1997) pp. vii–ix, Michael Omi and Howard Winant's (2012) "Racial Formation Rules: Continuity, Instability, and Change," in *Racial Formation in the Twenty-First Century*, Daniel Martinez HoSang, Oneka LaBennett, and Laura Pulido, editors (Berkeley: University of California Press, 2012) pp. 302–331, David Wellman's *Portraits of White Racism,* second edition (New York: Cambridge University Press, 1993), and Tim Wise's *Colorblind: The Rise of Post-Racial Politics and the Retreat from Racial Inequality* (San Francisco: City Lights Books, 2010).
11. There is considerable discussion about the number of youth of color in the foster care system, especially African American boys (Bell 2007; Chibnall et al. 2003).

12. See Angela Davis's (1997) "Race and Criminalization: Black Americans and The Punishment Industry," in *The House That Race Built: Black Americans, U.S. Terrain*, Wahneema Lubiano, editor (New York: Pantheon Books, 1997) pp. 264–279, Preston Elrod and R. Scott Ryder's *Juvenile Justice: A Social, Historical, and Legal Perspective* (New York: Jones & Bartlett Learning, 1999), Everette Penn, Helen Greene, and Shaun Gabbidon's "Introduction," in *Race and Juvenile Justice*, Everette Penn, Helen Greene, and Shaun Gabbidon, editors (Durham, NC: Carolina Academic Press, 2006) pp. 1–7, Everette Penn's "Black Youth: Disproportionality and Delinquency," in *Race in Juvenile Justice*, Everette B. Penn, Helen Taylor Greene, and Shaun L. Gabbidon, editors (Durham, NC: Carolina Academic Press, 2006) pp. 47–64, Robert Taylor and Eric Fritsch's *Juvenile Justice: Policies, Programs, and Practices* (Boston: McGraw-Hill, 2010), and D. Bishop and C. Frazier's (1988) "The Influence of Race in Juvenile Justice Decision-Making: Findings of a Statewide Analysis," *Journal of Research in Crime and Delinquency* 22 (1988): 309–328 for detailed discussions of this link between treatment centers and prison.
13. For more on the history of urban contexts and the Bronx in particular in relationship to hip hop see Jeff Chang's *Can't Stop Won't Stop: A History of the Hip Hop Generation* and Tricia Rose's *Black Noise: Rap Music and Black Culture in Contemporary America* (Middleton, CT: Wesleyan University Press, 1994).
14. What I mean by origin story is the common story that is told in a variety of texts (Chang 2005; Forman and Neal 2012).
15. Graffiti writing is often considered the fourth element of hip hop. Originally, graffiti was used in turf wars and in gang culture. However, graffiti artist known as TAKI 183 wrote his name all over subway stations and subway cars. All of a sudden graffiti was no longer about isolated gang tags but rather about elaborate, complex art pieces that could move and be seen throughout all of New York City. Graffiti themes included hip hop slang and cultural projects (e.g., b-boys and fashion). DJs soon began using the graffiti styles on their party advertisements thereby linking the antiestablishment of graffiti writing with hip hop music. In many ways, graffiti was the most visible element of the dynamic youth culture. For more on graffiti's history see Zeb.Roc.Zki's (2004) presentation of *Martha Cooper's Hip Hop Files: Photographs 1979–1984*, *Style Wars* a 1983 documentary directed by Tony Silver and produced by Tony Silver and Henry Chalfant, Martha Cooper and Henry Chalfant *Subway Art* (New York: Holt Paperbacks, 1988), and Craig Castleman's *Getting Up: Subway Graffiti in New York* (Cambridge, MA: The Massachusetts Institution of Technology Press, 1984).
16. For more comprehensive histories of Black popular music see Mark Anthony Neal's *What the Music Said: Black Popular Music and Black Public Culture* (New York: Routledge, 1999), Amiri Baraka and Amina Baraka's *The Music: Reflections on Jazz and Blues* (New York: William

Morrow & Co., 1987), Iian Chamber's *Urban Rhythms: Pop Music and Popular Culture* (New York: Macmillan, 1985), and Arnold Shaw's *Black Popular Music in America: From the Spirituals, Minstrels, and Ragtime to Soul, Disco, and Hip-Hop* (New York: Macmillan, 1986).

17. There is considerable discussion about the role of women, and female rappers in particular, in hip hop (Perry 2004; Rose 1994). Tricia Rose (1994) provides an exceptional discussion of the role of female rappers in the genre as well as the important power dynamics between men and women in hip hop, which often reflect patriarchal practices found in mainstream American life as well as African American culture. I focus my discussion on men simply because the young men of Havenwood listened to male rappers. I cannot say unequivocally that they only listened to male rappers, but not once did I hear rap music by female artists.

2 The Ethnographic Setting

1. Dwayne is one of over 250 youth discussed in the 70 intake meetings I observed. He is representative of the youth who are discussed at the meetings, those youth for whom the State is trying to find residential treatment placement.
2. Over the course of my research I collected all kinds of documents, including treatment manuals, meeting agendas, MHA/SH, goal sheets, weekly level tally sheets, and cottage programs. Others have analyzed how documents shape social order (Hull 2012) including in psychiatric contexts (Garfinkel 1974; Rhodes 2004). In this text, I do not examine these documents as a constitutive artifact using an analytical lens because the file was not read or used as a meaningful artifact by youth or cottage staff at Steele. I engage with the very significant regime of documentation in psychiatric custody, as well as the rejection of the file in other writing.
3. As with documents, I collected data from all kinds of meetings and do not engage with the constitutive aspects of these ethnographic events. David Buckholdt and Jaber F. Gubrium (1979) and Helen B. Schwartzman (1987) illustrate the importance of not overlooking the significance of meetings as disciplinary events or as constitutive of the social order. I absolutely agree. However, I chose to analyze other aspects of life in treatment in this book. As is the case with any ethnographic endeavor and text on the subject, something is always missing. While I understand how documents and meetings shape their lives and futures, I found that what emerged as meaningful to them was not this regimentation. However, I focus on the constitutive aspect of meetings and documents in another book.
4. I do not discuss differential diagnoses or medication regimens in this book due to the lack of discussion of mental illness diagnoses at the cottage level. I analyze these important aspects of psychiatric custody in

other writing, especially the cottage–institution divide as well as the shift in diagnosis, especially in relation to medication use.

5. There is a new version of the DSM (2013); the diagnoses used during my research were from the 2000 version of the DSM.
6. There was considerable overlap between cottages in terms of psychiatric diagnosis and sometimes youth were given a "bed" in one cottage that wasn't the best fit, due to time and space constraints. Therefore, this was the overarching logic rather than the definitive practice.
7. The Cottage Program was the official rule book of each cottage. Each youth was given one upon entering the cottage. I come back to the Program in chapter 3.
8. I was informed that no one ever earned a 5. In the numerical system, a 5 is equivalent to an A. When I asked why no one ever earned a 5, I was informed that no one was perfect and everyone had something to work on. No one at Havenwood could earn an "A" no matter how well he was doing.
9. Despite the ubiquity of the Conflict Cycle poster and the analysis of this aspect of the youth in meetings, and as with the analysis of medications and differential diagnosis, explicit analysis of the youth's conflict cycle will take place in other writing. Because it was not a useful tool at the cottage level or engaged with by the residents and their staff members, I do not focus on it in this book.
10. At Havenwood, *adult* emotional reaction was analyzed in addition to the residents'. This analysis was formulated into a model of treatment developed at Havenwood by leading psychologists and the president in 2001. This model was called "Counter Response." I analyze Counter Response and its use with adults at Havenwood in great detail (Hejtmanek 2014).
11. The week I participated in the training, a white male therapist who had been working at Havenwood for seven years was also enrolled but this was unusual. TCI trainers for Havenwood, pointed this man out to the group noting that he was the first therapist to be trained in TCI since they began using the strategy in 2000. Trainings were given once a month.
12. The majority of residents who identified with a religious tradition were Christian. However, if young people identified as Catholic, Jewish, or Muslim the director of religious services would try to find off-campus religious services for the youth to attend. Religious services and the role of religion in treatment and at Havenwood are not part of this text. However, they are the subject of other writing and analysis.
13. I do not analyze the difference between files and my life history interviews in this book. As with documents and meetings, I compare the various regimes of organization and construction of subjects in other writings.
14. These institutional documents were summaries of the foster care files, which are official accounts of the child's life used at the state level (i.e., justice system, education system, health and human services). I engage with these documents as constituting the social order in other writing.

15. Specific experiences are placed in these categories for the Child and Adolescent Needs and Strengths (CANS) scoring system developed by John Lyons (1999; see also Lyons, Howard, O'Mahoney and Lish 1997) at Northwestern University. His CANS scoring system was used to evaluate treatment needs and progress and to develop reachable goals and objectives.
16. I do not analyze the various roles and racial stratification linked to professional roles at Havenwood in this book. I write on that elsewhere.
17. I do not feature all 30 African American youth either. As mentioned in a note in the Introduction, I also merged some youth into composites.

3 Institutional Living

1. Most staff members did not eat from the dining hall, and if they did they did not have to pay for them. I paid $2.00 for each meal; I paid for my room and board with a National Science Foundation Dissertation Improvement Grant.
2. As mentioned in chapter 2, the role of documents is significant to the functioning of Havenwood as an institution. While this text does not focus on this process, but rather the lived experience of youth (which did not include files, documents, etc.), I do take up the role of documents in other writing.
3. Except during meetings, and I mentioned in an earlier note that I do not analyze these differences in this book. I take that on in other writing.
4. Also, for Christmas, each resident who stays on campus for the holiday is allocated $200 for his or her gifts.
5. In my notes on these seminars I did not write down what the therapy session was about. I decided it was not ethical to gather that data. I did, however, write down how the therapists talked about the session.

4 *Crazy Shit*

1. For descriptions of the panopticon prison see John Bender's *Imaging the Penitentiary*: *Fiction and the Architecture of Mind In Eighteenth-Century England* (Chicago: University of Chicago Press, 1987), Robin Evans's *The Fabrication of Virtue*: *English Prison Architecture, 1750–1840* (Cambridge: Cambridge University Press, 1982), Michel Foucault's *Discipline and Punish: The Birth of the Prison.* Trans. Alan Sheridan (New York: Vintage Books, 1977/1995), and Michael Ignatieff's *A Just Measure of Pain: The Penitentiary in the Industrial Revolution 1750–1850.* (New York: Puffin, 1989).
2. See van der Kolk, Bessel A., Susan Roth, David Pelcovitz, Susanne Sunday, and Joseph Spinazzola. "Disorders of Extreme Stress: The

Empirical Foundation of a Complex Adaptation to Trauma," *Journal of Traumatic Stress* 18 no. 5 (2005): 389–399, for a framework of understanding chronic trauma and social problem and mental disease. See James Masterson's *The Psychiatric Dilemma of Adolescence* (Boston, MA: Little, Brown and Company, 1967); *The Narcissistic and Borderline Disorders: An Integrated Developmental Approach* (New York: Routledge, 1981); and *The Personality Disorders Through the Lens of Attachment Theory and the Neurobiologic Development of the Self: A Clinical Integration* (Phoenix, AZ: Zeig, Tucker & Theisen, Inc., 2006) for a psychoanalytical approach to attachment problems and subsequent mental health problems. Also, Bruce Perry and Maia Szalavitz have an interesting take on dealing with acute trauma in their *The Boy Who Was Raised as a Dog: And Other Stories from a Child Psychiatrist's Notebook* (New York: Basic Books, 2006).

3. The Section 384.50 refers to the Department of Family and Children's Service's rule regulating manual restraints. All state residential facilities had to comply with this section of the rules.
4. Living in a residential treatment center might seem like a life-cycle ritual or rite of passage as the process includes a separation, transition, and reintegration, which Victor Turner (1967) explained. Even if living in residential treatment can be seen as a liminal stage, crises were not celebrated or encouraged as part of the process. Crises were tolerated and everyone's job—staff and resident—was to stop the crazy behavior. In this way, the crises or *crazy shit* was the reason for the social abjection into psychiatric custody to begin with, and its continued enactment was considered a limitation and hindrance to treatment progress and psychiatric healing.
5. This workbook is part of a training organized by Cornell University: Residential Child Care Project. 2001. *Therapeutic Crisis Intervention Student Workbook*. Family Life Development Center, College of Human Ecology, Cornell University. Ithaca, NY.
6. I provide an analysis of the clinical coercion to constrain emotional intimacy between staff and residents elsewhere (Hejtmanek 2014). I also analyze the various professional roles and institutional dynamics in other writing.
7. I discuss this divide in great detail elsewhere (Hejtmanek 2014).
8. For an abbreviated version of this vignette see "Caring Through Restraint: Violence, Intimacy, and Identity in Mental Health Practice," *Culture, Medicine, and Psychiatry* 34 (2010):668–674 (Hejtmanek 2010).
9. In training we were constantly reminded of the youth in residential treatment throughout the country who had suffocated and died during improper restraints. If one followed the official TCI procedures, the restraint would contain the resident, but would not allow them to suffocate themselves or bite you.
10. I decided early on in my research not to participate in any restraints. I did not want to be that closely aligned with staff members. However, it also meant that I did not help out during crisis or that residents could not "trust me" to not allow them to hurt themselves.

11. Other literature also suggests that African American parents use this framing to make sense of corporal punishment—"I would rather my child get a beating from me than from the police" (Whaley 2000; see also Lansford 2010).

5 A Keepin' It Real Group

1. For discussions of therapeutic communities see James Waldram *Hound Pound Narrative: Sexual Offender Habilitation and the Anthropology of Therapeutic Intervention* (Berkeley: University of California Press, 2012), J. Lees, N. Manning, and B. Rawlings *Therapeutic Community Effectiveness: A Systemic International Review of Therapeutic Community Treatment for People with Personality Disorders and Mentally Disordered Offenders* (York: National Health Service Centre for Reviews and Dissemination, University of York, 1999), Nancy Jainchill's "Therapeutic Communities for Adolescents: The Same and Not the Same," in *Community as Method: Therapeutic Communities for Special Populations and Special Settings*, George De Leon, editor (Westport, CT: Praeger, 1997) Pp. 161–178, Luhrmann's *Of Two Minds: An Anthropologist Looks at American Psychiatry* (New York: Vintage Books, 2000), Barbara Frankel's *Transforming Identities: Context, Power, and Ideology in a Therapeutic Community* (New York: Peter Lang Publishing, 1989), and Richard Almond's *The Healing Community: Dynamics of the Therapeutic Milieu* (New York: J. Aronson, 1974).
2. See for example Csordas's *The Sacred Self: A Cultural Phenomenology of Charismatic Healing* (Berkeley: University of California Press, 1997), Rebecca Lester's "Brokering Authenticity: Borderline Personality Disorder and the Ethics of Care in an American Eating Disorder Clinic," *Current Anthropology* 50 no. 3 (2009): 281–302., and James Waldram's *Hound Pound Narrative*.
3. This act of making group sessions sincere is different than Summerson Carr's (2011) "flipping the script." In her work, Carr argues that flipping the script is another layer of performance, manipulating the ritual speaking in addiction therapeutics to fool others, that these spoken words did not reflect inner states. I argue here that many of the youth at Havenwood did use group sessions to sincerely discuss their inner states and to be more sincere they reframed group sessions in a variety of ways, including using hip hop. They are trying to keep it "more" real with hip hop than what is desired by institutionally defined by group therapy sessions.
4. For a detailed history and dissection of authenticity in comparison to sincerity see Lionel Trilling (1972) and John Jackson (2005).
5. For an extensive analysis of the "Language of Hip Hop Culture" see linguist's H. Samy Alim's *Roc the Mic Right* (2006).

6 *Kickin' It*

1. For other work on nonsexual touch and close male relationships see Thomas Gregor's "The Men's House: Touching and Wrestling among Mehinaku Men," in *The Book of Touch*, Constance Classen, editor (Oxford: Berg Press, 2005) pp. 162–165. and Santanu Das's (2005) work on touch in the trenches of war.
2. See, for example, Philippe Bourgois's *In Search of Respect: Selling Crack in El Bario,* second edition (Cambridge, UK: Cambridge University Press, 2003), Daniel Hruschka's *Friendship: Development, Ecology, and Evolution of a Relationship* (Berkeley: University of California Press, 2010), and Alice Schlegel's "Cross Cultural Approaches to Adolescence," *Ethos* 23 no. 1 (1995): 15–32. See also Simon Coleman's "Making Friendship Impure: Some Reflections on a (Still) Neglected Topic," in *The Ways of Friendship: Anthropological Perspectives*, Amit Desai and Evan Killick editors (New York: Berghahn Books, (2013) pp. 197–206, for the anthropological neglect of this kind of relationship in lieu of other categories.
3. Anthropologists Daniel Mains's "Friends and Money: Balancing Affection and Reciprocity Among Young Men in Urban Ethiopia," *American Ethnologist* 40 no. 1 (2013): 335–346, Amit Desai and Evan Killick's *The Ways of Friendship: Anthropological Perspectives* (New York: Berghahn Books (2013), and Sandra Bell and Simon Coleman's *The Anthropology of Friendship* (Oxford: Berg Press, 1999). See also Ray Pahl's *On Friendship* (Malden, MA: Polity Press, 2000) and Niobe Way's *Deep Secrets: Boys' Friendships and the Crisis of Connection* (Cambridge: Harvard University Press, 2011).
4. This is often because categories of relatedness in many societies are not mutually exclusive. In fact, in some cases kinship words are used to signal close friendships that are not kin (Mains 2013; Obeid 2013; Rodgers 2013).
5. See for example Daniel Mains's "Friends and Money".
6. See for example Daniel Mains's "Friends and Money" as well as the classic text *The Gift: The Form and Reason for Exchange in Archaic Societies* (New York: W. W. Norton & Company, 1954) by Marcel Mauss.
7. Hruschka attempts the difficult task of quantifying these feelings. "Closeness" he determines is an idiom of proximity, a spatial metaphor that is used, even cross-culturally, to articulate what makes someone a friend rather than something else, such as an acquaintance (Hruschka 2010:30). Love is understood as a "direct description of feelings that we have towards others" (Hruschka 2010:34).
8. See also James Carrier's "People Who Can Be Friends: Selves and Social Relationships," in *The Anthropology of Friendship*, Sandra Bell and Simon Coleman, editors (Oxford: Berg Press, 1999) pp. 21–38.

9. Hruschka (2010) distinguishes "friendship-like relationships" from the colloquial "friendship" because the latter carries particular cultural expectations and meanings in the United States. As an anthropologist of US culture, I find that race, class, gender, age, and many other social factors shape meanings of friendship. Nonetheless, I think that friendship can be applied to the relationships among young men at Steele, forged in psychiatric custody.
10. Polsky also contributed significantly to the literature on residential treatment at the time (Polsky, Claster, and Goldberg 1968; 1970).
11. It might appear that women and girlfriends are absent or left out of my account here. This is indicative of the way that young people were allowed to interact at Havenwood, in general, and Steele Cottage, more specifically. Toward the middle of my research at Havenwood, a "Café" was opened. This special program was to teach youth to interact appropriately on dates, to encourage positive interactions between the genders. It was a pilot program at the time of my research and Steele Cottage did not participate in it. The Valentine's Day Dance allowed for youth to dance at a formal event, with girls in prom gowns and the boys in ties. However, intermingling or dating was strictly forbidden across the campus. Steele boys were allowed to "talk to girls," when they were at the skating rink or mall. However, talk about girls was restricted. Therefore, while sex was commented upon and I heard about "community girls," these were very rare occurrences. In addition, sexual activity among the boys (and girls) was not unheard of, but rare. If anything masturbation was a topic discussed more than sexual relationships. Most of the relationship focus was nonsexual in nature, focusing on teaching positive relationships outside of a sexual context. This was paramount because so many of the youth had been sexually abused as children and it was fear that all they knew was relating sexually.
12. In fact, Bourgois identifies that one of his main characters, Caesar, stayed in a "reform school" and psychiatric centers. Caesar describes a very different experience from what I am portraying here (Bourgois 2003:182–183, 190–191).
13. In his book, *Street Wise: Race, Class and Change in an Urban Community* (Chicago: University of Chicago Press, 1990), Elijah Anderson investigates race, class, and change in an urban community. He discusses drug culture, and one's fellow "gang boys" but friendship is not discussed, except for briefly mentioned as something across racial lines. Other African American scholars who discuss race, men, and the "state of Black America" focus on other factors that shape the lives of young Black men more than that of friendship. bell hooks' (2004) book on Black men and masculinity has a chapter on "gangsta culture," but has little to say about positive Black male friendships. See also Loïc Wacquant's *Urban Outcasts: A Comparative Sociology of Advanced Marginality* (Cambridge, UK: Polity Press, 2008).

7 Becoming Good Men

1. I return to a more in-depth analysis of types of meetings in the institution, but for a discussion of Staffings see David R. Buckholdt and Jaber F. Gubrium's "Doing Staffings," *Human Organization* 38 no. 3 (1979): 255–264.
2. Again, I analyze the file in other writing.
3. This conflation has a long and complex history. For an extensive analysis of how African American were vilified throughout American history as well as responses to this vilification in folklore and social banditry see William Van Deburg's *Hoodlums: Black Villains and Social Bandits in American Life* (Chicago: The University of Chicago Press, 2004) and Imani Perry's Chapter 4, "The Glorious Outlaw," in *Prophets of the Hood: Politics and Poetics in Hip Hop* (Durham, NC: Duke University Press, 2004).
4. This rejection has deep roots in racial oppression of Black men, especially by white men, see, for example, bell hooks's "Feminism Inside: Toward a Black Body Politic," in *Black Male: Representations of Masculinity in Contemporary American Art,* Thelma Golden, editor (New York: Whitney Museum of American Art, 1994) p. 127, and *We Real Cool: Black Men and Masculinity* (New York: Routledge, 2004).
5. This framework can be linked to the respectability narrative available for African American men (see Gordon 1997).
6. For more on basic trust between infant and caregiver, object relations, see the work of psychologist D.W. Winnicot. See also Paul Tillich for a philosophical approach to trust. Anthony Gidden's analysis of the relationships between self-identity, trust, risk, and anxiety, and modernity are the subject of his book *Modernity and Self-Identity: Self and Society in the Late Modern Age* (Stanford: Stanford University Press, 1991). My approach to "trust" is much like my approach to "love." It is not something that the young people give much to others, but what they are given, or feel they are given. This is the opposite direction of Winnicot's trust, which is when the child trusts the caregiver. William, and others, hope that they can earn the trust of their caregivers.
7. For an extensive survey of gangs, see *Youth Gangs in American Society,* fourth edition, (Stamford, CT: Cengage Learning, 2012) by Randall G. Sheldon, Sharon K. Tracy, William B. Brown. For a classic text on gangs, see Albert K. Cohen's *Delinquent Boys: The Culture of the Gang* (New York: The Free Press, 1955). See Victor Rios's *Punished: Policing the Lives of Black and Latino Boys* (New York: New York University Press, 2011) for a discussion of gang databases and the criminalization of young men of color.
8. See, for example, Bourgois's *In Search of Respect: Selling Crack in El Bario,* second edition (Cambridge, UK: Cambridge University Press, 2003).

9. See, for example, R. W. Connell's *Masculinities* (Berkeley: University of California Press, 1995) and *Gender* (Cambridge, UK: Polity Press, 2002) and Michael Messner's "Boyhood, Organized Sports, and the Construction of Masculinities," *Journal of Contemporary Ethnography* 18 (1990): 416–444. For a focus on Black masculinities, see Edmund Gordon's "Cultural Politics of Black Masculinity," *Transforming Anthropology* 6 nos.1 & 2 (1997): 36–53, Jafari Allen's *¡Venceremos?: The Politics of Black Self-making in Cuba* (Durham, NC: Duke University Press, 2011), Phillip Harper's *Are We Not Men?: Masculine Anxiety and the Problem of African-American Identity* (Oxford: Oxford University Press, 1996), David John's "Re-imagining Black Masculine Identity: An Investigation of the 'Problem' Surrounding the Construction of Black Masculinity in America," in *The State of Black America 2007: Portrait of the Black Male. An Official Publication of the National Urban League*, Stephanie J. Jones, editor (Silver Springs, MD: Beckham Publications Group, 2007) pp. 59–73, Nathan McCall's *Makes Me Wanna Holler: A Young Black Man in America* (New York: Vintage Books, 1995), bell hook's *We Real Cool*.
10. Philippe Bourgois (2003) also argues that crime and violence are ways in which the young men of the street prove their manhood and masculinity in a society that emasculates them in formal economic spheres. Anderson (2008) echoes this point. In addition to linking masculinity with criminality, Rios (2011) and Bourgois (2003) find that the young men they studied were socialized to meanings of manhood that were often in contrast to those of dominant social institutions. Rios (2011) states that "gender is one of the processes in which the criminal justice system and the youth control complex are involved in the reproduction of criminalization, social exclusion, and racial inequality" (141).

9 Mad Love: Theorizing and Politicizing Transformation

1. While I had considerable freedom to move around Havenwood, bestowed upon me by the president, Steve and a handful of other line staff members had much more power. The vice president, an African American man, and Steve were close, having come to Havenwood around the same time. The vice president had considerable power over minute details on campus and Steve would go to him if he needed anything. Therefore, Steve did not mobilize my white privilege at Havenwood.

Bibliography

Aichhorn, August. 1955. *Wayward Youth: A Psychoanalytic Study of Delinquent Children, Illustrated by Actual Case Histories*. New York: Meridian Books.

Alexander, Bryant Keith. 2006. *Performing Black Masculinity: Race, Culture, and Queer Identity*. Landam, MD: Altimira.

Alexander, Michelle. 2010. *The New Jim Crow: Mass Incarceration in the Age of Colorblindness*. New York: The New Press.

Alim, H. Samy. 2006. *Roc the Mic Right: The Language of Hip Hop Culture*. New York: Routledge.

Allen, Jafari. 2011. *¡Venceremos?: The Politics of Black Self-making in Cuba*. Durham, NC: Duke University Press.

Almond, Richard. 1974. *The Healing Community: Dynamics of the Therapeutic Milieu*. New York: J. Aronson.

American Psychiatric Association. 2013. *The Diagnostic and Statistical Manual of Mental Disorders V*. Washington, DC: American Psychiatric Press.

———. 2000. *The Diagnostic and Statistical Manual of Mental Disorders IV-TR*. Washington, DC: American Psychiatric Press.

Anderson, Elijah. 2008. "Against the Wall: Poor, Young, Black, and Male." In *Against the Wall: Poor, Young, Black, and Male*, Elijah Anderson, editor, pp. 1–27. Philadelphia: University of Pennsylvania Press.

———. 1990. *Street Wise: Race, Class and Change in an Urban Community*. Chicago: University of Chicago Press.

Ashby, LeRoy. 1997. *Endangered Children: Dependency, Neglect, and Abuse in American History*. New York: Twayne Pub.

Baraka, Amiri and Amina Baraka. 1987. *The Music: Reflections on Jazz and Blues*. New York: William Morrow & Co.

Barker, Philip, ed. 1974. *The Residential Psychiatric Treatment of Children*. Crosby, UK: Granada Publishing Limited.

Barth, Richard P. 2002. *Institutions vs. Foster Homes: The Empirical Base for the Second Century of Debate*. Chapel Hill: University of North Carolina, School of Social Work, Jordan Institute for Families.

Baugh, John. 1983. *Black Street Speech: Its History, Structure, and Survival*. Austin: University of Texas Press.

Bell, Sandra, and Simon Coleman, eds. 1999. *The Anthropology of Friendship*. Oxford: Berg Press.

Bell, William. 2007. "How are the Children?: Foster Care and African-American Boys." In *The State of Black America 2007: Portrait of the Black*

Male. An Official Publication of the National Urban League, Stephanie J. Jones, editor, pp. 151–157. Silver Springs, MD: Beckham Publications Group.

Bender, John. 1987. *Imaging the Penitentiary: Fiction and the Architecture of Mind In Eighteenth-Century England*. Chicago: University of Chicago Press.

Bettelheim, Bruno. 1955. *Truants from Life*. New York: The Free Press.

———. 1950. *Love Is Not Enough*. New York: The Free Press.

Bettelheim, Bruno, and E Sylvester. 1948. "A Therapeutic Milieu." *American Journal of Orthopsychiatry* 18: 191–206.

Biehl, João Guilherme, Byron Good, and Arthur Kleinman, eds. 2007. *Subjectivity*. Berkeley: University of California Press.

Billingsley, Andrew, and Jeanne M. Giovannoni. 1972. *Children of the Storm: Black Children and American Child Welfare*. New York: Harcourt, Brace, Jovanovich.

Bishop, D, and C Frazier. 1988. "The Influence of Race in Juvenile Justice Decision-Making: Findings of a Statewide Analysis." *Journal of Research in Crime and Delinquency* 22: 309–328.

Bolten, Catherine E. 2012. *I Did It to Save My Life: Love and Survival in Sierra Leone*. Berkeley: University of California Press.

Bonilla-Silva, Eduardo. 2003. *Racism without Racists: Color-Blind Racism and the Persistence of Racial Inequality in the United States*. New York: Rowman & Littlefield.

Bourgois, Philippe. 2003. *In Search of Respect: Selling Crack in El Bario*. 2nd ed. Cambridge, UK: Cambridge University Press.

Brendtro, Larry, and Mary Shahbazian. 2004. *Troubled Children & Youth: Turning Problems into Opportunities*. Champaign, IL: Research Press.

Brendtro, Larry K., Martin Brokenleg, and Steve Van Bockern. 2002. *Reclaiming Youth at Risk: Our Hope for the Future*, rev. ed. Bloomington, ID: National Education Service.

Brodwin, Paul. 2013. *Everyday Ethics in Community Psychiatry: Voices from the Front Lines of Community Psychiatry*. Berkeley: University of California Press.

Brown, Claude. 1965/2012. *Manchild in the Promised Land*. New York: Simon & Schuster.

Brown, Michael K., Martin Carnoy, Elliot Currie, Troy Duster, David B. Oppenheimer, Marjorie M. Shultz, and David Wellman. 2003. *Whitewashing Race: The Myth of a Color-Blind Society*. Berkeley: University of California Press.

Buckholdt, David R., and Jaber F. Gubrium. 1979. "Doing Staffings." *Human Organization* 38(3): 255–264.

Byrd, W. Michael, and Linda A. Clayton. 2000. *An American Health Dilemma: A Medical History of African Americans and the Problem of Race: Beginnings to 1900*. New York: Routledge.

Carr, E. Summerson. 2011. *Scripting Addiction: The Politics of Therapeutic Talk and American Sobriety*. Princeton, NJ: Princeton University Press.

Carrier, James. 1999. "People Who Can Be Friends: Selves and Social Relationships." In *The Anthropology of Friendship*, Sandra Bell and Simon Coleman, editors, pp. 21–38. Oxford: Berg Press.

Castleman, Craig. 1984. *Getting Up: Subway Graffiti in New York*. Cambridge, MA: The Massachusetts Institution of Technology Press.

Caudill, William A. 1958. *The Psychiatric Hospital as a Small Society*. Published for the Commonwealth Fund by Harvard University Press. Cambridge, MA

Chamber, Ilian. 1985. *Urban Rhythms: Pop Music and Popular Culture*. New York: Macmillan.

Chang, Jeff (with an introduction by D. J. Kool Herc). 2005. *Can't Stop, Won't Stop: A History of a Hip-Hop Generation*. New York: Picador.

Chibnall, Susan, Nicole Dutch, Brenda Jones-Harden, Annie Brown, Ruby Gourdine, Anniglo Boone, and Shelita Snyder. 2003. *Children of Color in the Child Welfare System: Perspectives from the Child Welfare Community*. Caliber and Associates and Howard University School of Social Work for the United States Department of Health and Human Services. Washington DC.

Chang, Jeff (with an introduction by D. J. Kool Herc). 2005. *Can't Stop, Won't Stop: A History of a Hip-Hop Generation*. New York: Picador.

Classen, Constance. 2005a. "Fingerprints: Writing about Touch." In *The Book of Touch*, Constance Classen, editor, pp. 1–9. Oxford: Berg Press.

Classen, Constance. 2005b. "Male Bonding." In *The Book of Touch*, Constance Classen, editor, pp.155–159. Oxford: Berg Press.

Cmiel, Kenneth. 1995. *A Home of Another Kind: One Chicago Orphanage and the Tangle of Child Welfare*. Chicago, IL: University of Chicago Press.

Coen, Anita S., Anne Libby, David Price, and Karen Silverman. 2003. *Inside the Black Box: A Study of the Residential Treatment Center Program in Colorado*. A Report Prepared for Child Welfare Services. Denver: Colorado Department of Human Services.

Cohen, Albert K. 1955. *Delinquent Boys: The Culture of the Gang*. New York: The Free Press.

Cohen, Cathy J. 2004. "Deviance as Resistance: A New Research Agenda for the Study of Black Politics." *DuBois Review* 1(1): 27–45.

Cohen, R. E., and L Grinspoon. 1963. "Limit Setting as a Corrective Ego Experience." *Archives of General Psychiatry* 8: 74–79.

Coleman, Simon. 2013. "Making Friendship Impure: Some Reflections on a (Still) Neglected Topic." In *The Ways of Friendship: Anthropological Perspectives*, Amit Desai and Evan Killick, editors, pp. 197–206. New York: Berghahn Books.

Connell, R.W. 2002. *Gender*. Cambridge, UK: Polity Press.

———. 1995. *Masculinities*. Berkeley: University of California Press.

Cooper, Martha, and Henry Chalfant. 1988. *Subway Art*. New York: Holt Paperbacks.

Cotton, Nancy S. 1993. *Lessons from the Lion's Den: Therapeutic Management of Children in Psychiatric Hospitals and Treatment Centers*. San Francisco, CA: Jossey-Bass.

Courtney, Mark E., and Darcy Hughes-Heuring. 2009. "Residential Care in the United States of America: Past, Present, and Future." In *Residential Care of Children: Comparative Perspectives*, Mark E. Courtney and Dorota Iwaniec, editors, pp. 173–190. New York: Oxford University Press.

Csordas, Thomas J. 1997. *The Sacred Self: A Cultural Phenomenology of Charismatic Healing*. Berkeley: University of California Press.

———. 1990. "Embodiment as a Paradigm for Anthropology." *Ethos* 18:5–47

Csordas, Thomas J., and Arthur Kleinman. 1996. "The Therapeutic Process." In *Medical Anthropology: Contemporary Theory and Method*, rev. ed. Carolyn F. Sargent and Thomas M. Johnson, editors, pp. 3–21. New York: Greenwood Press.

Das, Santanu. 2005. "The Dying Kiss: Intimacy and Gender in the Trenches of the First World War." In *The Book of Touch*, Constance Classen, editor, pp. 188–197. Oxford: Berg Press.

Davis, Angela Y. 1997. "Race and Criminalization: Black Americans and The Punishment Industry." In *The House That Race Built: Black Americans, U.S. Terrain*, Wahneema Lubiano, editor, pp. 264–279. New York: Pantheon Books.

De Genova, Nick. 1995. "Check Your Head: The Cultural Politics of Rap Music." *Transitions* 67: 123–137.

Desai, Amit, and Evan Killick, eds. 2013. *The Ways of Friendship: Anthropological Perspectives*. New York: Berghahn Books.

Dillard, Joey Lee. 1972. *Black English*. New York: Random House.

Dimitriadis, Greg. 2003. *Friendship, Cliques, and Gangs: Young Black Men Coming of Age in Urban America*. New York: Teachers College Press.

Du Bois, W.E.B. 2005[1903]. *The Souls of Black Folk*. New York: Pocket Books.

Duncan, Garrett Albert. 2002. "Critical Race Theory and Method: Rendering Race in Urban Ethnographic Research." *Qualitative Inquiry* 8(1): 85–104.

Duneier, Mitchell. 1992. *Slim's Table: Race, Respectability, and Masculinity*. Chicago: University of Chicago Press.

Duneier, Mitchell, with photographs by Ovie Carter. 1999. *Sidewalk*. New York: Farrar, Straus and Giroux.

Dureau, Christine. 2012. "Translating Love." *Ethos* 40(2): 142–163.

Dyson, Michael Eric. 1996. *Race Rules: Navigating the Color Line*. New York: Vintage Books

Elrod, Preston, and R. Scott Ryder. 1999. *Juvenile Justice: A Social, Historical, and Legal Perspective*. New York: Jones & Bartlett Learning.

Epstein, Richard A. 2005. "Beyond the Yellow Door: Outcome and Follow-up Studies of Students in a Residential Treatment Center." PhD Dissertation, University of Chicago.

Estroff, Sue E. 1981. *Making It Crazy: An Ethnography of Psychiatric Clients in an American Community*. Berkeley: University of California Press.

Evans, Robin. 1982. *The Fabrication of Virtue: English Prison Architecture, 1750–1840*. Cambridge: Cambridge University Press.

Fader, Jamie. 2013. *Falling Back: Incarceration and Transitions to Adulthood among Urban Youth*. New Brunswick: Rutgers University Press.

Fanon, Franz. 1963/2004. *The Wretched of the Earth*. Trans. Richard Philcox. New York: Grove Press.

———. 1952/2008. *Black Skin, White Masks*. Trans. Richard Philcox. New York: Grove Press.

Feagin, Joe R. 2006. *Systemic Racism: A Theory of Oppression*. New York: Routledge.

Fernando Jr., S. H. 1994. *New Beats: Exploring the Music, Culture, and Attitudes of Hip Hop*. New York: Anchor Books.

Field, Tiffany. 2003. *Touch*. Cambridge: MIT Press

Finnegan, Ruth. 2005. "Tactile Communication." In *The Book of Touch*, Constance Classen, editor, pp. 18–25. Oxford: Berg Press.

Forman, Murray. 2002. *The 'Hood Comes First: Race, Space, and Place in Rap and Hip-Hop*. Middleton, CT: Wesleyan University Press.

———. 2012. General Introduction. In *That's the Joint!: The Hip-Hop Studies Reader,* 2nd ed., Murray Forman and Marc Anthony Neal, eds. Pp. 1–8. New York: Routledge.

Forman, Murray, and Marc Anthony Neal, eds. 2012. *That's the Joint!: The Hip-Hop Studies Reader,* 2nd ed. New York: Routledge.

Foucault, Michel. 1977/1995. *Discipline & Punish: The Birth of the Prison*. Trans. Alan Sheridan. New York: Vintage Books.

———. 1988[1965]. *Madness and Civilization: A History of Insanity in the Age of Reason*. Trans. Richard Howard. New York: Vintage Books.

Frankel, Barbara. 1989. *Transforming Identities: Context, Power, and Ideology in a Therapeutic Community*. New York: Peter Lang Publishing.

Freud, Anna. 1969. *Research at the Hampstead Child-Therapy Clinic and Other Papers: 1956–1965*. Vol. 5. New York: International Universities Press.

Freundlich, Madelyn, and Rosemary J. Avery. 2005. "Planning for Permanency for Youth in Congregate Care." *Children and Youth Services Review* 27(2): 115–134.

Friedenberg, Jay, and Gordon Silverman. 2006. *Cognitive Science: An Introduction to the Study of Mind*. Thousand Oaks, CA: Sage Publications.

Gaines, Atwood D. 1992. "From DSM-I to III-R; Voices of Self, Mastery and the Other: A Cultural Constructivist Reading of U.S. Psychiatric Classification." *Social Science & Medicine* 35(1): 3–24.

Garfinkel, Harod. 1974. "'Good' Organizational Reasons for 'Bad' Clinical Records." In *Ethnomethodology*, Roy Turner, editor, pp. 109–127. Middlesex, UK: Penguin Education.

Geertz, Clifford. 1984. "'From the Native's Point of View': On the Nature of Anthropological Understanding." In *Culture Theory: Essays on Mind, Self, and Emotion*, Richard A. Shweder and Robert A. LeVine, editors, pp. 123–136. Cambridge, UK: Cambridge University Press.

George, Nelson. 2012. "Hip-Hop Founding Fathers Speak the Truth." In *That's the Joint!: The Hip-Hop Studies Reader,* 2nd ed., Murray Forman and Marc Anthony Neal, eds. Pp. 44–55. New York: Routledge.

Giddens, Anthony. 1992. *The Transformation of Intimacy: Sexuality, Love, and Eroticism in Modern Societies*. Oxford: Polity Press.

———. 1991. *Modernity and Self-Identity: Self and Society in the Late Modern Age*. Stanford, CA: Stanford University Press.

Gilmer, Micah. 2009. "'You Got to Have a Heart of Stone to Work Here': Coaching, Teaching, and 'Building Men' at Eastside High." PhD dissertation. Duke University.

———. 2008. "Don't Tell Nobody This But I Love Ya'll: The Not-So-Secret of Discussion of Feeling Among Black Men." Paper presented at the American Anthropological Association Meetings. San Francisco, CA, November 22.

Goffman, Erving. 1961. *Asylums: Essays on the Social Situation of Mental Patients and Other Inmates*. New York: Anchor Books.

Gordon, Edmund T. 1997. "Cultural Politics of Black Masculinity." *Transforming Anthropology* 6(1 & 2): 36–53.

Greenwood, Edward D. 1955. "The Role of Psychotherapy in Residential Treatment." *American Journal of Orthopsychiatry* 25(4): 692–698.

Gregor, Thomas. 2005. "The Men's House: Touching and Wrestling among Mehinaku Men." In *The Book of Touch*, Constance Classen, editor, pp. 162–165. Oxford: Berg Press.

Grier, William H., and Price M. Cobbs. 1969. *Black Rage*. New York: Bantam Books.

Grob, Gerald N. 1994. *The Mad among Us: A History of the Care of America's Mentally Ill*. New York: Free Press.

Guthrie, Robert V. 2004. *Even the Rat Was White: A Historical View of Psychology,* 2nd ed. New York: Pearson.

Hacker, Andrew. 1992. *Two Nations: Black and White, Separate, Hostile, Unequal*. New York: Charles Scribner's Sons.

Hacsi, Timothy A. 1997. *Second Home: Orphan Asylums and Poor Families in America*. Cambridge, MA: Harvard University Press.

Hadley, Susan and George Yancy, eds. 2012. *Therapeutic Uses of Rap and Hip-Hop*. New York: Routledge.

Hall, Stuart. 1997. "Subjects in History: Making Diasporic Identities." In *The House That Race Built: Black Americans, U.S. Terrain,* Wahneema Lubiano, editor, pp. 289–300. New York: Pantheon Books.

———. 1992. "What Is This 'Black' in Black Popular Culture?" In *Black Popular Culture*, Gina Dent, editor, pp. 21–33. Seattle: Bay Press.

———. 1986. "Gramsci's Relevance for the Study of Race and Ethnicity." *Journal of Communication Inquiry* 10(2): 5–27.

———. 1980. "Race, Articulation and Societies Structured in Dominance." In *Sociological Theories: Race and Colonialism*, pp. 305–345. Paris: UNESCO.

Hardt, Michael. 2011. "For Love or Money." *Cultural Anthropology* 26(4): 676–682.

Harper, Phillip. 1996. *Are We Not Men?: Masculine Anxiety and the Problem of African-American Identity*. Oxford: Oxford University Press.

Harrison, Anthony Kwame. 2009. *Hip Hop Underground: The Integrity and Ethics of Racial Identification*. Philadelphia: Temple University Press.

Hecht, Michael L., Ronald L. Jackson, and Sidney A. Ribeau. 2003. *African American Communication: Exploring Identity and Culture*. 2nd ed. Mahwah, NJ: Erlbaum.

Hejtmanek, Katie R. 2010. "Caring Through Restraint: Violence, Intimacy, and Identity in Mental Health Practice." *Culture, Medicine and Psychiatry* 34:668–674.

Hejtmanek, Katherine. 2014. "Practicing and Resisting Constraint: Ethnography of 'Counter Response' in American Adolescent Psychiatric Custody." *Culture, Medicine, and Psychiatry* 38(4): 578–596

———. 2013. "Residential Treatment for Young People." In *Mental Health Issues in America, an Encyclopedia*. Michael Shalley-Jensen, editor, pp. 683–690. Santa Barbara, CA: ABC-CLIO.

Hirsch, Jennifer, and Holly Wardlow. 2006. *Modern Loves: The Anthropology of Romantic Courtship and Companionate Marriage*. Ann Arbor: University of Michigan Press.

Hoffman, Leon. 1982. "An Historical View of Milieu Therapy." In *The Evaluation of Care of Severely Disturbed Children and Their Families*, Leon Hoffman, editor, pp. 1–8. Lancaster, UK: MTP Press Limited.

Hollan, Douglas, and C. Jason Throop. 2008. "Whatever Happened to Empathy?: Introduction." *Ethos* 36(4): 385–401.

hooks, bell. 2004. *We Real Cool: Black Men and Masculinity*. New York: Routledge.

———. 2000. *All about Love*. New York: William Morrow Inc.

———. 1994. "Feminism Inside: Toward a Black Body Politic." In *Black Male: Representations of Masculinity in Contemporary American Art*, Thelma Golden, editor, p. 127. New York: Whitney Museum of American Art.

Hruschka, Daniel J. 2010. *Friendship: Development, Ecology, and Evolution of a Relationship*. Berkeley: University of California Press.

Hull, Matthew S. 2012. *Government of Paper: The Materiality of Bureaucracy in Urban Pakistan*. Berkeley: University of California Press.

Hunter, Richard, and Ida Macalpine. 1963. *Three Hundred Years of Psychiatry 1535–1860*. London: Oxford University Press.

Ignatieff, Michael. 1989. *A Just Measure of Pain: The Penitentiary in the Industrial Revolution 1750–1850*. New York: Puffin.

Jackson, John L. Jr. 2008. *Racial Paranoia: The Unintended Consequences of Political Correctness*. New York: Basic Civitas Books.

———. 2005. *Real Black: Adventures in Racial Sincerity*. Chicago, IL: University of Chicago Press.

Jackson, Michael. 1998. *Minima Ethnographica: Intersubjectivity and the Anthropological Project*. Chicago: University of Chicago Press.

Jainchill, Nancy. 1997. "Therapeutic Communities for Adolescents: The Same and Not the Same." In *Community as Method: Therapeutic Communities for Special Populations and Special Settings*, George De Leon, editor, pp. 161–178. Westport, CT: Praeger.

Jankowiak, William R. ed. 2008. *Intimacies: Love and Sex across Cultures*. New York: Columbia University Press.

———. 1995. *Romantic Passion: A Universal Experience?* New York: Columbia University Press.

Jimenez, Mary Ann. 1987. *Changing Faces of Madness: Early American Attitudes and Treatment of the Insane*. Hanover, NH: University Press of New England.

Johns, David J. 2007. "Re-imagining Black Masculine Identity: An Investigation of the 'Problem' Surrounding the Construction of Black Masculinity in America." In *The State of Black America 2007: Portrait of the Black Male. An Official Publication of the National Urban League*, Stephanie J. Jones, editor, pp. 59–73. Silver Springs, MD: Beckham Publications Group.

Kelley, Robin D. G. 1994. *Race Rebels: Culture, Politics, and the Black Working Class*. New York: The Free Press.

Kennedy, Randall. 1997. *Race, Crime, and the Law*. New York: Pantheon Books.

Killick, Evan, and Amit Desai. 2013. "Introduction: Valuing Friendship." In *The Ways of Friendship: Anthropological Perspectives*, Amit Desai and Evan Killick, editors, pp. 1–19. New York: Berghahn Books.

Kitwana, Bakari. 2002. *The Hip Hop Generation: Young Blacks and the Crisis in African-American Culture*. New York: Basic Civitas Books.

Kleinman, Arthur. 1980. *Patients and Healers in the Context of Culture: An Exploration of the Borderland between Anthropology, Medicine, and Psychiatry*. Berkeley: University of California Press.

Kristeva, Julia. 1982. *Powers of Horror: An Essay on Abjection*. Trans. Leon S. Roudiez. New York: Columbia University Press.

Labov, William. 1972. *Language in the Inner City: Studies in the Black English Vernacular*. Philadelphia: University of Pennsylvania Press.

Labov, William, Paul Cohen, Clarence Robins, and John Lewis. 1968. *A Study of the Non-standard English of Negro and Puerto Rican Speakers in New York City*. Report on Co-operative Research Project 3288. New York: Columbia University.

Lansford, Jennifer E. 2010. "The Special Problem of Cultural Difference in Effects of Corporal Punishment." *Law and Contemporary Problems* 73: 89–106.

Lee, Bethany R., Charlottee L. Bright, Deborah V. Svoboda, Sunday Fakunmoju, and Richard P. Barth. 2011. "Outcomes of Group Care for Youth: A Review of Comparative Studies." *Research on Social Work Practice* 21(2):177–189.

Lee, Bethany R., and J. Curtis McMillan. 2007. "Measuring Quality in Residential Treatment for Children and Youth." *Residential Treatment for Children and Youth* 24(1/2): 1–17.

Lees, J., N. Manning, and B. Rawlings. 1999. *Therapeutic Community Effectiveness: A Systemic International Review of Therapeutic Community Treatment for People with Personality Disorders and Mentally Disordered Offenders*. York: National Health Service Centre for Reviews and Dissemination, University of York.

Lester, Rebecca J. 2011. "How Do I Code for Black Fingernail Polish? Finding the Missing Adolescent in Managed Mental Health Care." *Ethos* 39(4): 481–496.

———. 2009. "Brokering Authenticity: Borderline Personality Disorder and the Ethics of Care in an American Eating Disorder Clinic." *Current Anthropology* 50(3): 281–302.

———. 2007. "Critical Therapeutics: Cultural Politics and Clinical Realities in Two Eating Disorder Treatment Centers." *Medical Anthropological Quarterly* 21(4): 369–387.

———. 2005. *Jesus in Our Wombs: Embodying Modernity in a Mexican Convent*. Berkeley: University of California Press.

Levy, Robert I. 1984. "Emotion, Knowing, and Culture." In *Culture Theory: Essays on Mind, Self, and Emotion*, Richard A. Shweder and Robert LeVine, editors, pp. 214–237. Cambridge: Cambridge University Press.

———. 1983. "Introduction: Self and Emotion." *Ethos* 11(3): 128–134.

Long, Nicholas, James, Mary M. Wood, and Frank A. Fecser. 2001. *Life Space Crisis Intervention: Talking With Students in Conflict*, 2nd ed. Austin, TX: Pro-Ed.

Lubiano, Wahneema. 1997. "Introduction." In *The House That Race Built: Black Americans, U.S. Terrain,* Wahneema Lubiano, editor, pp. vii–ix. New York: Pantheon Books.

Luhrmann, T. M. 2006. "Subjectivity." *Anthropological Theory* 6(3): 345–361.

———. 2000. *Of Two Minds: An Anthropologist Looks at American Psychiatry*. New York: Vintage Books.

Lutz, Catherine A. 1998. *Unnatural Emotions: Everyday Sentiments on a Micronesian Atoll and their Challenge to Western Theory*. Chicago: University of Chicago Press.

Lyons, John. 1999. *Child & Adolescent Needs & Strengths: An Information Integration Tool for Children and Adolescents with Mental Health Challenges*. Chicago, IL: Praed Foundation.

Lyons, John S., Kenneth I. Howard, Michael T. O'Mahoney, and Jennifer D. Lish. 1997. *The Measurement & Management of Clinical Outcomes in Mental Health*. New York: Wiley.

Magellan Health Services Children's Services Task Force. 2010. *Perspectives on Residential Treatment and Community-Based Treatment for Youth and Families*. Tampa, FL: 23rd Annual Children's Mental Health Research & Policy Conference.

Mains, Daniel. 2013. "Friends and Money: Balancing Affection and Reciprocity among Young Men in Urban Ethiopia." *American Ethnologist* 40(1): 335–346.

Mansfield, Nick. 2000. *Subjectivity: Theories of the Self from Freud to Haraway*. New York: New York University Press.

Masterson, James F. 1981. *The Narcissistic and Borderline Disorders: An Integrated Developmental Approach*. New York: Routledge.

———. 1967. *The Psychiatric Dilemma of Adolescence*. Boston, MA: Little, Brown and Company.

Masterson, James F. ed. 2006. *The Personality Disorders through the Lens of Attachment Theory and the Neurobiologic Development of the Self: A Clinical Integration*. Phoenix, AZ: Zeig, Tucker & Theisen, Inc.

Mattingly, Cheryl. 2010. *The Paradox of Hope: Journeys through a Clinical Borderland*. Berkeley: University of California Press.

Mattingly, Cheryl, and Mary Lawlor. 2001. "The Fragility of Healing." *Ethos* 29(1): 30–57.

Mauer, Marc. 2006. *Race to Incarcerate*. 2nd ed. New York: W. W. Norton, Inc.

Mauss, Marcel. 1954. *The Gift: The Form and Reason for Exchange in Archaic Societies*. New York: W. W. Norton & Company.

Mayor, Morris F. 1955. "The Role of Residential Treatment for Children." *American Journal of Orthopsychiatry* 25: 667–668.

McCall, Nathan. 1995. *Makes Me Wanna Holler: A Young Black Man in America*. New York: Vintage Books.

Merleau-Ponty, Maurice. 1945/2003. *Phenomenology of Perception*. Trans. Colin Smith. London: Routledge.

Messner, Michael. 1990. "Boyhood, Organized Sports, and the Construction of Masculinities." *Journal of Contemporary Ethnography* 18: 416–444.

Metzl, Jonathan. 2009. *The Protest Psychosis: How Schizophrenia Became a Black Disease*. Boston, MA: Beacon Press.

Miller, William. 1997. *The Anatomy of Disgust*. Cambridge, MA: Harvard University Press.

Mitchell-Kernan, Claudia. 1972. "Signifying and Marking: Two Afro-American Speech Acts." In *Directions in Sociolinguistics: The Ethnography of Communication*, John Gumperz and Dell Hymes, editors, pp. 161–179. New York: Holt, Rhinehart & Winston.

Mody, Perveez. 2008. *The Intimate State: Love-Marriage and the Law in Delhi*. Delhi: Routledge.

Montagu, Ashley. 1971. *Touching: The Human Significance of the Skin*. New York: Harper and Row.

Mufwene, Salikoko S., and Nancy Condon. 1993. *Africanisms in Afro-American Language Varieties*. Athens, GA: University of Georgia Press.

Mufwene, Salikoko S., John Rickford, Guy Bailey, and John Baugh, eds. 1998. *African-American English*. New York: Routledge.

Neal, Mark Anthony. 2013. *Looking for Leroy: Illegible Black Masculinities*. New York: New York University Press.

———. 1999. *What the Music Said: Black Popular Music and Black Public Culture*. New York: Routledge.

Noshpitz, J. 1962. "Notes on the Theory of Residential Treatment." *Journal of the American Academy of Child Psychiatry* 1: 284–296.

Omi, Michael, and Howard Winant. 2012. "Racial Formation Rules: Continuity, Instability, and Change." In *Racial Formation in the Twenty-First Century*, Daniel Martinez HoSang, Oneka LaBennett, and Laura Pulido, editors, pp. 302–331. Berkeley: University of California Press.

———. 1994. *Racial Formation in the United States: From the 1960s to the 1990s*, 2nd ed. New York: Routledge.

Obeid, Michelle. 2013. "Friendship, kinship and Sociality in a Lebanese Town." In *The Ways of Friendship: Anthropological Perspectives*, Amit Desai and Evan Killick, editors, pp. 93–113. New York: Berghahn Books.

Ortner, Sherry. 2005. "Subjectivity and Cultural Critique." *Anthropological Theory* 5(1): 31–52.

Oshinsky, David M. 1997. *Worse Than Slavery: Parchman Farm and the Ordeal of Jim Crow Justice*. New York: Simon and Schuster.

Pahl, Ray. 2000. *On Friendship*. Malden, MA: Polity Press.

Penn, Everette B. 2006. "Black Youth: Disproportionality and Delinquency." In *Race in Juvenile Justice*, Everette B. Penn, Helen Taylor Greene, and Shaun L. Gabbidon, editors, pp. 47–64. Durham, NC: Carolina Academic Press.

Penn, Everette Burdette, Helen Taylor Greene, and Shaun L. Gabbidon. 2006. "Introduction." In *Race and Juvenile Justice*, Everette Penn, Helen Greene, and Shaun Gabbidon, editors, pp. 1–7. Durham, NC: Carolina Academic Press.

Perry, Bruce, and Maia Szalavitz. 2006. *The Boy Who Was Raised as a Dog: And Other Stories from a Child Psychiatrist's Notebook*. New York: Basic Books.

Perry, Imani. 2008. "'Tell us How It Feels to Be a Problem': Hip Hop Longings and Poor Young Black Men." In *Against the Wall: Poor, Young, Black, and Male*, Elijah Anderson, editor, pp. 165–177. Philadelphia: University of Pennsylvania Press.

———. 2004. *Prophets of the Hood: Politics and Poetics in Hip Hop*. Durham, NC: Duke University Press.

Polsky, Howard W. 1962/1977. *Cottage Six: The Social System of Delinquent Boys in Residential Treatment*. Malabar, FL: Robert E. Krieger Publishing Company.

Polsky, Howard W., Daniel S. Claster, and Carl Goldberg. 1968. *The Dynamics of Residential Treatment: A Social System Analysis*. Chapel Hill, NC: The University of North Carolina Press.

Polsky, Howard W., Daniel S. Claster, and Carl Goldberg, eds. 1970. *Social System Perspectives in Residential Institutions*. East Lansing, MI: Michigan State University Press.

Povinelli, Elizabeth. 2006. *The Empire of Love: Toward a Theory of Intimacy, Ggenealogy and arnality.* Durham, NC: Duke University Press.

Puzzanchera, Charles, Benjamin Adams, and Sarah Hockenberry 2012. *Juvenile Court Statistics 2009: Report*. National Center for Juvenile Justice.

Ray, George B. 2009. *Language and Interracial Communication in the United States: Speaking in Black and White*. New York: Peter Lang.

Rebhun, Linda. 1999. *The Heart Is Unknown Country: Love in the Changing Economy of Northeast Brazil*. Stanford: Stanford University Press.

Reid, Joseph H., and Helen R. Hagan. 1952. *Residential Treatment of Emotionally Disturbed Children: A Descriptive Study*. New York: Child Welfare League of America.

Residential Child Care Project. 2001. *Therapeutic Crisis Intervention Student Workbook*. Family Life Development Center, College of Human Ecology, Cornell University. Ithaca, NY.

Rhodes, Lorna A. 2004. *Total Confinement: Madness and Reason in the Maximum Security Prison*. Berkeley: University of California Press.

———. 2000. "Taxonomic Anxieties: Axis I and Axis II in Prison." *Medical Anthropology Quarterly* 14 (3): 346–373.

———. 1991. *Emptying Beds: The Work of an Emergency Psychiatric Unit*. Berkeley: University of California Press.

Rios, Victor M. 2011. *Punished: Policing the Lives of Black and Latino Boys*. New York: New York University Press.

Rivera, Raquel. 2003. *New York Ricans from the Hip-Hop Zone*. New York: Palgrave Macmillan.

Robinson, J. Frankin, George E. Gardner, Edward D. Greenwood, Helen R. Hagan, and Julius B. Richmond. 1957. *Psychiatric Inpatient Treatment of Children*. Washington, DC: American Psychiatric Association.

Rodgers, Graeme. 2013. "Friendship, Distance and Kinship-Talk amongst Mozambican Refugees in South Africa." In *The Ways of Friendship: Anthropological Perspectives*, Amit Desai and Evan Killick, editors, pp. 69–92. New York: Berghahn Books.

Rosaldo, Michelle. 1984. "Toward an Anthropology of Self and Feeling." In *Culture Theory: Essays on Mind, Self, and Emotion*, Richard A. Shweder and Robert LeVine, editors, pp. 137–157. Cambridge: Cambridge University Press.

Rose, Nikolas. 1999. *Governing the Soul: The Shaping of the Private Self*, 2nd ed. New York: Free Association Press.

Rose Tricia. 2008. *The Hip Hop Wars: What We Talk about When We Talk about Hip Hop—and Why It Matters*. New York: Basic Books.

———. 1994. *Black Noise: Rap Music and Black Culture in Contemporary America*. Middleton, CT: Wesleyan University Press.

Rothman, David J. 1971. *The Discovery of the Asylum: Social Order and Disorder in the New Republic*. Boston, MA: Little, Brown and Company.

Scarry, Elaine. 1985. *The Body in Pain: The Making and Unmaking of the World*. New York: Oxford University Press.

Schlegel, Alice. 1995. "Cross Cultural Approaches to Adolescence." *Ethos* 23(1): 15–32.

Schwartzman, Helen B. 1987. "The Significance of Meetings in an American Mental Health Center." *American Ethnologist* 14(2): 271–294.

Shaw, Arnold. 1986. *Black Popular Music in America: From the Spirituals, Minstrels, and Ragtime to Soul, Disco, and Hip-Hop*. New York: Macmillan.

Sheldon, Randall G., Sharon K. Tracy, and William B. Brown. 2012. *Youth Gangs in American Society*, 4th ed. Stamford, CT: Cengage Learning.

Shorter, Edward. 1997. *A History of Psychiatry: From the Era of the Asylum to the Age of Prozac*. New York: John Wiley & Sons, Inc.

Shweder, Richard A. 1995. "'You're Not Sick, You're Just in Love': Emotion as an Interpretive System." In *The Nature of Emotion: Fundamental Questions*, Paul Ekman and Richard J. Davidson, editors, pp. 32–44. New York: Oxford University Press.

Simmons, Russell, with Chris Marrow. 2007. *Do You! 12 Laws to Access the Power in You to Achieve Happiness and Success*. New York: Gotham Books.

Smitherman, Geneva. 2006. *Word from the Mother: Language and African Americans*. New York: Routledge, April.

Spears, Arthur. 2007. "African American Communicative Practices: Improvisation, Semantic License, and Augmentation." In *Talkin Black Talk: Language, Education, and Social Change*, H. Samy Alim and John Baugh, editors, pp. 100–110. New York: Teachers College Press.

Stanton, A. H., and M. S. Schwartz. 1954. *The Mental Hospital: A Study of Institutional Participation in Psychiatric Illness and Treatment*. New York: Basic Books.

Steinbugler, Amy C. 2012. *Beyond Loving: Intimate Racework in Lesbian, Gay, and Straight Interracial Relationships*. Oxford: Oxford University Press.

Taylor, Robert W., and Eric J. Fritsch. 2010. *Juvenile Justice: Policies, Programs, and Practices*. Boston: McGraw-Hill.

Tillich, Paul. 1954. *Love, Power, and Justice*. Oxford: Oxford University Press.

Toop, David. 1984. *Rap Attack: African Jive to New York Hip Hop*. London: Pluto Press.

Trieschman, Albert, Larry K. Whittaker, and Larry K. Brendtro. 1969. *The Other 23 Hours: Child-Care Work with Emotionally Disturbed Children in a Therapeutic Milieu*. Chicago, IL: Aldine Publishing Company.

Trilling, Lionel. 1972. *Sincerity and Authenticity*. Cambridge, MA: Harvard University Press.

Turner, Victor Witter. 1967. *The Forest of Symbols: Aspects of Ndembu Ritual*. Ithaca, NY: Cornell University Press.

Twine, France Widdance. 2000. Racial Ideologies and Racial Methodologies. In *Racing Research, Researching Race: Methodological Dilemmas in Critical Race Studies*, ed. France Winddance Twine and Jonathan Warren, 1–34. New York: New York University Press.

Twine, France Winddance, and Jonathan W. Warren, eds. 2000. *Racing Research, Researching Race*. New York: NYU Press.

U.S. Department of Health and Human Services' Administration for Children and Families, "Administration on Children, Youth and Families, Children's Bureau. 2013." *The AFCARS Report*, http://www.acf.hhs.gov/sites/default/files/cb/afcars_report15.pdf accessed September 27, 2013.

U.S. Department of Justice. 2013. "Juveniles in Residential Placement, 2010. Juvenile Offenders and Victims: National Report Series Bulletin." June. http://www.ojjdp.gov/pubs/241060.pdf accessed February 28, 2014.

Van Deburg, William L. 2004. *Hoodlums: Black Villains and Social Bandits in American Life*. Chicago: The University of Chicago Press.

van der Kolk, Bessel A., Susan Roth, David Pelcovitz, Susanne Sunday, and Joseph Spinazzola. 2005. "Disorders of Extreme Stress: The Empirical Foundation of a Complex Adaptation to Trauma." *Journal of Traumatic Stress* 18(5): 389–399.

Wacquant, Loïc. 2008. *Urban Outcasts: A Comparative Sociology of Advanced Marginality*. Cambridge, UK : Polity Press.

Wald, Elijah. 2012. *The Dozens: A History of Rap's Mama*. Oxford: Oxford University Press.

Waldram, James B. 2012. *Hound Pound Narrative: Sexual Offender Habilitation and the Anthropology of Therapeutic Intervention*. Berkeley: University of California Press.

Wallace, Maurice O. 2002. *Constructing the Black Masculine: Identity and Ideality in African American Men's Literature and Culture, 1775–1995*. Durham, NC: Duke University Press.

Washington, Harriet A. 2006. *Medical Apartheid: The Dark History of Medical Experimentation on Black Americans from Colonial Times to the Present*. New York: Doubleday.

Watkins, S. Craig. 2005. *Hip Hop Matters: Politics, Pop Culture, and the Struggle for the Soul of a Movement*. Boston: Beacon Press.

Way, Niobe. 2011. *Deep Secrets: Boys' Friendships and the Crisis of Connection*. Cambridge, MA: Harvard University Press.

Westbrook, Alonzo. 2002. *Hip Hoptionary: The Dictionary of Hip Hop Terminology*. New York: Harlem Moon Broadway Books.

Wellman, David T. 1993. *Portraits of White Racism*, 2nd ed. New York: Cambridge University Press.

Whaley, Arthur L. 2000. "Sociocultural Differences in the Developmental Consequences of the Use of Physical Discipline During Childhood for African Americans." *Cultural Diversity and Ethnic Minority Psychology* 6(1): 5–12.

Wikan, Unni. 1993. "Beyond the Words: The Power of Resonance." In *Beyond Boundaries: Understanding, Translation and Anthropological Discourse*, G´ısli P´alsson, editor, pp. 184–209. Oxford: Berg Press.

Winnicott, D. W. 1992. *Babies and Their Mothers*, reprint ed. Cambridge, MA: Da Capo Press.

Wise, Tim. 2010. *Colorblind: The Rise of Post-Racial Politics and the Retreat from Racial Inequality*. San Francisco: City Lights Books.

Wolfram, Walter. 1969. *A Sociolinguistic Description of Detroit Negro Speech*. Washington, DC: Center for Applied Linguistics.

Wool, Zoë H., and Seth D. Messinger. 2012. "Labors of Love: The Transformation of Care in the Non-Medical Attendant Program at Walter Reed Army Medical Center." *Medical Anthropology Quarterly* 26(1): 26–48.

Zeb.Roc.Ski. 2004. *Martha Cooper's Hip Hop Files: Photographs 1979–1984*. Berlin, Germany: From Here to Fame Publishing.

Zigon, Jarrett. 2013. "On Love: Remaking Moral Subjectivity in Post-rehabilitation Russia." *American Ethnologist* 40(1): 201–215.

Index

CPSIA information can be obtained
at www.ICGtesting.com
Printed in the USA
LVHW080911091221
705729LV00001B/1